Why Washington Won't Work

Chicago Studies in American Politics

A SERIES EDITED BY BENJAMIN I. PAGE, SUSAN HERBST,
LAWRENCE R. JACOBS, AND ADAM J. BERINSKY

Also in the series:

Additional series titles follow index

Why Washington Won't Work

Polarization, Political Trust, and the Governing Crisis

MARC J. HETHERINGTON

THOMAS J. RUDOLPH

THE UNIVERSITY OF CHICAGO PRESS   CHICAGO AND LONDON

MARC J. HETHERINGTON is professor of political science at Vanderbilt University. He is the author of *Why Trust Matters* and coauthor, with Jonathan D. Weiler, of *Authoritarianism and Polarization in American Politics*.

THOMAS J. RUDOLPH is professor of political science at the University of Illinois at Urbana-Champaign and coauthor of *Expression vs. Equality*.

The University of Chicago Press, Chicago 60637
The University of Chicago Press, Ltd., London
© 2015 by The University of Chicago
All rights reserved. Published 2015.
Printed in the United States of America

24 23 22 21 20 19 18 17 16 15   1 2 3 4 5

ISBN-13: 978-0-226-29918-1 (cloth)
ISBN-13: 978-0-226-29921-1 (paper)
ISBN-13: 978-0-226-29935-8 (e-book)
DOI: 10.7208/chicago/9780226299358.001.0001

Library of Congress Cataloging-in-Publication Data

Hetherington, Marc J., 1968– author.
    Why Washington won't work : polarization, political trust, and the governing crisis / Marc J. Hetherington, Thomas J. Rudolph.
        pages ; cm
    Includes bibliographical references and index.
    ISBN 978-0-226-29918-1 (cloth : alk. paper)—ISBN 978-0-226-29921-1 (pbk. : alk. paper)—
ISBN 978-0-226-29935-8 (ebook)   1. Politics, Practical—United States. 2. Trust—
Political aspects—United States. 3. Polarization (Social sciences)—United States.
4. United States—Politics and government—2009–. 5. Political parties—United States.
I. Rudolph, Thomas J., author. II. Title.
    E893.H48 2015
    324.20973—dc23

                                                                                    2015010765

Contents

Acknowledgments

Marc J. Hetherington owes more debts than the Bible has psalms (apologies to House of Pain). Starting with the professional ones, Larry Bartels provided so much help and advice along the way that it is impossible to catalog. He provided us with the means to do the data collection that appears in chapter 7, which was incredibly generous but was perhaps the least of his contributions. What was most helpful was the fact that his door is always open. Larry is the LeBron James of political science and not just because of his towering physical stature. He is always the best player on the court, but what makes him even more valuable is that he makes all the players around him better.

We benefited from a remarkable editorial team. John Tryneski gave us terrific direction at various points, which helped us mesh together the various moving parts of our analysis. We were fortunate to have two remarkable series editors as well. The project would not have gotten off the ground if not for the tireless work of Jamie Druckman. He made every one of our ideas crisper. And although we were unlucky to lose Jamie partway through, we were lucky to gain Adam Berinsky. He pushed us to be both more rigorous and more accessible. Although that might sound like contradictory advice, Adam provided us clear ideas about how to accomplish both. In addition, Rodney Powell was incredibly adept at moving the manuscript through the process. This group also secured two extraordinarily helpful reader reports that allowed us to put together a final manuscript that is both technically better and significantly more interesting than the draft we first submitted.

There are so many scholars who have helped us improve the final product. Jonathan Weiler—both a great friend and great coauthor—provided tons of guidance without even knowing he was doing it. As often seems to be the case, someone comes on the scene to make an unanticipated contribution. Jenny Mansbridge was that person for us. She e-mailed us a question about trust in government and got a draft of the book in response, surely not what she hoped for or expected. The feedback and encouragement she provided proved invaluable. Others read or commented on various drafts or engaged our ideas over the years. These people include Mike Nelson, Larry Evans, Ted Carmines, Bruce Larson, Alan Abramowitz, Jeremy Pope, Margie Hershey, Mike MacKuen, Dietlind Stolle, David Karol, Eric Belanger, Rick Wilson, John Alford, Tom Mann, Bill Jacoby, Frances Lee, and Jim Thurber. Numerous talks over the last few years at College of William and Mary, University of Maryland, University of Illinois, University of North Carolina, American University, McGill University, Rice University, University of Alabama, and Indiana University provided a bevy of great ideas as well.

Not among the names in the list above but a person especially important to us is Mo Fiorina. His book *Culture War?* is the starting place for every book and article that has been written on polarization in the past decade. As readers will see in the pages that follow, we share Mo's view on some things but not on others. The key point here is that the clarity and cogency of his original argument inspired us to think for years about what is really going on in the mass public. We suspect that we are not alone in appreciating that inspiration.

Colleagues at Vanderbilt were also a big help, even fundamentally important at times. James Booth provided friendship and kept our eye on the big picture. Josh Clinton helped us solve every methodological problem we encountered. Josh and Dave Lewis were generous to allow us room on the Vanderbilt Poll to test our ideas about agency-specific trust, which appear in chapter 9. Bruce Oppenheimer was, as always, a great source of wisdom and information when it came connecting our public opinion story with what is happening in Congress. Other colleagues, such as Emily Nacol, Michaela Mattes, Zeynep Somer-Topcu, Monique Lyle, Giacomo Chiozza, and Carol Atkinson, provided enthusiasm and encouragement, which was at least as important as all the other stuff. A raft of graduate students helped with various parts of the book. Carrie Roush read multiple drafts of the complete manuscript and consistently provided useful ideas. She also tamed Microsoft Excel for us during the artwork phase of the project, which was critical in heading off an emotional breakdown. In addition, Drew Englehardt, Meri Long, Brielle Harbin, Scott Limbocker, and Camille Burge were a big help. Also important to acknowledge is a terrific group of undergraduate students from the fall 2013 semester who took Hetherington's honors seminar about the public in American politics. They were great guinea pigs to try out some of the ideas that we were developing at that point, some of which they indicated worked and some of which they indicated did not.

Several people were not directly involved in this particular project, but it still bears their imprint. Bill Keefe, the best ever undergraduate teacher of political science, inspired Hetherington to go to graduate school, making his first steps in the profession possible. (In keeping with Bill's style, we want to make clear that, given the large number of people who have been involved in the process, any mistakes that remain in the book are surely their fault, not ours.) Those first steps led Hetherington to Bob Luskin, the best ever dissertation supervisor. None of this would be possible without Bob's careful and tireless training. Finally, Jon Hurwitz has been the most generous of friends over the years, reconnecting him to his academic roots at the University of Pittsburgh. He was also an important sounding board for matters both big and small.

The number of people to whom Hetherington owes personal debts probably approaches infinity. He is lucky to have the best family imaginable. His parents, Bob and Terry Hetherington, provided the best political education in the world. Taking part in conversations at their dinner table from his earliest days forward gave him whatever unique insights he might have. Now into their mid-eighties, Bob and Terry still provide the same gifts—advice, support, determination, and love—to their kids. In addition, it is impossible to begin to measure all that his sister, Beth, provided through this process. Her generosity and willingness to lend an ear knows no boundaries. Bryan, Susan, and Kathy never failed to be there either.

Hetherington also wants to thank his two great kids, Ben and Sammy. Their interests could sometimes not seem more different, but they are similarly and singularly wonderful. It would be much harder to write books if it weren't for all the opportunities they provide to listen to Benny Goodman and Jimi Hendrix and to play catch and shoot baskets.

Finally, the most important person in all this is Suzanne Globetti. The many years that this book has been in the works have featured a few more trials and tribulations than usual. Having a partner so adept and picking you up and dusting you off is a tremendous blessing. Having a partner who can do that *and* make all your work better because she is a better political scientist than you places her in a category all her own. Without Suzanne, Thomas J. Rudolph would have been on his own.

Collectively, we also would like to thank Wiley and University of Chicago Press Journals for granting us permission to use parts of articles that we published with them in years past. A previous version of chapter 3 appeared in the *Journal of Politics* in 2008. We thank Wiley for allowing us to update it. In addition, a previous version of chapter 6 appeared in the *American Journal of Political Science*. We thank the University of Chicago Press for allowing us to update it.

Rudolph has also accumulated a number of personal debts over the years. His parents, Dr. and Mrs. James T. Rudolph, both of whom worked as educators, provided a supportive environment that encouraged intellectual curiosity. A special debt is owed to Dr. Erwin P. Rudolph, Rudolph's grandfather and professor emeritus from Wheaton College. A retired professor of medieval English, Erwin has been a wonderful role model and example of what living the life of the mind should be like. Although nearing his ninety-ninth birthday at the time of this writing, he remains intellectually curious and has followed this book's development with great interest.

Colleagues at Illinois have been equally supportive. Jim Kuklinski, in particular, read the entire manuscript and offered both encouraging words and constructive criticisms. Members of Rudolph's Political Psychology seminar also offered useful feedback on certain chapters.

Rudolph also wishes to thank the many members of his brood: Timothy, Luke, Andrew, Clara, Louisa, Thaddeus, Matthias, and Elsa. They help to keep life in proper perspective daily. Between their various athletic and musical pursuits, they never fail to provide interesting distractions from work.

Most of all, Rudolph would like to thank his best friend and soul mate, Heather. For more than twenty years, she has been an unfailing source of encouragement and inspiration. Whether serving as a sounding board for new research ideas or keeping the inmates from taking over the asylum at home, her support has been invaluable. Very little of what Rudolph manages to accomplish in this world would be possible without Heather.

CHAPTER ONE

Why Extreme Leaders Don't Listen to a Moderate Public

We face more than a deficit of dollars right now. We face a deficit of trust—deep and corrosive doubts about how Washington works that have been growing for years. —Barack Obama, 2010 State of the Union Address

American politics is dysfunctional. With no ideological overlap left between the parties and moderates going the way of the dinosaur (e.g., Theriault 2008), cross-party compromises on important matters are increasingly rare. Unlike congressional representatives, American citizens are moderate, if ideological at all (e.g., Fiorina, Abrams, and Pope 2005). Why, then, do citizens continue to allow their representatives to do such a poor job representing them? That is what this book is about. We endeavor to explain why the public has become an inert force in American politics. The short answer is that partisans whose party is out of power have almost no trust at all in a government run by the other side. This is a striking departure from the past. Absent this supply of trust, public consensus on issues rarely forms. Lawmakers, in turn, feel little pressure from their constituents to rise above their basest partisan instincts. Ultimately, little gets done, but partisans blame only the other side for the lack of productivity.

Recent events tell the story. While polarization in Washington has been high, congressional productivity has been low. The 112th and 113th Congresses, which served from 2011 to 2014, were the least productive ones since scholars began to measure congressional productivity in the 1940s (Binder 2014; Terkel 2012). Mark Twain aphorisms notwithstanding, unproductive political institutions can be costly. Since 1917, Congress and the president have agreed nearly one hundred times, mostly without incident, to increase the country's ability to borrow money for obligations already incurred. In the 2010s, however, the routine became anything but. With Republicans ascendant after sweeping midterm victories in 2010 and congressional parties as polarized as any time in the last one hundred years, Congress and the president repeatedly failed to reach an agreement on raising the debt ceiling. As a result, one of the three major credit rating agencies downgraded US debt, a stunning and—to that point— unthinkable outcome.

Over the next two years, these partisan clashes continued, with an increasing price tag to the American public. First came the sequestration of $85.4 billion during the 2013 fiscal year. Sequestration included a mandatory 7.9 percent cut in the defense budget, a 5.3 percent cut in discretionary domestic spending, and a 2 percent cut in Medicare.[1] These across-the-board cuts, especially damaging during fragile economic times, were actually designed the year before to be so odious that the prospect of implementing them would force Republicans and Democrats to compromise on spending cuts and revenue increases. Yet in the polarized environment inside the Beltway, compromise never emerged, and an economically injurious policy was enacted by default. In the fall of 2013, partisan brinksmanship over funding Obamacare, the federal budget, and the need to again increase the debt ceiling led to a sixteen-day government shutdown, the first in seventeen years. Its economic costs were high. Standard and Poor's estimated that the shutdown cost the economy about $24 billion, reducing projections for gross domestic product (GDP) growth from 3 percent to 2.4 percent.[2] The Council of Economic Advisors estimated that the shutdown cost about 120,000 jobs as well. Although Congress eventually did agree on a debt limit increase just hours before the country would have defaulted, political dysfunction carried tangible costs.

Ideologically committed congressional representatives are unlikely to depolarize on their own because they strongly believe that their approach is correct. Indeed, that is probably why most sought office in the first place (Aldrich 1995; Cohen et al. 2008). Furthermore, the minority party has strong incentives not to compromise when party margins in Congress are close (Lee 2009). What is puzzling is why the American public has sat idly by as the congressional parties, particularly the Republicans, have lurched toward ideological extremes. The electorate is uniquely positioned to force representatives toward the political center. Representatives need public support at election time, so they have incentives to listen to public opinion, particularly when the public is angry. And the public has been angry: congressional approval has registered consistently below 25 percent since 2010 and plummeted to 9 percent at the end of 2013.[3] Yet the public has done little to rein in ideological and partisan excesses in Washington. Although the public's quiescence could be evidence that it is just as thirsty for ideological combat as members of Congress, public opinion surveys have repeatedly shown that the *policy preferences* of ordinary Americans, unlike those of Congress, are not particularly extreme (Fiorina et al. 2005; Clinton 2006; Bafumi and Herron 2010). This is quite a puzzle.

Why, then, do American citizens put up with—even reward—such excess? We argue that ordinary Americans are, in fact, increasingly polarized, just not in their policy preferences or ideology.[4] Instead, we focus on the fact that partisans are now polarized in their feelings about their political opponents. Republicans and Democrats simply do not like each other to an unprecedented degree.

As an example of what we mean by a polarization of feelings, consider the response when, in September 2009, the Obama administration announced that the president would mark the new school year by giving a speech to students to challenge them "to work hard, set educational goals, and take responsibility for their learning" (Obama 2009). When people think about "hot button" issues that deeply divide Americans, neither education nor hard work is usually among them. Furthermore, a Department of Education spokeswoman made clear that the speech was not a policy address; its viewing would be entirely voluntary, with each individual school making a decision on whether to broadcast the speech during school hours.[5] The ensuing furor must have taken the administration by surprise. It is perhaps not a shock that Republican officials took the president to task because that is, arguably, their job. For example, the president of the Florida Republican Party, Jim Greer, wrote a letter in which he charged that "President Obama has turned to American's [sic] children to spread his liberal lies, indoctrinating American's [sic] youngest children before they have a chance to decide for themselves" (Greer 2009).

But it was not only political leaders who had strong feelings about the president's speech; ordinary Americans did, too. Angry phone calls and letters poured into superintendents' offices across the country with parents threatening to keep their children home from school if Obama's address was aired. One Colorado parent, in tears, told CNN, "Thinking about my kids . . . sorry . . . in school having to listen to that just really

upsets me. I'm an American. They are Americans, and I don't feel that's
OK. I feel very scared to be in this country with our leadership right
now."[6] If this Colorado woman felt this strongly about her child simply
being exposed to a video recording of a Democrat, we suspect she is going
to place little pressure on her favored party leaders to compromise with
that Democrat regardless of the issue.

It is important to note that negative feelings have not always run so
deep. When, on September 8, President Obama made his speech, urging
students to take responsibility for their education, no matter their circumstances, and to "get serious this year . . . put your best effort into everything you do," many school districts, overwhelmed by parental complaints,
opted not to share it.[7] When George H. W. Bush addressed public school
students in a similar fashion in 1991, however, it did not cause a stir.[8]

Americans' strong, negative feelings about their political opponents
have led to another, even more consequential, development in public
opinion: the polarization of political trust. Political trust is critical because it helps create consensus in the mass public by providing a bridge
between the governing party's policy ideas and the opinions of those who
usually support the other party. Consensus is important because research
tells us that policy makers respond to the wishes of the public when consensus develops (see, for example, Page, Shapiro, and Dempsey 1987).
When both Republicans and Democrats (or liberals and conservatives)
in the electorate support an item on the policy agenda, Congress and the
president usually respond with laws.[9]

We show again and again in this book that the recent polarization of
political trust stands in the way of the emergence of public consensus on
public policy. The reason is simple: people who distrust government are
unwilling to make what we call "ideological sacrifices." For a conservative
citizen to go along with a liberal policy idea like health care reform, for
example, it requires him or her to sacrifice his or her general principles
that smaller government is better government. For a liberal citizen to go
along with a conservative policy idea like privatizing Social Security, it requires him or her to sacrifice his or her general principles that big government in this realm works. Those who trust government are apt to make
ideological sacrifices. Those who distrust the government are not. Strong
dislike and deep distrust of the governing party means that partisans from
the out party in the electorate will not nudge their representatives toward
compromises with the governing party.

To illustrate our thinking about trust and sacrifices, consider the following: Suppose that Harry and Louise, a newly married couple, wish to

adopt a pet for their new home. Since they only have enough room for one, they must agree on which type. Louise is the proverbial "cat person." She grew up in an apartment with cats and assures Harry that they have a number of desirable qualities. Cats, she argues, are intelligent, independent, low maintenance, and keep rodents away. In short, Louise is predisposed to see the virtues of cat ownership. Harry, by contrast, is a "dog person." His family had a dog when he was a child. Dogs make better pets, he believes, because they are affectionate, playful, loyal, and protective. For Harry to agree to adopt a cat rather than a dog, he must be willing to sacrifice his own pet preferences. The same is true for Louise to go along with a dog adoption. If neither agrees to sacrifice, however, consensus will not develop, no adoption will occur, and there will be yet another lonely pet in the world. Both Harry and Louise are more likely to make such a sacrifice if they trust their partner's vision of what the future might hold. If they question this vision, or question each other's motives, they will not yield. And, in turn, they will not adopt.

Pet preferences are like ideological preferences. They may be strongly held, yet, under the right circumstances and with enough trust in one's negotiating partner, people can be persuaded to sacrifice them. As the following chapters will demonstrate, trust is most necessary to conservatives when asked to support a liberal policy initiative or to liberals when asked to support a conservative one. In both cases, political trust, if it exists, has the potential to dampen ideological conflict and forge policy consensus. Its absence ensures dissensus.

Considered in this way, trust can serve as a reservoir that policy makers draw on to cause those not ideologically predisposed to follow them to give their ideas a shot.[10] That reservoir has run dry. As evidence, consider the following data. In 2010, we asked one thousand respondents a version of a trust-in-government question that has been asked by survey organizations since the 1950s. Our question read, "How much of the time do you think you can trust the government in Washington to do what is right? Just about always, most of the time, only some of the time, or never?" During the first fifty years that survey researchers have asked this question, Republicans and Democrats have rarely differed by much. Democrats expressed a few percentage points more trust than Republicans did under a Democratic president and Republicans expressed a few percentage points more trust than Democrats did under a Republican president (Hetherington 2005).

That tendency toward slight partisan differences has changed fundamentally of late. In figure 1.1, we have broken down the distribution of

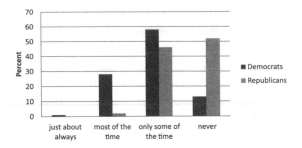

FIGURE I.I. Trust in government by party, 2010

Source: CCES, 2010, Vanderbilt Module.

responses to our 2010 survey by party identification. The findings are remarkable. A stunning 52 percent of Republicans reported that they "never"
trusted the government in Washington to do what is right. Another 46 percent said they trusted it "only some of the time." A vanishingly small
2 percent reported trusting the government "most of the time," and not
one Republican identifier said he or she trusted government "just about
always." If we are correct that trusting, out-party partisans are the bridge
to overcoming partisan gridlock, these results make clear that the bridge
has washed away. The absence of trust among Republicans all but elimi-
nates the development of public consensus. Instead, Republicans in the
electorate will do what comes naturally: follow the cues of Republicans
in Washington and oppose everything that Democrats propose. Without
consensus, public opinion will not nudge representatives toward moderation and compromise. Instead, the public will reinforce polarization in
Washington. In short, the polarization of political trust has rendered an
ideologically moderate (or perhaps nonideological) mass public an inert
force in overcoming polarization in Washington. Without public trust in
government, the lawmaking process in Washington has ground to a halt.

A Tale of Two First Terms

Contrasting the beginning of George W. Bush's presidency with the beginning of Barack Obama's helps illustrate the central importance of political
trust to policy outcomes. After the 9/11 terrorist attacks, political trust
surged to levels not seen since the 1960s. In the month before the attacks,
only 30 percent of Americans said they trusted the government to do what

was right either "almost always" or "most of the time." Just a month later, 64 percent did. This reading was twenty points higher than any taken in the twenty-five years prior to the attacks. With trust remaining relatively high through his first term, Bush usually got what he wanted despite relatively narrow congressional majorities. For example, trust in government was important to securing public support for restrictions on civil liberties like the PATRIOT Act and other domestic security enhancements (Davis and Silver 2004) along with, as we show in this book, the wars in Afghanistan and Iraq (see also Hetherington and Husser 2012).

Two things are important to understand here. First, political trust was very high during the early Bush years—stratospherically so right after 9/11. A key reason, which we detail in this book, is that politics was consumed by foreign affairs and war. Despite the fact that Americans often express little trust in the government as a whole, they actually like and trust certain parts of it. For example, almost everyone these days likes the military, which is part of the government, too. As a result, trust tends to be higher when foreign policy is salient and lower when more partisan domestic concerns that make use of less popular parts of the government are salient. When people evaluate the government's trustworthiness, that evaluation bears the imprint of the part of the government that is on their minds when they are asked about it.

The second thing that is important to understand is that, especially in 2002 and 2003, political trust had not yet polarized by party. With the focus on keeping the country safe from terror and fighting the popular part of wars in Afghanistan and Iraq, Democrats were very likely to say they trusted the government, too. For example, in 2002, 63 percent of Republicans and 49 percent of Democrats said they trusted the government in Washington to do what is right at least "most of the time." Historically speaking, these percentages are extremely high. As a result, broad public consensus existed for early Bush era policy changes. Many Democrats in Congress, some of whom had misgivings about the challenges to civil liberties embedded in the PATRTIOT Act, felt they needed to support it because their constituents did. Although people can debate the merits of the PATRIOT Act, the critical fact here is that consensus in public opinion helped nudge Congress, including some of its recalcitrant members, and the president toward policy change.

What a difference six or seven years can make. During the first years of Barack Obama's presidency, trust reached, by far, its nadir since survey organizations first started asking about it in the 1950s, with only 9 percent expressing trust in an October 2011 *New York Times* poll. The reasons for the drop were numerous. Most important, the central task of governing changed relative to most of the Bush years. No longer was government mostly working on consensual matters, such as keeping Americans safe from terrorists and taking the fight to them. Instead, government was dealing with a financial crisis more severe than any since the Great Depression. Unemployment and budget deficits were high, the stock market and economic optimism were low, and Americans were unhappy. When people perceive performance to be poor, trust in government evaporates (Citrin and Green 1986). Moreover, party leaders did not pull together as they often do when facing a crisis. Perhaps because the crisis was economic and not foreign, the public was treated to a lot of angry sniping between Republicans and Democrats in Washington. Finally, Americans had even grown weary of the things that tended to unify them. Specifically, people increasingly questioned whether the wars in Afghanistan and Iraq were worth the cost.

With political trust lower than ever before, Obama's experience starkly demonstrates how profoundly low trust can affect policy support. Programs that started out as very popular with the public, such as health care reform, economic stimulus, and financial industry regulation, quickly became political lightning rods. Only bruising and seldom-used legislative tactics ensured their passage. In the end, legislators received no leeway from constituents for their efforts to stanch the bleeding from the financial crisis. Massive midterm losses for the majority Democrats ensued in 2010, even though most experts agreed that the roots of the calamity were to be found in the policies of George W. Bush and Republican congressional majorities in the early 2000s. In the Tea Party, low trust spawned a virulently antigovernment political movement. After the midterm elections, government time and again teetered on the brink of shutdown. In the view of many commentators, the nation's political institutions became all but ungovernable.

The contrasting experiences of Bush and Obama are amplified examples of a general trend: trust is notably higher during Republican administrations. The American National Election Study (ANES) has regularly asked a question to tap how "much people trust the government in Washington to do what is right" since 1964. Americans can choose between three categories: "just about always," "most of the time," and "only some of the time." In figure 1.2, we graph the percentage of Democrats and Republicans who report trusting the government either just about always or most of the time (see also Haidt and Hetherington 2012). To simplify

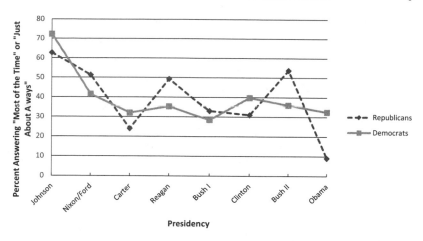

FIGURE 1.2. Partisan differences in trust in government by presidential administration

Sources: American National Election Study, 2011, Cumulative Data File; CCES, 2010; American National Election Study, 2012.

its presentation, we group together all the ANES surveys that were taken under a given president.[11] For example, trust in government during the Clinton years is the average score from the surveys taken in 1994, 1996, 1998, and 2000. For George W. Bush, it is the average score from surveys taken in 2002, 2004, and 2008 (no ANES survey was administered in 2006).

The results are striking. Democrats have not varied all that much in how much they report trusting government. Since the 1970s, the percentage of trusting Democrats has fluctuated between 30 percent and 40 percent, regardless of the president's party. Most of the change over time has been in Republicans' trust in government. These data explode one myth right away: it is not true that Republicans do not trust government. In fact, they trust it quite a lot when one of their own occupies the White House. What Republicans do not trust is government headed by Democrats. This is the key reason that trust is higher during Republican presidencies. Democrats trust government during Democratic and Republican presidencies at basically the same rate, whereas Republicans trust it much more when their party is in power.

It is the people who trust government but who identify with the party opposite the president who are the key to our story of political dysfunction. They decide whether or not public consensus develops, which, in turn, can push policy makers toward action. On most (but not all) issues, presidents and other party elites can convince their own party faithful in the electorate to support their positions. Consensus requires significant buy-in from independents and partisans of the opposite party. It is *trusting* out-party partisans who are most likely to provide such a bridge. They are the most willing to make the ideological sacrifice necessary for consensus to develop (Rudolph and Popp 2009).

Considered through this lens, the data in figure 1.2 suggest that, historically, between 30 percent and 40 percent of Democrats have been willing to make ideological sacrifices insofar as that percentage of Democrats has tended to trust the government. Such relatively high levels of trust in government from the Nixon to early Bush years facilitated policy making for Republican presidents. Although Democratic presidents Carter and Clinton worked in a somewhat more difficult environment than their Republican counterparts, the percentages of trusting Republicans during their times in office were not nearly as vanishingly low as they were during Obama's presidency. Back then, consensus building across party lines in the electorate was still possible.

Lately, changes in the trust environment have made consensus building more complicated regardless of which party is in power. Figure 1.3 tells the story. Democrats' trust in government when run by a Republican president and Republican majorities in both houses of Congress was relatively high through 2004. Starting in 2005, however, Democrats' trust in government nosedived, though Republicans continued to trust it quite a lot, at least into 2006. In February 2005, for example, 55 percent of GOP identifiers reported that they trusted the government to do what is right at least "most of the time" even as the economy began to slow and the wars in Iraq and Afghanistan trudged on. In contrast, only 21 percent of Democrats did—much lower than the historical norm for Democrats. Bush's agenda began to founder. It was at this point in his presidency that Bush failed to accomplish much of anything, with signature initiatives like Social Security privatization and comprehensive immigration reform dying in Congress. Low trust among Democrats was particularly germane to the failure of Social Security privatization (Rudolph and Popp 2009). With the percentage of potential ideological sacrificers among mass-level Democrats dwindling, there was little to push elite-level Democrats toward action.

When Barack Obama assumed the presidency with Democratic majorities in both houses of Congress, Democratic partisans returned to their usual level of trust, with between 30 percent and 40 percent trusting the government in Washington to do what was right at least most of the time.

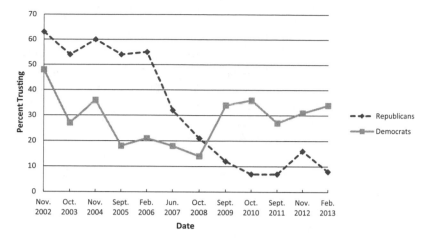

FIGURE I.3. Political trust by partisanship, 2002–12

Trust among Republicans, however, reached unprecedentedly low levels. Consistent with the snapshot we showed in figure 1.1, political trust among Republicans during Obama's first term was often in the single digits. The near complete absence of Republicans who would be good candidates to make an ideological sacrifice during the period placed a brake on policy making that remains in place to this day. Although the situation has been particularly difficult for a Democratic president, readers will see throughout the book that an absence of government trust hamstrings Republican presidents just as it does Democratic ones, as George W. Bush learned in the last three years of his presidency. Chronically low levels of trust along with its polarization are central to the story of political dysfunction.

Plan of the Book

In the chapters that follow, we further explore this partisan polarization of trust and its costly consequences. We start in chapter 2 by defining our key terms: "polarization," "political trust," and "institutional responsiveness." Although we agree with Fiorina et al. (2005) and others that Americans' ideological predispositions and policy preferences are not polarized, we argue that this is not the only way that polarization might manifest itself in the public. We go on to show that Americans' feelings about their opponents have, in fact, polarized. These polarized feelings are, in turn, central to why trust in government has polarized.

To understand why trust became polarized, we must first establish what causes it to change. In chapter 3, we employ time-series analysis to this end. Our results point to the central importance of issue salience. Trust is much higher when the public is focused on international rather than domestic problems. In addition, we find that since fewer people think the economy is important during good times than they do during bad times, good economies increase trust less than poor economies diminish it. Taken together, the results in chapter 3 imply that it is unlikely that political trust will ever return to 1960s levels for any length of time.

Although partisans of the governing party have always tended to trust government a little more than out-party partisans, the gap is very large today, with distrust of government among out-party partisans being nearly universal. In chapter 4, we use the lessons from chapter 3 as clues in our search for the causes of this recent polarization. We identify two key factors. First, we find that partisans' more negative feelings about the other party are central to the rise of polarized trust. Second, consistent with theories of motivated reasoning (Kunda 1990; Lodge and Taber 2000, 2013; Rudolph 2006; Taber and Lodge 2006), we find that partisans of different stripes perceive the political world increasingly differently depending on whether their party is in power. What's more, partisans now update their trust evaluations based on different criteria from each other, selectively focusing on information that favors their allies and disfavors their adversaries.

The next four chapters demonstrate the consequences of low and polarized trust. In chapter 5, we further leverage the importance of what parts of government become salient to people to demonstrate that the potential range of trust's effects is much wider than previously believed. Specifically, the *effects* of political trust on policy support depend on which issues are made salient to people before being asked how much they trust the government. In chapter 6, we further test our thinking by using survey data from a random cross section of Americans. With 9/11 serving as a natural experiment, we show that political trust did not affect attitudes about race-targeted programs in the years after the attack, as it usually does (Hetherington and Globetti 2002), but instead affected a range of foreign policies and national defense preferences that it had not affected before. Ironically, our results suggest that Republicans, the antigovernment party, appear to benefit from a deeper reservoir of trust-based support when they are in office. We also begin to explore the important real-world implications of the *polarization* of trust. Specifically, we find that the gradual, then rapid, drop in trust among liberals during the middle-to-late Bush years is central to understanding why they stopped supporting the wars, ultimately turning Iraq into the most polarized conflict of the survey era (Jacobson 2006).

Although trust started to drop and polarize during the George W. Bush years, it would become still lower and more polarized during Barack Obama's presidency, with profound consequences. In chapter 7, we demonstrate that those who hope to use the machinery of government to jumpstart a reeling economy face an uphill climb. When the economy most needs stimulus (namely, when it is poor), trust in government tends to be low, which undermines support for running deficits and increasing government spending, particularly among conservatives. However, we find that low trust has no effect on support for using tax cuts as stimulus. To the extent that tax cuts have a less powerful effect than do spending increases in stimulating the economy, this knot of relationships appears to harm policy efficacy. In chapter 8, we establish the centrality of trust to explaining the ebb of public support for the Affordable Care Act (a.k.a. Obamacare). Using a unique series of tracking polls, we demonstrate that declining support for health care reform resulted from three interrelated trends: the decline of political trust, the increase in people who thought health care reform would affect their families negatively, and a surge in conservative self-identification. Collectively, these trends combined to make the idea of a national health plan unpalatable to the American public, which, in turn, helps explain the brutal end game to the legislative process.

In chapter 9, we provide some ideas about what might increase and depolarize trust. Specifically, we find that polarization about government shrinks if we focus people on its specific parts rather than the whole. People always view the specific parts of government as more trustworthy than the government as a whole, which helps explain why Americans say they hate government but want to do away with precious little of it. In a second survey experiment, we find that reminding people about some of the things that government does well can increase political trust to some degree. However, we find that these effects are strongest among Democrats and liberals, which means that increasing trust with positive information about government will not do anything to mitigate its polarization.

Finally, we recap the main points of the book. We explore whether polarization based on deep dislike and severe distrust of the other side

is perhaps even worse than polarization based on ideological or policy differences. We suspect it is. In addition, we explain why scholars have tended
to underestimate the importance of political trust. Up to now, finding relationships between political trust and variables of normative import has
depended a lot on studying the phenomena at the "right" time—when it is
salient. Finally, we question how likely it is that circumstances will change
for the better any time soon.

Polarization, Political Trust, and Institutional Responsiveness

Embedded in our argument about the causes of political dysfunction lay several key, interrelated terms: "polarization," "political trust," and "institutional responsiveness." The meanings of these terms all seem straightforward, but they are more elusive than one might first imagine. We therefore define and explain each in detail in this chapter. We argue that, taken together, they help explain the roots of political dysfunction in the United States. Partisans today are polarized not in their policy preferences but rather in their feelings about each other. As a result, political trust has polarized by party, leading to an absence of policy consensus and a gridlocked political system with little incentive to compromise. This is why Washington does not work right now.

We begin by discussing polarization with a particular emphasis on whether the mass public is polarized in a meaningful way. We realize that the existence of polarization must seem self-evident to many, but it turns out that it is not. Indeed, scholars have, to date, turned up strikingly little firm evidence of polarization in the electorate. In this section, we explain why. And, more important, we present evidence that polarization actually does exist among ordinary Americans, just not where scholars have typically been looking. Because trust is one of the areas where polarization in the electorate manifests itself, we next define political trust and explain why it is an important influence in causing people to support government programs. In addition, we explain the key role it can play in helping citizens overcome ideological differences to forge consensus in their opinions about public policy. We then discuss the difficulties inherent in the legislative process and the role that public opinion has played in the past to nudge the legislative process forward. We argue that it is a role that it is much less likely to play in a polarized political environment. We conclude with a methodological digression that is critically important to supporting the scholarly contribution of our argument. Here we tackle issues about causality and how the multiple methodological tools we employ help us make reliable inferences throughout the book.

On Polarization

Some readers might be shocked to learn that a controversy exists about whether the electorate is polarized. Of course it is, or so it seems. But the reality is not so simple. As is the case with many scholarly debates, whether or not one thinks the electorate is polarized depends on what one means by polarization or where one looks for it. If polarization means that most Americans are staunch liberals or conservatives, like the people who represent them in Congress, then the answer is a resounding no. Consider the data in figure 2.1. As it has done since 1972, the American National Election Study (ANES) asked people in 2012 to place themselves on a seven-point scale arrayed from "extremely liberal" to "extremely conservative." Moderate or middle of the road occupies the midpoint of the scale. People can also opt out of placing themselves by answering that they "haven't thought much about it." The figure makes clear that nearly

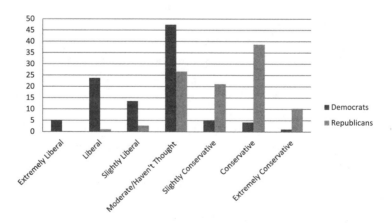

FIGURE 2.1. Ideological self-identification by party identification

Source: American National Election Study, 2012.

half of Democrats and plenty of Republicans, too, either consider them-selves "moderate" or say they haven't thought enough about it to place themselves on the ideological spectrum. In fact, these counterintuitive re-sults appear so clear that one might be tempted to assert that polarization is a media-driven myth (Fiorina et al. 2005).

Before embracing the seemingly counterintuitive notion that polariza-tion does not exist in the American electorate, it is probably useful to keep in mind that polarization connotes something more than how a picture looks. Moreover, it might be found in places other than people's ideo-logical leanings and policy preferences. As for how a picture looks, some dismiss polarization claims based on two features of the distribution: (1) the bars in the middle are too tall and (2) the bars in the tails are not sufficiently "fat." We address both these concerns below.

As for the presence of many people clustered in the middle of the dis-tribution, it is very clearly true. That said, we wonder whether the center of distributions regarding Americans' preferences and evaluations about *anything*—political or otherwise—would look markedly different. In explaining why Americans pay little attention to politics, scholars often cite "rational ignorance" (Downs 1957). The idea is that people do not care much about politics because they get so little payoff from caring. The story goes that people do care about other things, such as work, fam-ily, and, let's say, baseball. We suspect that if one were to ask a random sample of Americans about their "policy preferences" about the national pastime, the value of advanced statistics (so called sabermetrics) would arouse the deepest divisions. Younger, mathematically inclined fans think they are indispensable. Older, more traditional fans think they are worth-less. It seems there would be potential for polarization. Yet, a 2007 Gallup Poll found that only 45 percent of Americans called themselves baseball fans.[1] That probably means the 55 percent of Americans who do not call themselves baseball fans would cluster in the middle of any distribution of preferences for sabermetrics or almost anything else that has to do with baseball. This is a lot like opinions about politics.

One might argue that baseball is a silly example. Its popularity is on the wane, and not everyone is expected to follow it to be a good citizen. Fair enough. Everyone has to eat, so perhaps food would attract more noncentrist evaluations. In 2012, the Huffington Post published a feature on the ten most polarizing foods.[2] Cilantro occupied the top spot. Ap-parently there are physiological reasons that help explain why people ei-ther love or hate cilantro. However, we suspect that a large percentage of

Americans would have no opinion about cilantro. If asked about their cilantro sentiments, these people would be most inclined to report that they
were either neutral about it or had not thought enough about cilantro to
form an opinion, just like in politics.

The point here is that it is hard to imagine a preference distribution
that would not be heavily weighted in the middle. As it relates to politics, specifically, we know that, among the less informed, survey responses
tend to cluster in the middle of the scale (Delli Carpini and Keeter 1996).
This is because people do not want to appear ignorant when a survey
interviewer asks them a question. As a result, they provide answers about
things they do not fully understand, and these answers tend to be in the
middle of the scale because that is the safest haven between two alternatives that they cannot make much sense of.

The other concern that skeptics of polarization raise is the absence of
fat tails. "Fat tails" indicate that a substantial number of people have opinions near the polar extremes. Defining polarization as such requires a very
literal understanding of polarization. However, the problem with such a
literal definition as it relates to public opinion data, specifically, is that it,
too, may be a standard that is impossible to meet. Whereas a high percentage of the uniformed will tend toward the middle, we suspect that many
among the well informed would rather not think of *themselves* as extreme
ideologically or extreme in their policy preferences. Extremity carries a
negative connotation in American political life. Just ask Barry Goldwater,
circa 1964.[3] When the news media identifies friends and foes in foreign
policy, the line of demarcation is usually presented as moderate good guys
versus extremist bad guys. Not surprisingly, then, Americans would rather
think about their political opponents than their own side as extreme. As
evidence, the percentage of Democrats who classify the Republican Party
as "extremely conservative" has climbed from 8 percent in 1972, the first
time this question was asked by the ANES, to 38 percent in 2012. The percentage of Republicans who classify the Democratic Party as "extremely
liberal" has climbed from 5 percent to 31 percent over the same period.
In contrast, only 9 percent of Democrats and 15 percent of Republicans
see their own parties as extreme (Hetherington and Roush n.d.). Taken
together, these two simple regularities about survey research and American public opinion all but guarantee that pictures of public opinion about
issues or ideology like the one in figure 2.1 will never *look* particularly
polarized, even if polarization, perhaps considered differently, does exist.

Scholars have employed alternatives to a literal definition of polarization in their examination of policy preferences. They possess certain

advantages over the literal definition, but they are not perfect either. The most common alternative is to consider polarization in terms of a *growing distance* between the preferences of people who identify with the political parties. Such a reckoning suggests Democrats are pulling to the left and Republicans to the right—that polarization is a process, not just a state. By this definition, significant evidence of polarization exists. There is more distance between partisans on policy preferences today than a few decades ago. For example, the Pew Research Foundation released a report in the summer of 2012 that many scholars and journalists used as evidence of growing polarization in the electorate. In it, Pew revealed that, on a battery of forty-eight policy and values items they have tracked since 1987, the average Republican and average Democrat were eighteen percentage points apart. The difference was only about 10 percentage points when Pew first started to ask these questions in the 1980s, so it appears that the US electorate is in the *process* of polarizing.

There are, however, problems with thinking about polarization this way, too. Although we like the notion that polarization might be best thought of as a process rather than a state, what if the increase in distance between Republicans and Democrats was from 1 percentage point to 5 percentage points? Given that the distance could theoretically be 100 percentage points, such a relatively small difference, even if growing, seems to suggest something other than polarization. Even 18 percentage points might not seem like much to many. For the process to rise to the level of polarization, how far apart do the average Republican and the average Democrat have to be? As a practical matter, the emphasis on "how far apart" can encourage a Potter Stewart–esque approach to assessing whether polarization exists. Stewart, readers might recall, was the Supreme Court Justice in the 1960s who said that he could not define obscenity but that he knew it when he saw it. Just as with experts at an art exhibit, two scholars can look at that the same data and reach different conclusions about how much difference is enough to claim that polarization in the electorate exists.

In addition, the larger average distances between partisans have most often developed from people sorting themselves into the correct party (conservative Democrats becoming Republicans and liberal Republicans becoming Democrats) without many in either party taking a more extreme position on much of anything (Fiorina et al. 2005; Levendusky 2009). Although we have argued above that scholars should not be overly focused on how fat the tails of distributions are, it still seems to us that something about people's opinions must become more extreme to merit the term "polarization." It is possible to identify groups in the electorate that do show evidence of more extreme position-taking. In fact, among the most knowledgeable 10–15 percent of the electorate, the distribution of preferences of Republicans and Democrats looks much like the picture of polarization in Congress that we show below in figure 2.2b (Lauderdale 2013). But 10–15 percent of the electorate seems a small sliver indeed.

Another alternative that polarization proponents have pursued is to demonstrate a greater consistency of opinion. Specifically, Democrats and Republicans today give more consistently liberal and conservative responses, respectively, when asked their opinions about various issues than in decades past (Abramowitz and Saunders 2008; Abramowitz 2010). Converse (1964) labeled this understanding of "what goes with what" *constraint*. Although we agree that constraint has increased dramatically, greater constraint and greater extremity are not synonymous. Consider a Democrat who, on five issues, places himself one point to the left of center of a seven-point scale. He would score a maximum five points. Consider a second Democrat who, on the same five issues, places herself at one on four of the issues and at the scale's midpoint on one of them. That respondent would receive a score of only four points. It would be hard to argue, however, that the opinions of the second respondent are not more extreme, or polarized, than those of the first.

Moreover, we wonder how *meaningful* people's opinions on a matter are if they are willing to change their position on it simply because they have come to learn their party leaders believe a certain thing. People tend to change opinions on things that are peripheral to who they are politically and hold fast to the things that matter to them (Converse 1964). This is important because polarization conceptually suggests people care deeply about something. People who change their minds about an issue because of a party cue do not seem particularly intense in their preference about that issue to us.[4]

In sum, we perceive problems with assessing polarization in the electorate based on a literal definition because, as it relates to policy and ideology, it is a standard that is impossible to meet. We are somewhat more satisfied with the notion that polarization is best thought of as a process, with increasing average distances between groups over time. But we are unsettled by the fact that the process of polarization in Americans' policy preferences and ideology is mostly driven by party sorting rather than people taking increasingly extreme positions. Some indication of a greater extremity of beliefs seems conceptually critical in the term "polarization."

Hence we believe that further alternatives to thinking about how polarization in the electorate might manifest itself must be explored.

Is Polarization in Washington Exclusively Ideological?

In focusing their search on ideology and policy preferences for evidence of polarization in the electorate, we believe scholars might be looking in the wrong places. Our thinking is, in part, driven by the belief that the nature of the divide between Republicans and Democrats in Congress is somewhat less ideological than is commonly believed. What members of Congress definitely do much more today than they used to is vote the same way as other members of their party caucus. Scholars and congressional observers have many different ways to measure party unity (see, for example, Carson et al. 2010; Crespin, Rohde, and Vander Wielen 2013; Krehbiel 2000; Rohde 1991). All tell the same story. The parties in Congress vote *en bloc* much more often today than before, and the two caucuses disagree much more often today than before.

The most common interpretation of this change in congressional behavior is that congressional parties are *ideologically* polarized today. The evidence for the emergence of ideological polarization is usually depicted in graphs like those presented in figures 2.2a and 2.2b. They capture two snapshots of the apparent ideology of Republican and Democratic House members, one taken in the 1970s and the other in the 2000s. Keith Poole and Howard Rosenthal developed the measure of ideology we use in the figures, called a DW-NOMINATE score. They use all available roll call votes to generate an estimate of each House member's ideology in such a way that they can be compared over time. Figure 2.2a displays the distribution of House ideology in 1973–74, broken down by party. Figure 2.2b displays the distribution using data from 2011 to 2012.

It is readily apparent that the middle has disappeared from Congress. In the 92nd Congress, 108 members, nearly a quarter of the House, had scores between −0.2 and 0.2. Indeed, 80 or so conservative Democratic and liberal Republican House members would have fit comfortably in the other party back then. The most common category for Republican members of the House to fall into was between 0.2 and 0.3 on this scale, and the most common category for Democrats was between −0.4 and −0.5.

Compare these data with those from the present day. In the 112th Congress, which is the most recent for which data are available, only 15 of the 435 members of the House had DW-NOMINATE scores between −0.2

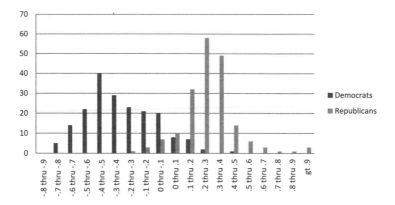

FIGURE 2.2A. "Ideology" of members of House of Representatives, 92nd (1973–74) Congress by party, DW-NOMINATE scores

Source: Voteview.com, http://www.voteview.com.

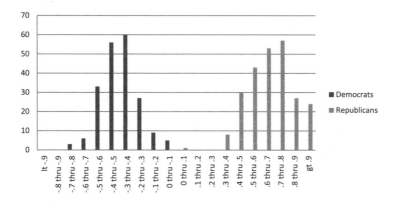

FIGURE 2.2B. "Ideology" of members of House of Representatives, 112th (2011–12) Congress by party, DW-NOMINATE scores

Sources: American National Election Study, 2011, cumulative data file; American National Election Study, 2012, YouGov survey.

and 0.2. Whereas fewer than 30 Republicans had ideology scores of 0.4 or more in the 92nd Congress, all but 9 of them had scores at least that high in the 112th Congress. In fact, as recently as the 110th Congress, only 7 Republicans had DW-NOMINATE scores of greater than 0.8, but that number reached 51 only 4 years later.[5] Regardless, the key point here is that there is complete ideological separation between the parties in Congress these days.

In the scholarly debate about polarization in the electorate, skeptics point to how different the distribution of ideology in the public depicted in figure 2.1 looks compared with the distribution of ideology in the House of Representatives depicted in figure 2.2b. The complete separation of Republicans from Democrats in Congress, combined with more members now near the poles, is all but universally interpreted as ideological polarization in Congress. The absence of such a picture as it relates to ideology in the electorate causes many scholars to argue that the public is not polarized.

We believe the story is more complicated as it relates to polarization both in Congress and, as a consequence, in the electorate. First, congressional polarization is likely not exclusively ideological. Recall that the measure of ideology that we used to create figures 2.2a and 2.2b (and all the other measures of ideology that scholars and congressional observers use) was derived from the votes cast by members of Congress. It is just an assumption that members' votes are driven by their ideology as opposed to some other motivation. In general, such an assumption makes sense. Scholars have known for decades that office holders are much more ideological than ordinary Americans are (Converse 1964; McClosky and Brill 1983; Sniderman, Brody, and Tetlock 1991). In fact, there is plenty of evidence that members are more ideologically motivated now than when the landmark studies comparing representatives and the represented were carried out (Cohen et al. 2008).

We suspect, however, that something in addition to ideology drives congressional voting behavior at times. How else can conservative ideas become liberal ideas in the space of fewer than twenty years? In a June 2012 *New Yorker* article titled "Why Republicans Oppose the Individual Health-Care Mandate," Ezra Klein traces how a number of policies that Democrats pursued in Barack Obama's first term were born in conservative think tanks such as the Heritage Foundation. For example, the most controversial part of Obamacare, the individual mandate, was the conservative key to lowering rates by increasing the risk pool to include healthy people while generating lots of new business for insurance companies, a frequent ally of Republican lawmakers. Similarly, insurance exchanges for those not covered by their employer rely on a market approach to pooling risk, which is designed to lower rates for the self-employed and those who work for businesses too small to provide group insurance plans. Conservatives tend to like markets more than liberals do. Republican governor of Massachusetts Mitt Romney championed what is widely considered the state-level pilot program that Obamacare would later be based on. He received almost unanimous support from Republicans in both the state house and state senate. Fewer than ten years later, however, only a single Republican voted for the Affordable Care Act (ACA) when it came before Congress.

Obamacare is not the only example. Republicans universally argued against greatly increased government spending as stimulus after financial sector panic of 2008–9, but Ronald Reagan, the great touchstone of modern American conservatism, governed as a Keynesian in the early 1980s when economic times were tough. George W. Bush apparently had no fear of deficit spending in the early 2000s either. We don't mean to suggest that only Republicans are guilty of ideological hypocrisy. When Republicans during George W. Bush's presidency adopted several Democratic ideas, such as a Medicare prescription drug plan and a national approach to education testing, Democrats in Washington provided little support. These examples all suggest that even the more ideological parties of today are not rigidly ideological.

Rather than ideology, perhaps a central reason Obama's approach to health care (or cap and trade or any number of other proposals) became unacceptable to Republican lawmakers in the 2000s was that Democrats advocated it. In other words, the GOP's motivation to oppose it was partisan, not ideological. Indeed, scholars have shown that a large number of the votes that make up measures of congressional ideology come from votes on procedure; they are not solely votes on policy matters (Theriault 2008). Even when the vote in question does involve a policy matter, it is possible that there is a partisan advantage to be gained from holding such a vote. For example, in the 2011–12 Congress, the measures of congressional ideology that apparently reveal so much ideological polarization include no fewer than forty separate votes in the House to repeal health care reform (Clinton, Katznelson, and Lapinski forthcoming). Holding all those votes was clearly a partisan tactic employed by Republicans to remind their base just how strongly they opposed President Obama.

The politics of the late-1800s provide a good illustration of our thinking. The "Gilded Age" Congresses from 1876 to 1896 appear, by measures of ideological polarization like the DW-NOMINATE score, to be among the most polarized ever. During this period, however, the substance of party disagreements was rarely ideological. Instead, they most often revolved around patronage and how government benefits would be distributed (Lee n.d.). In a similar vein, the New Deal Congresses reveal among the lowest levels of party polarization, despite the fact that huge ideological principles about the proper role of government were at stake, and pitched battles were waged across party lines (Clinton, Katznelson, and Lapinski forthcoming). One reason that the measures of polarization might not pick up what they are supposed to is that the Gilded Age Congresses featured close partisan margins, which encouraged more party-line voting. In contrast, the New Deal Congresses featured enormous Democratic majorities, which allowed a fair number of members to buck party leadership without endangering final passages of bills.

Indeed, research increasingly suggests that the close partisan margins in the House and Senate drive much of the acrimony in Washington today (see especially Lee 2009). When caucus leaders from the minority party believe the next election could put them in the majority, they are loath to cooperate with their adversaries. The minority does not want to provide the majority with accomplishments that they can run on in the next election (Lee 2009; Mann and Ornstein 2012). The close margins also produce a team mentality among caucus members that creates more pressure to toe the party line.[6] Combined with the stronger powers that contemporary congressional leaders wield, close margins in Congress contribute to party line voting. The key point here is that, in such cases, there is nothing inherently philosophical or ideological about the disagreements between Republicans and Democrats.[7]

In making this distinction between partisanship and ideology, we are not arguing that congressional polarization is devoid of ideology. We fully believe that there is an important ideological component to congressional polarization. Many, perhaps even most, party disagreements do have the age-old conflict between activist and limited government at their core. However, it is equally clear to us that at least some of what *appears* to be ideological polarization in Congress is simply partisanship, in that it is motivated by a desire to rob the other party of victory. As such, disagreements between congressional parties are not always the result of overarching philosophical differences about what government ought to do, even though our measures of ideology in Congress tacitly treat them as such.

The reason we have explored the basis of polarization among office holders is because we think it suggests the need for a wider search for polarization in the electorate. If congressional polarization is not solely about ideology, then perhaps ideological preferences are not the only, or even best, places to look for polarization in the electorate. Based on research about the survey response and the apparent nature of conflict between the parties in Washington, it is little wonder to us that ordinary Americans fail to line up consistently on the far right and far left on policy questions or in their ideological predispositions. Whether out of disinterest, dispassion, or an inability to keep up with party elites' latest zigs and zags, ordinary Americans' preferences will always tend to cluster toward the middle and lack extremity. This, however, does not mean that polarization doesn't exist.

Our Approach to Polarization

To recap, we have argued that ideology and issue preferences might not be the best place to search for polarization in the electorate, particularly when using a literal definition of polarization in assessing its presence or absence. Because a substantial percentage of Americans do not know much about political issues or what an ideology is, a substantial percentage of their responses will cluster in the center of distributions. And because people would rather think of themselves as moderate and their opponents as extreme, distributions of opinion about policy matters and ideology will rarely produce fat tails. That much we know from decades studying how people respond to public opinion polls. Not only that, but the cues that party elites provide are not exclusively ideological. Much of it is raw political conflict driven by desire to gain political advantage.

If ideological predispositions and issue preferences are the wrong places to look, then what is the right place? We believe indications of polarization ought to be rooted in how people *feel* rather than in how they think or where they stand. Because it takes much less expertise to express strong feelings than it takes to express strong policy preferences, a smaller percentage of Americans will disqualify themselves from appearing polarized because of their political ignorance. Consider, for example, the iconic Tea Party member carrying a sign warning the federal government to keep its hands off her Medicare ("don't steal from Medicare to pay for socialized medicine"). She might have a hard time expressing to a survey interviewer where she stands ideologically, even though she clearly cares very deeply about something political; however, we suspect she would have no trouble expressing her dislike and distrust of the Democratic Party and President Obama.

Much has happened during the past generation that might polarize political feelings. First and foremost, the polarization of elite-level politics is critical. The opinions that ordinary Americans express almost always reflect how those in Washington behave (Key 1966). When elites are more partisan, the masses are, too (Hetherington 2001). As we detailed above, officeholders today provide the impression that partisans of different stripes do not agree on anything, big or small. This provides partisans in the electorate a sense that the ideas of the other side are not worth considering—that those on the other side are flawed and do not possess the right values and goals. Ordinary Americans will follow these cues as best they can, with expressions of negative feelings being the most likely manifestation.

The way politics is presented to people has also changed over the past generation to encourage stronger affective reactions. Iyengar and his various collaborators place much of the blame on increasingly negative political campaigns (see Iyengar, Sood, and Lelkes 2012; Iyengar and Westwood 2014). But that is not all that has changed. The emergence of cable news outlets like Fox News and MSNBC, along with websites such as Red State and Talking Points Memo, allow people to live inside information bubbles that constantly remind them that their side is good and, especially, that the other side is bad. This departs from a bygone era when most everyone, regardless of political predispositions, watched the same three national news programs and read newspapers that adhered to the same neutrality norms. Similarly, political talk shows these days are purposefully presented in an uncivil manner that violates social norms and, as a consequence, sharpens feelings (Mutz and Reeves 2005). The O'Reilly Factor of today is not at all like the Meet the Press of yesteryear. Although a surprisingly small percentage of Americans view these programs and read these blogs themselves (Prior 2013), those who do will tend to be opinion leaders for others in their peer groups. This means that the changed media environment could have an important indirect effect on a large cross section of the public.

In addition, the contemporary issue agenda is ripe to produce stronger feelings. Carmines and Stimson (1989) suggest that only easy, symbolic issues that operate at the gut level, such as race, have the power to polarize. Race is not alone among salient issues with such power. Another is abortion rights (Adams 1997). Although it is true that the majority of Americans have a "pro-choice-but" position on the issue (Fiorina, Abrams, and Pope 2010), that reality might be less important than how people perceive it. Abortion is polarizing because of what it stands for—for example, what it says about the proper role of women in society and the values that accompany that position (Luker 1985) or how the unborn ought to be considered. Such symbolic conflicts may transcend specific issues. Hetherington and Weiler (2009) argue that the American political system has evolved such that a central element of party identification hinges on fundamental views of how a good society ought to operate. Should it be more hierarchically organized and authority based, or should it be more horizontally organized and authority questioning? They suggest that political conflicts are more polarizing when issues that touch on this worldview divide become salient. Of consequence, a plethora of such issues are central to party conflict today, including race, feminism, crime and punishment, sexual orientation, immigration, and how to deal with terrorism.

Because so many easy, symbolic issues now occupy considerable space on the political agenda, we suspect that, increasingly, those on one side of the divide have come to view their political opponents as nefarious characters with dangerous ideas. Hence polarized feelings might be more likely to show up in assessments of enemies rather than of friends. Even if people do not see those on their own side as angels, they may see those on the other as devils. Such assessments of the other side, however, probably will not manifest as extreme policy preferences or ideological predispositions, which is where scholars have been looking for polarization. People are motivated to see their own positions as moderate and responsible. It is those on the other side who are extreme. It is in their feelings about the other side that polarization ought to manifest.

Evidence of Affective Polarization

When scholars have looked for polarization in feelings (so-called affective polarization), they have often found it (see, for example, Haidt and Hetherington 2012). Iyengar, Sood, and Lelkes (2012) turn up many indications of polarized feelings, none more interesting than the increased discomfort partisans express in the proposition that a family member might marry a person who identifies with the other party. Back in the 1960s, almost no Americans, neither Republicans nor Democrats, expressed any concern at all about "partisan intermarriage." In 2010, however, a third of Democrats and nearly half of Republicans expressed at least moderate concern about nuptials across party lines. In a follow-up paper, Iyengar and Westwood (2014) demonstrate that feelings about parties are sufficiently strong today to produce both implicit and explicit biases that are stronger than even those attached to race. For example, partisans

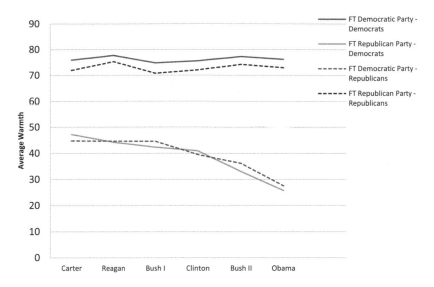

FIGURE 2.3. Feelings about the parties by partisanship

Sources: American National Election Study, 2011, cumulative data file; American National Election Study, 2011 and 2012, YouGov survey.

were much more likely to favor the résumés of people who had the same partisanship than those who had the same race. Partisan bias persisted, moreover, even when the résumés of their copartisans were not impressive. Similarly, a 2014 Pew Research Center study revealed that more than a quarter of Democrats and more than a third of Republicans viewed the other party as "a threat to the nation's well-being." It is hard to imagine a more extreme manifestation of negative feelings. More generally, Pew found that partisans' "very unfavorable" attitudes toward the other party more than doubled between 1994 and 2004 (Pew Research Center 2014).

To explore more systematically how people's feelings about political combatants have changed over time, we turn again to the ANES. It has been asking people since the 1970s to place the major political parties on what they call "feeling thermometers." People can rate groups they like as high as one hundred degrees and groups they dislike as low as zero degrees. If people have neutral feelings toward a group, they are instructed to rate them at fifty degrees.

Figure 2.3 reveals that Democrats' feelings about the Republican Party and Republicans' feelings about the Democratic Party have grown much more negative of late, while their feelings about their own party have remained constant over time. This is much as we expected and what others have also shown (see, for example, Haidt and Hetherington 2012; Iyengar, Sood, and Lelkes 2012). We group the data in the figure by presidential administration to smooth out some of the year-by-year noise. Although specific years do not appear in the figure, it is sometimes useful to reference them, which we do below.

Early in the time series, those who identified with a party did not express much distaste for the other party. Over the course of the Reagan years, for example, the average score that a Republican rated the Democratic Party was forty-five degrees, and the average score that a Democrat rated the Republican Party was forty-four degrees. These are not exactly balmy temperatures, but they are warm enough to allow students in Maine to break out the Bermuda shorts in March.[8] Fast forwarding to 2000, partisans, particularly Republicans, had grown somewhat more negative toward the other side. Republicans rated the Democratic Party at an average of thirty-eight degrees, whereas Democrats in 2000 rated the Republicans at forty-one degrees—a little lower than they did during the Reagan years.

By 2008, partisans' feelings toward the other party had dropped more noticeably, especially, this time, among Democrats. They rated the Republican Party at an icy thirty degrees. Republicans' average rating of the Democrats also dropped in 2008 to a barely liquid thirty-four degrees. To put those scores into perspective, the average score that all Americans gave to "illegal immigrants"—no one's favorite group—was forty degrees. Feelings about gays and lesbians among Americans during the height of the AIDS epidemic in the mid-to-late 1980s were about the same as those that partisans expressed about the other party during the George W. Bush years.

Partisans' feelings about the other party would only grow more negative during Obama's first term. Although the ANES did not ask feeling thermometer questions in 2010, YouGov, an Internet-based survey firm that gathers and weights data from national samples, did in 2011.[9] That survey found that Republicans gave the Democratic Party an average reading of only eighteen degrees; Democrats gave the Republican Party the same Lambeau Field in December-like temperature reading.[10] Although ANES data indicate that feelings about the other side warmed a bit in 2012, the averages were still unprecedentedly low relative to the rest of the ANES time series.

Because opinion extremity is often considered an important component of polarization, we examine how the distributions of responses from Democrats and Republicans to the party feeling thermometers have changed over time. Do these distributions show movement toward the poles that those who champion a literal definition of polarization require as evidence? To answer this question, we break the one-hundred-degree political party thermometers into ten separate ten-degree wide intervals and compare two snapshots, one taken in 1980, the first presidential election year the ANES asked the party thermometers, and the other taken in 2012, the most recent presidential election year that the ANES asked the thermometers. Recall from the data in figure 2.3 that we are unlikely to see change in the distribution of how partisans feel about their own party. Those have remained relatively constant over time. Our focus is on the distributions of feelings that partisans express about the other party. That said, partisans' feelings about their own party have always been pretty positive, with a definite clustering of responses toward the favorable pole of the distribution in both snapshots.

The results appear in figure 2.4. Unlike people's ideological self-placement or how they place themselves on issue scales, we see significant movement toward the feeling thermometer poles, specifically as it relates to partisans' increased negativity toward the other party. Back in 1980, only about 7 percent of Republicans and Democrats, respectively, provided the other party feeling thermometer scores of ten degrees or fewer. And a little more than 10 percent of Republicans and Democrats provided scores of twenty degrees or fewer to their political adversaries. For partisans of both stripes, the most common score they provided for the other party fell in the interval between forty-one and fifty degrees.

The story was fundamentally different in 2012. Fully 30 percent of Democrats provided the Republican Party a feeling thermometer score of ten degrees or fewer—about twice the percentage that falls into any other interval. The other two most highly populated intervals other than the most negative one were those between eleven and twenty degrees and twenty-one and thirty degrees. Indeed, more than 60 percent of Democrats' responses about the Republican Party fell in the three intervals at or closest to the unfavorable pole. Increasingly polarized feelings about the Democratic Party are also occurring among Republican partisans. In 2012, the most common Republican rating of the Democratic Party was between zero and ten degrees. Similar to the Democrats, about 58 percent of Republican responses fell into the coolest three intervals, those representing scores of thirty degrees or fewer. In sum, Republicans and Democrats are abandoning the middle and heading for the poles in their negative feelings about the other party.[11]

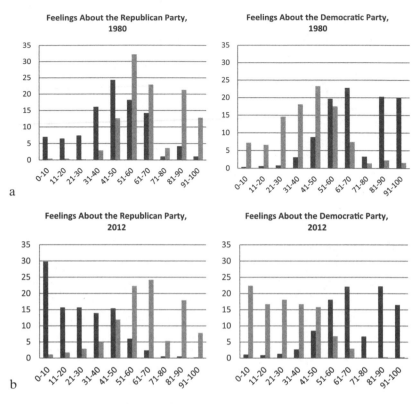

FIGURE 2.4. Increasingly negative feelings about the other party, 1980 and 2012

Sources: American National Election Study, 2012, cumulative data file; American National Election Study, 2012.

Is it of consequence that partisans today dislike the other side so much more intensely? We suspect it has had pernicious, indirect effects that bear directly on the thesis of this book. Specifically, we argue that increased dislike of the opposition party is central to understanding the decrease in trust in government expressed by partisans of one side when the other side is in power. This is so because people generally do not tend to trust things they do not like. Hence, when the government is run by a party that a person strongly dislikes—a condition that is now the norm—he or she will be unlikely to express much trust in government. We provide evidence for our contention in chapter 4.

For now, we again emphasize the extreme partisan nature of trust responses. Recall from chapter 1 that, in 2010, more than 50 percent of self-identified Republicans said that they *never* trusted the government in Washington to do what is right. Never. They could have said "almost always," "most of the time," or even just "some of the time." But when we gave them the option to say "never," more than 50 percent of out-party partisans availed themselves of the opportunity to offer this evaluation. "Never" is an extreme word. Indeed, many of us are brought up to "never say never." Like with feelings that people express about people or groups, it also makes sense that we might find evidence of polarization in trust evaluations. Trust in government is an easy concept to understand. Unlike with issues and ideology, people do not have to be experts to know how much they trust something. Almost everyone has experience forming trust judgments in their everyday lives. Trust in government is just an extension of a familiar task.

In sum, we believe a central reason scholars have struggled to turn up evidence of polarization in the electorate is that they have been looking in the wrong places. The focus has most often been on areas that are notoriously difficult for many Americans to understand. Because less knowledgeable people tend to place themselves in the middle categories when asked about policies and ideology (e.g., Delli Carpini and Keeter 1996; Treier and Hillygus 2009), a focus on such areas will bias findings toward moderation. Feelings about the parties and simple heuristics like trust are different. They require little political expertise. In that sense, we find polarization in the place it is most likely to manifest itself in the electorate.

We next turn to an in depth treatment of what political trust is, when it should matter, and for whom it should matter. This section will lay the foundation for why its polarization causes Washington to accomplish less.

On Trust

The concept of political trust has captured the interest of social scientists for more than a half century. Scholars believed political trust was important because it contributed to the legitimacy and longevity of governments, providing a "reservoir of support" for leaders even during hard times (Easton 1965). Much to the dismay of scholars of the time, political trust in the United States entered a period of sharp decline soon after scholars started to measure it in 1958. In 1964, 76 percent of Americans trusted the government to do what is right at least most of the time. That figure fell to 35 percent by 1974 and to 25 percent by 1980. Early research on political trust was motivated by a desire to understand and explain this precipitous decline (cf. Citrin 1974; Miller 1974). Not only was this important because trust was declining, but it was also important because, despite the troubling decline in political trust, neither the legitimacy nor longevity of American institutions seemed to be in much doubt. To be sure, Americans protested for civil rights and women's rights and against the Vietnam War, but significantly changing the structure of government was never on the table, even as trust dropped to unprecedentedly low levels.

What, then, do people mean when they say they do or don't trust the government? A common definition of political trust is a feeling that people have about government based on their perceptions of its performance relative to their expectations of how it ought to perform (Hetherington 1998, 2005; Miller 1974; Stokes 1962). This definition places a spotlight on government *performance* in understanding how much a citizenry trusts its government and what, in the future, might cause it to rise and fall. When people perceive that government performance meets expectations, political trust ought to flourish. When they do not, trust ought to decay.

Other scholars have rightly argued that a wholly performance-based definition of trust is incomplete. Instead, they suggest that citizens care not only about outcomes but also about the *processes* through which those outcomes emerged (Hibbing and Theiss-Morse 2002). In particular, Americans do not like to see democracy in action, even though they profess loving democracy in theory. The conflict inherent in the "sausage-making" process is not attractive to most because they mistakenly believe commonsense solutions to political problems are obvious and readily available; their representatives should simply come together to implement them. As evidence of this argument's wisdom, consider how much more confidence Americans have in the Supreme Court, an institution in which political conflict is private, than in Congress, an institution in which conflict is public. According to the 2012 General Social Survey, 29 percent of Americans express at least "a great deal of confidence" in the Supreme Court, whereas only 6 percent express that much confidence in Congress (Smith, Hout, and Marsden 2012). In general, when people perceive the governing process to be fair and responsive, political trust rises, and, when they do not, it falls.

Still other research suggests that levels of political trust are a reflection of governmental *probity* or, more precisely, the absence of it. Political trust tends to decline during periods of government scandals (Chanley, Rudolph, and Rahn 2000; Hetherington and Rudolph 2008; Keele 2007) and rises in its absence. Although scandals often carry a high profile and, as a consequence, seem devastating to public trust, it is best not to overestimate their importance. Trust continued to decline for years after Richard Nixon resigned after Watergate, and it actually rose in the midst of the Monica Lewinsky scandal during the Clinton presidency. Scandals have an effect, but their impact is most often short lived.

Why Should Trust Matter?

Up to this point, our focus has been on what contributes to how much people trust government. But perhaps an even more important question is, why should we expect trust to matter and in what ways?

Our reasoning as to why trust matters starts from a time-honored perspective in the study of American politics. Most people do not know much about most things political (e.g., Converse 1964). Thinkers of a bygone era might have hoped ordinary citizens in modern democracies would approach the sophistication we attribute to the ancient Athenians. But Stimson (2004) puts it best in explaining what levels of citizen competence are actually like: "Such a view [of competence] survived a couple thousand years of speculation about the public. Its death was quick and brutal when early students of public opinion actually went out and interviewed ordinary people in surveys" (13). These surveys revealed that Americans know shockingly little about public affairs.

Because people's knowledge of political matters is far from encyclopedic, they need to employ rules of thumb to get by. Trust in government can provide one such rule of thumb or, to use the social science term, "heuristic." Heuristics are mental shortcuts that enable people to make judgments more effortlessly and, as a result, more efficiently than gathering all available information about a topic. The concept of heuristics is premised on the assumption that people prefer to expend as little effort as possible when trying to make judgments or decisions.

Examples of heuristic reasoning abound, both in life and in politics. When dining out, a person might encounter a dessert tray that has unfamiliar offerings but familiar ingredients. If, for example, a person likes chocolate and orders an unfamiliar chocolate-based dessert because he or she surmises from past experience with chocolate that he or she will like it, that person has employed a heuristic. Although heuristics can lead people astray at times (e.g., a chocolate-lover might be quite disappointed by German chocolate cake), people use them all the time to good effect in navigating a complex world.

Our story about chocolate desserts illustrates the "representativeness heuristic." The representativeness heuristic enables people to make in-ferences about whether a person or object belongs to a particular cat-egory without paying the cost of gathering and analyzing a great deal of information. We can apply heuristics to politics as well. A voter seeks to determine whether an unknown candidate appearing in a television ad is a Republican or a Democrat. The ad mentions that the candidate is a pro-life member of the National Rifle Association who wants to repeal Obamacare. Based on what the voter in question knows about the stereo-typical traits of each political party, he or she might reasonably conclude that the unknown candidate is a Republican. Although the representa-tiveness heuristic can lead people to make occasional errors, it generally allows them to make good inferences through a relatively simple and ef-ficient process.

Because people are not always (or perhaps not often) willing or able to sort through the complex details of a new policy initiative, they natu-rally search for ways to simplify decision making when they are asked to decide where they stand on it. Using political trust as a heuristic, people can decide their support for new government policies or actions with rela-tive ease. The decision to endorse or reject a proposed policy turns on the question of trust: "other things equal, if people perceive the architect of policies as untrustworthy, they will reject its policies; if they consider it trustworthy, they will be more inclined to embrace them" (Hetherington 2005, 51). The trust heuristic is a powerful predictor of policy support because it is based, in part, on citizens' satisfaction with its past actions.

Of course, our reasoning suggests that trust, in addition to being back-ward looking, also signals citizens' willingness to believe government promises about the future consequences of a proposed policy or action (Rudolph 2009). This occurs, psychologists contend, because trust in-creases the likelihood that messages will be accepted and, ultimately, will be persuasive (Hovland, Janis, and Kelley 1953; Hovland and Weiss 1951). Consider, for example, a newly married couple that must decide between purchasing a small but affordable two-bedroom house and a larger but more expensive three-bedroom house. A well-intentioned but unknown realtor urges the young couple to purchase the larger home because it is located in a nicer neighborhood and is a better long-term investment than the two-bedroom house. But the realtor, the couple recognizes, would also stand to earn a bigger commission on the purchase of the more ex-pensive house. Without trust, it may be difficult for the couple to accept the realtor's arguments and be persuaded to purchase the larger home.

Instead, suppose that the bride's parents advocate the purchase of the larger house because it will offer more room and a bigger yard for the grandchildren they hope will soon be forthcoming. If the couple trusts the bride's parents, which is probably more likely than them trusting the realtor, they are more likely to accept the parents' arguments and be persuaded to purchase the larger home. In short, trust can affect whether people internalize others' arguments and, in turn, subscribe to their ideas.

Given its implications for building support for future policies, political trust serves as a meaningful indicator of public opinion. It provides an important signal to lawmakers about whether the public is likely to back certain types of initiatives at any particular moment. In this respect, it is not unlike other indicators of public opinion, such as ideology. Indeed, it would seem on the surface that someone who is distrustful of government and someone who is conservative would want the same things. Despite some similarities, however, political trust is distinct from ideology, the latter with more philosophical objections to government than the former. "While the distrustful distrust *this* government and thus want to minimize its involvement in certain areas, they might embrace government involvement in [other] areas if they trusted it would do a good job. This is not true of conservative ideologues. Outside of national defense and law and order issues, they oppose government on philosophical grounds, no matter its quality" (Hetherington 2005, 60).

Political trust is also distinct from political approval. Presidential approval, for example, is typically measured by asking citizens whether they approve or disapprove of how the president is handling his or her job. In other words, it is clearly linked to past or current performance-based considerations. It is an indicator of support for what the president has done or is doing. Although political trust is partly a function of performance-based considerations, it is also an indicator of future support based on that which is unobservable. Political trust is, in this respect, not unlike religious faith. If faith is "the assurance of things hoped for, the conviction of things not seen,"[12] then political trust is the belief that government will do rightly in the future. Political trust is, from this perspective, a kind of faith in the government.

In sum, political trust is a barometer of citizens' feelings toward government. It is shaped by a blend of considerations concerning government performance, processes, probity, and, we will argue in subsequent chapters, more. It functions as a useful heuristic, or shortcut, that helps citizens make decisions about what government should do. It, therefore, ought to have a profound effect on people's preferences across a broad range of issues.

For Whom Should Trust Matter?

One central argument of ours is that trust is not equally necessary for all Americans. Some people will support or oppose policies regardless of how much they trust government. Trust, however, will have a particularly strong influence on the preferences of the very people who are most central to understanding whether or not public consensus on an issue develops and, in turn, whether public opinion encourages policy makers toward action. Specifically, political trust is important when government intervention requires people to make either material (Hetherington and Globetti 2002; Hetherington 2005) or ideological (Rudolph and Evans 2005; Rudolph 2009) sacrifices. When government programs require even perceived sacrifices, those asked to make them need to trust government to support such programs. In contrast, the beneficiaries of such programs do not need to trust government to support those policies because they do not pay the costs; they only reap the benefits.

Most important to our argument is the notion of ideological sacrifice. An ideological sacrifice is required for a liberal to follow a conservative leader's ideas or for a conservative to follow a liberal leader's ideas. Because almost no trust in government exists these days among those ideologically opposite the governing administration, few ordinary Americans are willing to make ideological sacrifices any longer. We argue that this has enormous implications for the role of public opinion in policy making. Republicans in the electorate will not support Democratic ideas when Democrats run the government, and Democrats in the electorate will not support Republican ideas when Republicans run the government. In a polarized environment in Washington, minority party members in Congress will, in turn, feel little pressure from their constituents to reach compromises on policy matters with the governing party. As a result, political gridlock remains the order of the day.

To sum up the ground we have covered so far, we find evidence of polarization in partisans' feelings about the other party. This has caused trust in government to polarize because people do not tend to trust things that are run by people they do not like. (We provide empirical evidence for this in chapter 4.) The polarization of trust is particularly consequential because so few out-party partisans are willing to make ideological sacrifices, so consensus on issues now rarely develops. (We provide empirical evidence for this in chapters 6–8.) As we discuss below, political institutions were designed to work slowly. The existence of policy consensus in the electorate can give institutions a nudge. But without it, those who occupy those institutions need not be particularly concerned with public opinion.

On Institutional Responsiveness

The Framers conceived a set of governing institutions designed to frustrate change. Compared with most other democracies, the legislative process in the United States is a labyrinth with so many potential choke points that it is something of a miracle that legislative accomplishments occur at all. Bills must traverse two houses of Congress. They can (and usually do) die in subcommittees, committees, or on the floor in either the House or Senate. If bills successfully navigate the legislative process, the president can veto them. Courts can find acts of Congress unconstitutional. Although it might seem counterintuitive, the Framers actually had a certain level of institutional unresponsiveness in mind when they wrote the Constitution. They did not want to make change easy.

That said, they also wanted a federal government that could provide vigorous leadership when it was called for. And, historically, Washington has produced that vigor. Despite all the potential roadblocks, the government has usually managed to make laws. A complete treatment of how elected officials have been able to overcome the barriers to lawmaking would require a book of its own. But a couple regularities are particularly noteworthy. First, the present situation confirms that unified party control of government facilitates lawmaking (Binder 2003). Barack Obama's agenda enjoyed much more success during his first two years in office when Democrats held relatively large majorities in both houses of Congress than it did in the next four when the Republicans controlled the House. Overcoming institutional barriers to legislative success is particularly manageable when the majority party has a *very* large majority of seats in both houses of Congress. Think about the early New Deal Congresses of the 1930s. Periods with large congressional majorities and a president belonging to that party, however, are quite rare in American history. Hence greasing the wheels of the lawmaking apparatus has most often required other means.

A second way to overcome the institutional barriers built into the law-making process is to build cross-party coalitions. The presence of a large number of conservative Southern Democrats from the 1950s through the 1980s, for example, made life easier for Ronald Reagan and other Republican presidents of this era. Especially in the case of Reagan, building cross-party coalitions often involved what Samuel Kernell dubbed "going public." This refers to the president appealing directly to the public for support of his or her program and using that support as leverage to get those in Washington to follow his or her lead. In considering this process, it is important to remember that not all opinions are equally important to legislators. Those from whom they do not expect to receive a vote at election time ought to matter much less than those from whom they expect to receive support. That means that the opinions of Republicans will matter more to Republican members and the opinions of Democrats will matter more to Democratic members. By going over the heads of majority House Democrats and appealing directly to Democrats in the mass public in the early 1980s, Reagan enhanced his ability to pressure Democratic lawmakers to vote for his program even if their first instinct as Democrats might have been to oppose the Republican president (Kernell 1986).

Among all the forces in American political life, the public is one of the few that could plausibly encourage elites to rise above their worst partisan instincts. Indeed, that is one of the reasons that scholars study the American electorate. In a healthy and vibrant republic, the preferences of the people should be reflected in policy outputs made by their representatives (Miller and Stokes 1962). Hence understanding what ordinary Americans want and why they want it is an important endeavor. Reassuringly, scholars have found that, at least in the past, lawmakers respond with new laws when public consensus emerges on an issue (Page, Shapiro, and Dempsey 1987). When the public mood shifts to the left, those laws tend to be more liberal, and when it shifts to the right, those laws tend to be more conservative (Erikson, MacKuen, and Stimson 2002). The fact that members would seek to satisfy constituent demands is not only normatively reassuring; it also makes electoral sense. Elected officials who wish to be reelected have a powerful incentive to reflect constituents' preferences, especially those they expect to be part of their reelection constituency. Importantly, when public consensus exists, the reelection constituencies of both majority and minority party politicians support a position.[13]

Few obvious and consistent areas of public consensus on specific policy issues exist today, however (Abramowitz 2012). On the big issues, such as spending on the social safety net, climate change, gay marriage, and many others, the public appears nearly as hopelessly split as those who govern them. One of the leading suspected sources of public dissensus is elite dissensus. Despite the link between mass preferences and public policy, scholars of public opinion have repeatedly shown that citizens' *initial* policy preferences are quite sensitive to how their elites talk about politics (Zaller 1992). This implies that citizens' policy preferences are first *led* by political elites and only later *lead* the decisions of political elites. We would like to think that the relationship between the governed and their governors is largely bottom up: the people start with strong beliefs and preferences about a political matter, and their representatives work to reflect it. This is seldom how the process actually works in the real political world, however.

Instead, public opinion formation tends to be top down. Most Americans do not care much about political matters and do not carry crystallized beliefs in their heads. Doing their jobs, caring for their families, and entertaining themselves occupies far more time and energy than does following political matters. Baseball fans tend to know all nine starters on their favorite team. Only the most devout political junkies (1 percent of the population, according to a recent Pew study) know all nine members of the Supreme Court (Pew Research Center 2010a). Hence most people do not develop their political preferences by thinking long and hard about the ins and outs of each issue and considering how they fit into an overall political philosophy. Instead, they look to their favored elites—heuristics again—to help them fill things in. Those who represent ordinary Americans do think long and hard about the ins and outs of the issue and how they fit together. On most matters, ordinary Americans observe their party elites and parrot as best they can muster the opinions and beliefs expressed by those elites.

This tendency is problematic today because of how polarized party elites are. For Republicans in Washington, Democrats always play the villain, and for Democrats, the reverse is true. Elite polarization breeds problems at the mass level. Recent research suggests that partisanship is so strong today that partisans in the electorate fail to learn certain facts that are inconvenient truths for their party (Jacobson 2006). When they agree on the facts, partisans of different stripes interpret them differently (Gaines et al. 2007). And partisans are swayed by even weak arguments made by their party leaders and reject strong arguments made by the other party in a polarized political environment (Druckman, Peterson, and Slothuus 2013). As a result, rather than countering the polarization in Washington, the public increasingly reinforces it.

Such a set of circumstances renders a going public strategy ineffective. Implicit in the success of a going public strategy is the presence of a fair number of partisans in the electorate who are willing to go along with the other party's president's policy goals. Those are the people the president is trying to activate when he goes public. The polarization of political trust makes finding such people all but impossible. Because almost no out-party partisans trust government these days, few, if any, will be inclined to step outside party orthodoxy to support the president's ideas. As a result, consensus in the public will not tend to form, rendering public opinion something of an inert force in nudging policy makers toward action. Political elites now lack the potentially critical push from the public that might cause them to rise above the polarization that infects Washington. The fact that trust in government is both historically low and more polarized by party than ever before explains why Washington does not work in the early twenty-first century. In the end, problems remain unresolved; a governing crisis persists.

On Causation: A Note about Our Multimethod Approach

Among the most vexing problems in the study of mass politics since the inception of survey research has been establishing causation—knowing what causes what. The earliest forays into the field occurred before the advent of scientific polling methods. Hence they relied on aggregate-level election outcome data. V. O. Key's (1955) work on realignment is an example of this kind of work at its best. By examining changes in precinct-level voting results in heavily Catholic areas during Herbert Hoover's two presidential elections, Key demonstrated that the earthquake election of 1932 actually had its roots in 1928 when the Democrats nominated Al Smith, the first major-party Catholic candidate, for president. Heavily Catholic precincts, which were often resolutely Republican before 1928, voted more for the Democrats starting in 1928. This process only accelerated in 1932.

The problem with making inferences about individuals with aggregate-level data is that researchers cannot be certain that individuals from the hypothesized group are actually the ones who changed their behavior. This leads to the so-called ecological inference problem. Returning to the example from Key's work, was it really Catholics who voted more Democratic in 1928, or was it instead non-Catholics who lived in a predominantly Catholic precinct? Theories of social identity tell us that it was almost certainly Catholics, with a Catholic candidate topping the Democratic ticket. But without knowing both the religion and the voting behavior of specific *individuals* during this time period, Key could not know for certain.

In our view, the best way to demonstrate causation convincingly is to employ multiple methods, which we do throughout the book. Pairing individual-level survey data analysis with the results from aggregate-level analysis is our first step. In chapter 3, we use aggregate-level data to show that trust increases when the percentage of Americans focused on international issues grows. Based on these results, however, we cannot conclude that specific types of individuals trust government more when international issues are salient to them. We can only conclude that a focus on international issues increases trust. Fortunately, we have available to us individual-level survey data. Those data allow us to show that the specific individuals who identify international issues as most important to them also express more trust in the government than those who identify domestic policy issues as most important.

Although individual-level data are helpful, they are not a magic bullet in demonstrating causation. Establishing causality using cross-sectional survey data—these are data that are collected at one specific time—is always tricky business. Based solely on the analysis of cross-sectional data, we cannot conclusively assert that variable x is a cause of variable y. Statistically, the best we can show is that a correlation exists. It is possible that variable y is actually a cause of variable x. To establish causal ordering, we can build a *verbal theory* that suggests a certain set of causal dynamics. And we can use statistical controls to account for other potential causes of variable y in addition to variable x, which will give us more confidence that any correlation we find between x and y actually exists and is not spurious. However, cross-sectional data alone do not allow researchers to establish a clear temporal ordering of variables—that is, what comes first and what comes second—because all the potential x's and y's are collected at the same time.

Panel data can help researchers make stronger claims about causation than cross-sectional data allow. By panel data, we mean that the *same* survey respondents are asked questions at multiple points in time. Because panel data are expensive and difficult to collect, they are rare in the social sciences. Fortunately, the ANES has carried out panel studies several times in the sixty-plus years it has been doing academic surveys.

When possible, we employ such data throughout the book as a means of establishing causation. For example, in chapter 4, we use panel data to demonstrate that Republicans and Democrats weighted the importance of different performance evaluations differently, thus producing a polarization of political trust in the early 2000s. Panel data allow us to account for how much trust people expressed in 2000, how much these same people expressed in 2002, and what evaluations intervened between these two times to explain the change that occurred (or didn't occur) between these two measurements.

Unfortunately, even panel data do not solve all the problems of causation. Sometimes the panel waves are so far apart that a multitude of factors, some that either could not be or were not measured, intervened to cause change in y. Or, it could be that common tests of causation in the analysis of panel data yield results that suggest causal dynamics more complicated than x causes y or y causes x. Both potential problems suggest the need for still other means of establishing causation.

We therefore turn at times to nonsurvey-based methods to make our case. Specifically, we employ experimental methods, an increasingly popular avenue for hypothesis testing in political science. Experiments are useful for addressing questions of causality because they allow researchers to carefully control or manipulate the effects of independent variables. If an explanatory variable is truly the cause of a dependent variable, then a manipulation of the independent variable should produce a change in the value of the dependent variable. An experiment allows a researcher not only to manipulate the independent variable in question but also to hold constant the effects of other possible independent variables through randomization.

We employ experimental methods in two ways. In chapter 5, for example, we bring subjects into a lab and manipulate issue attention by having randomly chosen groups read news stories about selected issues. Immediately after reading these stories, we ask subjects how much they trust government. This allows us to control what issues people are thinking about at the particular moment that they express their political trust. This, in turn, allows us to demonstrate that making different issues salient has the potential to change not only how much trust people express but also what policy preferences trust affects. Although experiments have limited external validity, we are able to overcome these shortcomings by pairing these results with those in chapter 6, which demonstrates the same process at work using the ANES's cumulative data collection over decades.

Of course, these data are limited in their internal validity for many of the reasons we have articulated above, which the use of our experiment helps us to overcome.

The second way we use experiments is to embed them in national probability samples, taking advantage of the positive qualities of both surveys and experiments at the same time. Specifically, in chapter 9, we conduct a simple survey experiment in which we explore the pliability of political trust. Of central interest in the experiment is the question of whether those who initially distrust government can be persuaded to trust government by receiving additional information. After collecting pretest measurements of political trust, we randomly assign distrustful respondents to receive information about government's (1) efficiency, (2) programmatic benefits, or (3) regulatory protections. We then collect a posttest measure of political trust. The experiment is designed to show whether respondents can be persuaded to trust government and, if so, which types of arguments are most persuasive. In sum, our multimethod approach is designed to increase confidence in the causal inferences that we make throughout the book about the sources and consequences of political trust. Critics might not like one or another of the methods that we use to buttress our argument. Hopefully, the fact that multiple methods all tell a similar story will help mollify their concerns.

CHAPTER THREE

What Moves Political Trust

O ur explanation for why public opinion is a greatly weakened force in nudging representatives toward action places the primary focus on the recent polarization of political trust by party. Because trust among those who identify with the party outside the White House has all but evaporated, consensus in the electorate rarely develops, which, in turn, diminishes public opinion's potential effect on policy makers.[1] Before we explore polarization's effects, however, we must identify the sources of trust in government and what causes them to change over time. It is these sources that, when combined with the contemporary political context, have produced trust's polarization by party.

Our treatment of what moves political trust over time yields important new insights. As we reviewed in chapter 2, others have found that the three Ps—government's *performance*, its *processes*, and its *probity*—influence political trust. But these factors fail to account fully for trust's fluctuations over the last half-century. We search for and find new explanations— namely, *priming* and *polarization*.

A central argument of this book is that political trust is, in significant measure, driven by the criteria that citizens use to judge their government at the time they are asked about it. This is *priming*. The information environment frequently focuses attention on different criteria at different times. One factor that ought to guide and concentrate public attention on different criteria is issue salience. The visibility and prominence of issues on the national agenda is not fixed over time. Whether prompted by elite cues, real-world events, or personal experience, the public will sometimes view the economy as the most important issue facing the nation. At other times, it might be international issues. And still at other times, specific policies such as Social Security or health care will occupy public attention. We argue that changes in issue salience trigger changes in the criteria people use to evaluate government. This, in turn, affects the level of trust that people report.

Another of our core arguments is that polarization in Washington may impede effective governance by both eroding and polarizing political trust among those in the electorate. There are several reasons to suspect that *polarization* might have this impact. Polarized parties produce more conflict, which, in turn, ought to undermine trust because people become disenchanted with the conflict inherent in government processes (Hibbing and Theiss-Morse 2002). In addition, a polarized government accomplishes less than a government in which the parties are closer together ideologically (Binder 2003), which might undermine trust because citizens perceive government to be underperforming expectations. Finally, polarization ought to have an asymmetric effect by party, which will both decrease trust in the aggregate and polarize it among individuals. Specifically, the results that we presented in the first two chapters suggest that satisfaction with the governing party among those belonging to that party is no higher now that parties are polarized than it was before polarization's onset; however, satisfaction with the governing party is a lot lower among out-party partisans now that parties are polarized than before. Taken together, this ought to lower trust, which we demonstrate in this chapter, and polarize it by party, which we demonstrate in the next chapter.

A final insight this chapter offers is that political trust is unlikely to return to the level it achieved when scholars first started to measure it in the 1950s and 1960s. Since those high readings were also the first readings, scholars tended to think that high levels of political trust were the norm. The last forty years of chronically low political trust suggests otherwise. Our analysis in this chapter explains why low levels of political trust are probably here to stay. It is these chronically low levels of trust that have important negative implications for building public support for government action itself, implications that are only made more problematic by trust's recent polarization.

In the next section, we review the trust literature and identify a lingering puzzle. Why has political trust not rebounded to the heights it enjoyed during the Great Society era? We discuss conventional explanations of trust and explain why they offer an incomplete account. We then present our theory of how issue salience and polarization ought to influence political trust. After describing our data and measures, we test our hypotheses by estimating a time-series analysis of political trust. A time-series approach allows us to avoid some of the endogeneity concerns (those about what causes what—the proverbial chicken versus egg concerns) that have plagued individual-level analyses of the sources of political trust. We find that political trust increases when the public identifies international issues as most important. We also find that the effects of economic performance on political trust are asymmetric: weak economies harm trust more than strong economies help it. This is because the economy becomes more salient when it is bad than when it is good, which means that more people are judging the government based on the economy in bad times than good. Finally, our analysis provides preliminary evidence that greater polarization depresses political trust.

The Puzzle of Persistently Low Trust

In the mid-to-late 1960s, trust in the federal government began a dramatic decline that lasted more than a decade and a half. In 1964, 76 percent of Americans said they trusted the government in Washington to do what is right at least most of the time. By 1980, only 25 percent did. Levels of trust briefly crossed the 60 percent mark in the immediate aftermath of the tragedy on September 11, 2001. A decade later in 2011, however, trust had fallen well below 20 percent, lower than ever before. Since the 1980s, trust has both risen and fallen, yet it has never come close to regaining the heights that it experienced during the Great Society era. Why? In this section, we review traditional accounts of trust and explain why they provide incomplete answers to this question.

With trust in free fall throughout the late 1960s and 1970s, scholars turned their attention to explaining the decline, identifying three important factors. Perhaps the leading account of trust is rooted in government performance. Received wisdom suggests that performance drives trust (e.g., Citrin 1974; Hetherington 1998; Chanley, Rudolph, and Rahn 2000), with economic considerations being particularly important (Citrin and Green 1986; Citrin and Luks 2001; Weatherford 1984). Fluctuations in economic outcomes appear to covary with movements in political trust over time. Trust declined throughout the 1970s, a decade marked by declining real income, high unemployment, and skyrocketing inflation. Trust then increased with the economic resurgence of the middle Reagan years, only to decline dramatically in the early 1990s during a recession. When a long, uninterrupted economic expansion occurred under Bill Clinton, trust in government rebounded, despite the president's persistent and intense scandal problems. Taken together, a strong link appears to exist between political trust and the economy.

The empirical evidence, however, suggests a more complicated story. At the individual level, citizens' economic perceptions sometimes have large effects on trust, but sometimes they have no effect (Citrin and Green 1986; Hetherington 1998; Miller and Borrelli 1991). Although time-series analyses have generally found more consistent evidence for the importance of the economy (Chanley 2002; Chanley, Rudolph, and Rahn 2000; Keele 2007), these models treat the effect of the economy as constant over time and, hence, may overestimate its effect in some years and underestimate it in others.

Moreover, any well-specified dynamic theory of political trust ought to explain its increases, decreases, and stasis, but government performance fails in this regard. The United States effectively vanquished its Cold War nemesis with the demise of the Soviet Union in the early 1990s. Yet, on the heels of this success, political trust reached its minimum up to that point as measured by the American National Election Study (ANES). The length and breadth of the economic expansions in both the Reagan and Clinton years produced economies that were sometimes even stronger than those of the post–World War II years. Although the mid-1980s and late 1990s both saw increases in political trust, in neither period did trust approach the level it had attained in 1972, much less in 1958 or 1964. Simply put, a performance-based account is, by itself, incomplete.

In addition to performance, a second line of reasoning suggests that trust in government is shaped by perceptions about political processes, particularly those relating to Congress. Congress is unpopular relative to the presidency and judiciary because its processes are so public (Hibbing and Theiss-Morse 1995). Although Americans like democracy in theory, they are troubled by it in practice, disliking the sometimes bitter partisan disagreement inherent in the legislative process. Moreover, the public tends to think that members of Congress typically play ordinary Americans for suckers by abusing legislative perquisites while ignoring what is best for the country as a whole (Hibbing and Theiss-Morse 2002). Because of the public's aversion to partisan bickering in the legislative process, exposure to legislative conflict has a negative impact on congressional approval (Durr, Gilmour, and Wolbrecht 1997).[2]

If trust in government is partially a function of process-related concerns, then congressional approval ought to move trust. It does (Citrin and Luks 2001; Hetherington 1998; Hetherington and Rudolph 2008). Yet we have reason to doubt that a process-based account can adequately explain all of trust's movement over the last several decades. For example, partisan conflict reached a fever pitch during the Clinton impeachment battle. Yet despite this intense institutional conflict, trust experienced no meaningful decline during this period. In fact, it increased. Indeed, trust has often increased during periods of divided government (e.g., the early 1980s and late 1990s) despite the fact that conflict is probably highest during such periods.

A third set of findings suggests that trust in government will rise and fall in accordance with public perceptions of government probity. When people perceive that government is honest and acting with integrity, trust in government should flourish. Concerns about corruption, malfeasance, or illegality, by contrast, ought to cause political trust to suffer. There exists some empirical support for this expectation. Political trust tends to fall during periods of government scandal (Chanley, Rudolph, and Rahn 2000; Keele 2007; but see Miller and Borrelli 1991). One must take care, however, not to overestimate the importance of scandals. Watergate did less to lower trust in the 1970s than a poor economy did (Weatherford 1984), and trust actually increased during Clinton's second term despite the Monica Lewinsky scandal and his subsequent impeachment.

All three P's (performance, process, and probity) are probably important to some degree, but, even taken together, they do not provide a satisfactory explanation for movements in political trust over the last half-century. We offer other explanations below.

Priming and the Dynamics of Political Trust

We add another P to the mix: priming. Priming refers to people's tendency to change the criteria that they use to evaluate leaders or relevant conditions, depending on what is salient at a given point in time (see Iyengar and Kinder 1987). To illustrate how priming can affect overall evaluations, consider the former Major League baseball player Steve Sax, a second baseman for the Los Angeles Dodgers who won the National League Rookie of the Year Award in 1982. Sax was a pretty good hitter and a great base runner during much of his playing career. If baseball fans had been asked to evaluate him after seeing him hit and run, they would have given him high marks. Starting in 1983, however, Sax developed a malady that became known as Steve Sax Syndrome. He could no longer throw the ball consistently to first base, causing people sitting behind the first base dugout to don helmets lest he uncork a wild throw.[3] The same fans who might have evaluated him positively when thinking about his offensive skills would likely evaluate him negatively when thinking about him in the field. Sax, of course, was the same player, but the criteria on which people might be "primed" to evaluate him could change, which would, in turn, affect their overall evaluation of him.

Priming applies to evaluations in politics as well as baseball. Perhaps the clearest example of priming occurred during the George H. W. Bush presidency. So much went right for Bush in his early years as president, almost all in the realm of foreign affairs. The Berlin Wall came down, the Soviet Union imploded, and the US military under Bush's direction expelled Saddam Hussein from Kuwait. With the criteria people were using to evaluate him firmly focused on foreign affairs, Americans admired Bush. In fact, in March 1991, his approval rating reached 89 percent, the highest percentage ever recorded by the Gallup Organization to that date. Many thought his reelection was assured. Within a year, however, his approval rating plummeted into the low 30s, setting the stage for Bill Clinton's victory in the 1992 presidential race. Bush, of course, was the same person, and his foreign policy accomplishments remained impressive. But public attention had turned from foreign affairs to an economy buffeted by recession in late 1991 and 1992. When people stopped evaluating him based on foreign policy success and started evaluating him based on economic policy weakness, his approval rating nosedived (Krosnick and Brannon 1993). It was priming that ended the first Bush presidency after one term.

We suspect that people decide how much they trust government based, in part, on which issues they think are important at a particular moment in time. Put another way, people are primed to evaluate the government on different criteria depending on identifiable circumstances. Because people like certain parts of government more than others, this process can affect the level of trust that people report. Priming, we expect, offers untapped theoretical insight into the question of why trust moves and, importantly, why it has never returned to Great Society–era levels.

Following Miller and Krosnick (2000), we view priming as the second half of a two-stage process. The first stage is agenda setting, which is the "process by which problems become salient as political issues" (Erbring, Goldenberg, and Miller 1980, 16–17). Although the mass media plays a prominent role in the agenda-setting process, public concerns often come from other sources. Indeed, scholars have shown that the public's national importance judgments are shaped by a diverse set of sources, including media coverage, personal experience, real-world cues, interpersonal communication, and presidential rhetoric (Behr and Iyengar 1985; Erbring, Goldenberg, and Miller 1980; Iyengar and Kinder 1987; MacKuen 1984; MacKuen and Coombs 1981; Mendelsohn 1996; Miller and Krosnick 2000; Yang and Stone 2003).

Priming is a related but distinct phenomenon that occurs after agenda setting has taken place. Priming effects occur when public attention to an issue influences the weight assigned to it when political evaluations are formed (Druckman 2004; Krosnick and Kinder 1990; Miller and Krosnick 2000). For example, people would weight evaluations of Steve Sax's offensive prowess greater than they would weight evaluations of his defensive prowess in their overall evaluations of Sax if they thought the former was most important at that particular time. Although priming has long been thought to work through the mechanism of accessibility (Price and Tewksbury 1997), subsequent work suggests that it is, instead, mediated by judgments of importance (Miller and Krosnick 2000). So conceived, we can investigate priming as an aggregate-level phenomenon by tracking public perceptions of the nation's most important problem over time and examining their impact on political evaluations (see also Behr and Iyengar 1985; Edwards, Mitchell, and Welch 1995; Johnston et al. 1992).

Shifts in national importance judgments are significant because they prime the public to focus its performance evaluations in particular domains. We predict that performance evaluations concerning a given issue will exert a greater impact on political trust as the proportion of the public naming that issue as nationally important increases. The argument that national importance judgments can produce priming effects already enjoys empirical support in the study of presidential approval (Edwards, Mitchell, and Welch 1995). We believe that these theoretical insights can be fruitfully applied to the study of more global attitudes toward government, such as political trust.[4]

The economy is unique in the study of political trust because we can measure people's perceptions of its performance in the aggregate with some precision by using the Index of Consumer Sentiment. Obviously, people ought to trust government less when they perceive the economy to be doing worse and vice versa. But decades of scholarship suggest the effects of good and bad economies ought to differ. Campbell et al. (1960) were the first to hypothesize such an asymmetry in explaining why party fortunes change over time. Starting from the assumption that politics carries low salience for most people most of the time, they argued that good performance would do "little to motivate the electorate to connect events of the wider environment with the actors of politics." In contrast, "economic . . . calamity can force events across the threshold of political awareness" (556). The same asymmetry exists in presidential approval (Mueller 1970) and in models of aggregate- (Bloom and Price 1975) and individual-level (Cover 1986, but see Radcliff 1994) voting behavior. Evidence of a more general negativity bias also appears in evaluations of the character of presidential candidates (Goren 2002) and confidence in the Supreme Court (Grosskopf and Mondak 1998), with further scholarly evidence suggesting that such biases are pervasive in politics (e.g., Lau 1985) and beyond (e.g., Jordan 1965).

We anticipate, then, that the public's assessments of economic importance ought to condition the effect of economic performance on political trust. Since human beings tend to overweight negative information (Tversky and Kahneman 1974; Tversky and Kahneman 1981), more people will identify the economy as an important problem when it is relatively bad (see also Bloom and Price 1975). When the economy is relatively good, however, salience will be lower. By implication, fewer people will judge the government based on how it is performing during good times than bad ones.[5]

As we noted, the economy is unique in that it provides an aggregate measure (consumer sentiment) of the public's perception of its performance. No such measures exist for performance on the international front or in the vast majority of domestic issue areas. When data are not available to tap public perceptions of government performance, we expect that certain national importance judgments will exert a direct impact on political trust. In particular, we expect that greater concern about international issues will increase political trust. Our thinking starts from the notion that most Americans have little reason to consider the foreign world unless the country is facing a crisis. During a crisis, people are more inclined to think collectively because only government can respond to the crisis (Alford 2001; Mueller 1973). Indeed, research in social psychology shows that external intergroup threat increases perceptions of both in-group and out-group homogeneity (Rothgerber 1997). As a result, patriotism rises during international crises, which helps explain the rally in approval ratings that the president typically receives (Mueller 1973).

In addition, the government is likely to receive less negative media coverage when confronting international problems as compared to domestic ones. This is, in large part, the result of the executive branch's information advantage. The media are less able to present opposing interpretations of international crises than domestic problems because the most sensitive information about the crisis is available only from the executive branch (Baker and Oneal 2001). In addition, presidents are typically able to maintain high levels of approval even when performance in confronting the threat is poor because competing elites often mute their criticism so as not to seem unpatriotic (Brody 1991). Even when media coverage of the government on foreign affairs turns negative, as was the case toward the end of the war in Iraq, people still evaluate the president more favorably on foreign affairs than they do on domestic concerns like the economy. For example, even though Americans' approval of President Bush on Iraq deteriorated toward the end of 2004, their average approval of his performance with regard to Iraq and terrorism was always significantly higher than their approval of his handling of the economy, which, arguably, was performing quite well.[6] In fact, even though a majority of Americans turned against the Iraq war for the first time at the end of 2004, political trust increased sharply that quarter, likely reflecting the marked increase in concerns about international problems, a point we take up in more detail below.

Higher trust in government when international issues take center stage also ought to result from the striking asymmetries in the feelings that citizens have about different parts of government. Americans have particularly positive feelings toward the parts of government that might combat a foreign threat. In the 2012 ANES, for example, the average feeling thermometer score that Americans provided for the military was eighty-three degrees, by far the highest score for any part of the government. In contrast, the average feeling thermometer score for Congress, the part of government that most Americans have in mind when they think about government (Feldman 1983; Williams 1985), was forty-seven degrees. The average feeling thermometer for "people on welfare"—the group that Americans think receives the bulk of government money (Gilens 1999) and is hence critical to explaining people's evaluation of government (Hetherington 2005, chapter 2)—was fifty-two degrees. This suggests that people will likely express more trust in government when the part of government they are thinking about is the military than when it is Congress or government agencies that redistribute money.

Our theorizing about priming and political trust has some empirical support. In an ABC News poll taken on January 9, 2002, half the sample was invited to judge the government's trustworthiness after being encouraged to think about government in the realm of the economy, health care, Social Security, and education while the other half was encouraged to think about the government in the realm of national security and the war on terrorism. Among those primed to think about domestic concerns, only 38 percent provided trusting responses. In contrast, 69 percent of those primed about national security did. There is more general, but still descriptive, evidence that political trust increases when international concerns are salient. During the first Gulf War, trust increased for a time along with President Bush's popularity (Parker 1995; Hetherington and Nelson 2003). In the months after the 9/11 terrorist attacks, the percentage of people citing terrorism, Iraq, or foreign affairs was correlated positively with aggregate levels of political trust (Hetherington 2005, chapter 8). According to the biennial ANES time series between 1958 and 1996, a positive correlation exists between the percentage of people citing an international problem as most important and levels of political trust (Alford 2001).[7] Evidence from time-series analyses has been supportive of these conclusions as well (Chanley 2002) but not consistently so (Chanley, Rudolph, and Rahn 2000).

Polarization and the Dynamics of Political Trust

In addition to priming, we suspect that another P, polarization, may help explain movement in political trust over time. By polarization, we mean movement by party elites toward the ideological poles. The notion of polarized politics is anathema to the American political culture. Two-party politics, with its logical pull toward the political middle (Downs 1957), has been the norm through its history. When Americans have complained about their representatives in Washington, their complaints have rarely been about them being too moderate. Rather, the political culture has tended to be nonideological and centrist compared to its European counterparts, perhaps owing to the fact that feudalism never existed in the United States (Hartz 1957).

As evidence of Americans' distaste for ideological extremity, the larger the constituency is, the bigger the problem political elites have when they are perceived as extreme. Purists might flourish in low-turnout primary elections, but when elections include larger numbers of people, most politicians find it useful to at least appear to be moderate. For example, Barack Obama did not win two elections by telling Americans he is extremely liberal on health care and the environment. Instead, he worked to make his proposals sound as moderate as possible. When, during the 2012 Republican primaries, Mitt Romney inartfully described himself as "severely conservative," pundits considered it a grave blow to his general election prospects. Indeed, officeholders often find it useful to use ideological terms to describe their opponents. For the last twenty-five or thirty years, Democrats have regularly used the term "extremist" pejoratively to describe Republicans. Republicans have hung the term "liberal" around the necks of Democrats for decades as well, never more famously than during the 1988 presidential election between George H. W. Bush and Michael Dukakis. The reason such tactics work is because Americans, on average, do not like extremeness.

We anticipate that more polarization will reduce political trust among the mass public for two principal reasons: it creates unattractive processes and encourages poor performance. First, elite polarization carries negative implications for legislative processes, making them uglier and more contentious than when common ground across party lines exists. In a polarized environment, partisan elites are far apart in terms of both what they think ought to be on the legislative agenda and their preferences for the best way to solve the problems that eventually emerge on the agenda. More distance makes it very difficult to forge legislative compromises or reach consensus on much of anything. In the absence of consensus and compromise, partisan conflict reigns, and contentious legislative processes are on full display. Much research has shown that people do not like government that bickers publicly; Americans tend to believe that solutions to the nation's problems are obvious and commonsense (Hibbing and Theiss-Morse 1995, 2002). They do not have much appreciation for the fact that competing ideological outlooks champion different approaches to solving problems and that partisan conflict is part of any policy making process. As a result, exposure to such conflict leads to more negative evaluations of government.

More and less polarized times are clearly different in terms of the amount of conflict they produce. The 1970s were, historically speaking, a very unpolarized time by any measure of congressional behavior. Because Republicans of the period had little to no chance of winning majorities in the House and Senate, they needed to cooperate with majority Democrats to get at least part of what they wanted. This led to a distinct approach to legislating—one that squares with the public's idealized view of lawmaking. For example, in the early 1970s, the top staff people for Senate Majority Leader Mike Mansfield (D-MT) and Senate Minority

Leader Hugh Scott (R-PA) met for breakfast in the Senate dining room nearly every day that the Senate was in session to discuss the business that would come before the Senate.[8] Moreover, Mansfield and Scott shared a strong mutual respect for one another, even socializing regularly. As a result, partisan backstabbing was kept to a minimum, with the parties in Congress tending to work together in crafting solutions on legislative matters. That did not mean the parties agreed on all or even most issues. Vietnam certainly springs to mind, although the conflict on this issue occurred not only between parties but also within them. Regardless, the cooperative model of lawmaking that emerged in the post–World War II period and ran through the beginning of the Reagan presidency is the ideal that most Americans have in mind.

What they do not have in mind is petty partisan politics carried out over an ideological divide that hamstrings even members' best efforts to legislate. Of course, that is what characterizes the politics of today. Contrast the breakfast sessions between top staff across party lines from the 1970s with what makes the headlines about the legislative process in today's polarized environment. Present day Senate leaders, Harry Reid and Mitch McConnell, seem to have nothing but contempt for each other. As a result, partisan shenanigans rule the day. There have been occasions when majority party members have failed to alert minority party members of important congressional meetings (Mann and Ornstein 2012). Bill markups, once a device that ensured thoughtful and bipartisan deliberation (Sinclair 1997), are now nothing but a sham. The political dialogue, such that it is, is demonstrably courser these days. For example, Representative Joe Wilson (R-SC) famously blurted out "You lie!" at Barack Obama during a 2009 address to Congress on the benefits of health care reform. It is hard to imagine such a thing happening when Dwight Eisenhower or John Kennedy was president. Times have changed regarding legislative processes, and not for the better. We expect that Americans will trust the government less under such circumstances.

In addition to concerns about process, elite polarization apparently carries negative implications for government performance. As polarization in Congress has reached its maximum, congressional productivity has reached its minimum. Even when problems exist that require the government to act, polarization can stand in the way. Recall our treatment in chapter 1 of the debt ceiling debacle from 2010 to 2012 and the budget fiasco of 2013, which ultimately led to a government shutdown. Why would Americans feel positively about a government that can't act even when it absolutely must? Polarized environments that are rife with legislative conflict between partisan elites make compromises and, in turn, passing major pieces of legislation nearly impossible. Congressional scholars have shown that polarized governments produce more legislative gridlock and fewer important laws (Binder 2003). If polarized governments are less likely to succeed in passing legislation to deal effectively with the nation's social and economic challenges, then why would Americans trust them?

Finally, part of our thinking about why more polarization in Washington ought to drive down trust is just math. The survey data suggest that polarized politics makes people feel worse about the other side without making them feel any better about their own side. Recall from chapter 2 in particular that the average feeling thermometer scores that partisans give the other party have nosedived as politics has polarized. At the same time, however, their evaluations of their own parties have remained relatively constant. The first trend suggests that trust among partisans will go down more when their party is out of power in a polarized environment than in an unpolarized one. The second trend suggests that trust among partisans will not go up more when their party is in power in a polarized environment than in an unpolarized one. Taken together, these two trends will result in a lower average level of trust during polarized times.

In sum, polarization at the elite level ought to contribute to less political trust for two reasons. Loud disagreements between party elites will raise public concerns about legislative processes. In addition, polarization decreases the likelihood that Congress will produce a meaningful record of legislative accomplishment. For both reasons, polarization ought to cause political trust to decline.

Time-Series Data and Measures

The theory outlined above is dynamic in the sense that we predict that, over time, changes in the public's national importance judgments will lead to changes in political trust. Testing this priming hypothesis thus requires a time-series analysis of longitudinal (over-time) data. In this section, we describe our data and explain how we constructed our time-series measures.

Political Trust

We measure political trust by using an updated version of the quarterly trust series constructed by Hetherington and Rudolph (2008). We created

TABLE 3.1 **Correlations of indicators with overall political trust index**

Item name	Item wording	Correlation
Trust 1	How much of the time do you think you can trust the government in Washington to do what is right: just about always, most of the time, or only some of the time? (e.g., Gallup, CBS News, *New York Times*) ($n = 150$, asked in 89 quarters)	0.99
Trust 2	How much of the time do you think you can trust the government in Washington to do what is right: just about always, most of the time, only some of the time, or hardly ever? (e.g., *Los Angeles Times*) ($n = 19$, asked in 19 quarters)	0.91
Trust 3	How much of the time do you think you can trust the government in Washington to do what is right: just about always, most of the time, only some of the time, or never? (e.g., CBS News) ($n = 12$, asked in 11 quarters)	0.93
Trust 4	How much of the time do you trust the government in Washington to do what is right: just about always, most of the time, or only some of the time? (e.g., ABC News, *Washington Post*) ($n = 35$, asked in 29 quarters)	0.90
Trust 5	Thinking about the government in Washington, how much trust do you have in the federal government to do what is right: a lot of trust, some trust, only a little trust, or none at all? (e.g., *Time*, Yankelovich) ($n = 3$, asked in 3 quarters)	0.64
Percent variance explained		91.80

Note: Data are quarterly and cover the period from 1976:1 to 2011:4.

this quarterly trust measure by using Stimson's (1999) "dyad ratios" algorithm. Stimson's method overcomes the problem of intermittent time-series data in public opinion by allowing researchers to treat similarly (but not identically) worded instruments as indicators of a single underlying construct based on their common movement over time. Using variants of the ANES's familiar trust instrument (i.e., "How much of the time do you think you can trust the government in Washington to do what is right: just about always, most of the time, or only some of the time?"), we used Stimson's method to create a quarterly trust series that extends from the first quarter of 1976 (1976:1) through the fourth quarter of 2011 (2011:4).[9] For descriptive purposes, we also create an annualized version of the series from 1958 to 2011.

Five different series contributed to the construction of the political trust index. The question wording and frequencies for each of these series is reported in table 3.1. Table 3.1 also reports the loading (correlation) between each component series and the overall index. Each of the individual series loads quite well, and the implied measurement model performs admirably, with the quarterly trust index explaining more than 90 percent of the variance in the individual series.

National Importance Judgments

To test for priming effects, we measure and track public perceptions about the most important problem facing the nation. To measure national importance judgments, we rely principally on responses to the question "what do you think is the most important problem facing this country today?" This question, and subtle variants of it, has been asked by survey houses more than 650 times since 1976. Using these data and Stimson's algorithm, we create two quarterly most important problem (MIP) series.[10] The *MIP International* series represents the proportion of the public who named international issues or concerns (e.g., foreign policy, national defense, terrorism, war, the Middle East, or specific foreign nations/leaders) as the nation's most important problem. The *MIP Economy* series reflects the proportion who named economic issues (e.g., economy, unemployment, inflation, prices, or interest rates) as most important. Details concerning the construction of these three measures are reported in table 3.2. The eight component series load quite well on the two indices, and the measurement models perform well, as each index explains at least 87 percent of the variance in its component series.

Polarization

To examine the effects of partisan polarization on political trust over time, we require a time-series measure of polarization that can be assessed at quarterly intervals. Because elite behavior affects public opinion, it would be ideal to employ a quarterly measure that taps elite polarization. Unfortunately, data that tap elite behavior tend to be gathered for each two-year congressional session. Because the observations in our analysis are gathered quarterly, such measures of elite behavior are ill suited to our purposes. Public opinion data provide us the most practicable avenue to measure polarization. Although imperfect, we expect it ought to work reasonably well given that mass opinion tends to follow elite behavior (Key 1966; Zaller 1992). To this end, we collected the 993 Gallup polls that measured presidential approval between 1976 and 2011 and disaggregated them by political party. We then used Stimson's (1999) dyad ratios

TABLE 3.2 **Correlations of indicators with overall most important problem index**

Item name	Item wording	MIP international	MIP economy
MIP 1	What do you think is the most important problem facing this country today? (e.g., Gallup) (n = 216, asked in 115 quarters)	0.99	0.99
MIP 2	What do you think is the most important problem facing the country today? (e.g., CBS News, *New York Times*) (n = 179, asked in 96 quarters)	0.97	0.96
MIP 3	What do you think is the most important problem facing this country today? (e.g., ABC, *Washington Post*) (n = 39, asked in 34 quarters)	0.90	0.94
MIP 4	Which of the following do you think is the most important problem facing this country today? (e.g., Associated Press) (n = 8, asked in 7 quarters)	0.98	0.98
MIP 5	What is the most important problem facing this country today? (*Los Angeles Times*) (n = 29, asked in 26 quarters)	0.72	0.85
MIP 6	What is the most important problem facing the country today? (PSRA) (n = 39, asked in 38 quarters)	0.98	0.96
MIP 7	What would you say is the single most important problem facing the United States today, that is, the one that you, yourself, are most concerned about? (Wirthlin) (n = 30, asked in 18 quarters)	0.72	0.92
MIP 8	What do you think is the single most important problem for the government—that is, the President and Congress—to address in the coming year? (CBS) (n = 28, asked in 15 quarters)	0.85	0.81
Percent variance explained		87.83	90.54

Note: Data are quarterly and cover the period from 1976:1 to 2011:4. Because the response categories reported for open-ended questions and the number of accepted responses varies across survey houses, we treat identically worded questions from different survey houses as separate entries.

algorithm to create a quarterly time-series measure of presidential approval among Republicans and a quarterly time-series measure of presidential approval among Democrats. Finally, we calculated the absolute value of the difference between these two approval series to create a quarterly measure of partisan polarization. In the analyses to follow, we expect that increases in polarization will reduce political trust.

Performance, Process, and Probity

As a measure of economic performance, we employ the Index of Consumer Sentiment from the University of Michigan's Survey of Consumers. This composite measure reflects public perceptions of personal and national economic conditions and is composed of indicators that are both retrospective and prospective in nature. While we anticipate that economic sentiment will influence political trust, we expect that its effects will depend on the extent to which the public views economic concerns to be important. The effect of consumer sentiment will be larger when more people think the economy is important, and it will be smaller when fewer people do.

We also include measures of presidential and congressional approval. Presidential approval is a clear indicator of performance, generally rising and falling with national conditions. Some research finds that people tend to trust the government more when they approve of the president (Citrin and Luks 2001; Citrin 1974; Citrin and Green 1986; Miller and Borrelli 1991). We measure presidential approval using the quarterly mean response to Gallup's familiar question "Do you approve or disapprove of the way President _____ is handling his job as president?"

Although few Americans know enough about politics to gauge the performance of Congress, its effect on trust is, somewhat curiously, even stronger than that of presidential approval (Feldman 1983; Williams 1985; Hetherington 1998). This suggests that congressional approval taps more than performance. Variation in congressional approval is largely a function of discord in the lawmaking process, such as the occurrence of veto overrides, conflict within Congress, and major bill passage (Durr, Gilmour, and Wolbrecht 1997). These are many of the elements that Hibbing and Theiss-Morse (1995) identify as manifestations of the political process that Americans intensely dislike, so we view this as a measure of process as well.[11] We measure congressional approval using an updated version of the quarterly series developed by Durr, Gilmour, and Wolbrecht (1997) and modified by other studies of trust (Chanley, Rudolph, and Rahn 2000; Hetherington and Rudolph 2008).

Economic perceptions are, of course, strongly tied to both presidential approval (MacKuen, Erickson, and Stimson 1992) and congressional approval (Durr, Gilmour, and Wolbrecht 1997; Rudolph 2002). As a consequence, we create distinctly political measures of performance by purging both approval series of their economic variance.[12]

Scandals ought to matter, too, so we must account for them. To that end, we create a dummy series that assumes a value of one during quarters in which a scandal was highly visible. The scandals we include are drawn from the literature on political trust (Chanley, Rudolph, and Rahn 2000) and political approval (Durr, Gilmour, and Wolbrecht 1997). Our series includes the following scandals: Koreagate (1977:1), Abscam (1980:1), Iran-Contra (1986:4), Jim Wright (1989:2), Keating Five (1990:4), House banking (1991:3), House post office (1992:2), White House travel office (1993:2), Whitewater (1994:2), Filegate (1996:2), the Clinton impeachment proceedings (1998:4), Tom Delay resignation (2006:2), Mark Foley (2006:3), and Larry Craig (2007:3–2007:4).

Descriptive Analysis

To offer the broadest possible historical perspective, we first examine the annualized versions of the time series, which we can extend back to the 1950s, in figure 3.1. Political trust enjoyed its highest recorded levels in the 1950s and 1960s. The heights of the 1960s, however, were soon followed by the depths of the 1970s. After a temporary rebound in the 1980s, trust resumed its decline through the early 1990s, reaching a local minimum in 1994. Political trust began a slow ascent in the late 1990s and surged after 9/11. But trust lost its post-9/11 momentum relatively quickly and by 2005 had begun to decline again. Indeed, the last observations we gathered for this analysis are the lowest that have been recorded since scholars began to measure political trust. It is also worth noting that at no point in the annual series did levels of trust approach the heights of the 1950s and 1960s.

Annualized versions of the two MIP series (*Economy* and *International*) also appear in figure 3.1. Each series appears to follow a course that is broadly consistent with its hypothesized impact on political trust. Like political trust, *MIP International* was relatively high in the 1950s and 1960s, declined in the 1970s, but rebounded somewhat during the Reagan years. Also, like political trust, *MIP International* bottomed out in the mid-1990s, started to grow in the late 1990s, and jumped dramatically after 9/11. It has fallen sharply since the Great Recession of 2008, along with political trust. The path of *MIP Economy*, by contrast, follows a much different, but still anticipated, course. Suggesting a negative association with political trust, *MIP Economy* reached its heights in the 1970s and

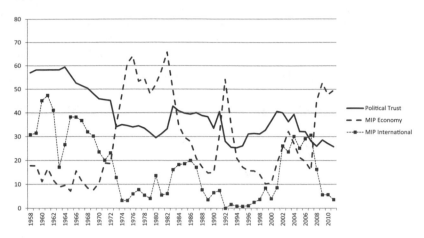

FIGURE 3.1. Political trust and national importance judgments: Annual data, 1958–2011

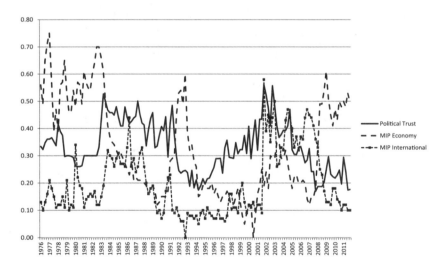

FIGURE 3.2. Political trust and national importance judgments: Quarterly data, 1976:1–2011:4

was declining rapidly during the Reagan years. It increased sharply during
the recession of the early 1990s but dropped soon after and remained low
for the rest of the decade. Not surprisingly, the *MIP Economy* series shot
upward in 2008 and has remained quite high through 2011. This pattern
is broadly consistent with our expectation that more people will think the
economy is important when it is bad than when it is good, which suggests

that bad economies will drive trust down more than good economies will cause it to increase.

The quarterly versions of these three series appear in figure 3.2. In some respects, the quarterly and annual series tell much the same story for the period they share in common. The quarterly series, however, adds much greater precision to the tale. In the case of political trust, for example, it shows that the Gulf War interrupted the steep descent that began in the early 1990s. It also shows that in the immediate aftermath of 9/11, political trust approached, albeit temporarily, levels not seen since the pre-Watergate era. Importantly, all three series exhibit considerably more short-term variation than their annual counterparts. In the analyses that follow, we exploit this variation to test whether fluctuations in performance, polarization, and national importance judgments have meaningful consequences for political trust.

A Dynamic Model of Political Trust

Our theory anticipates that political trust changes as our measures of performance, process, probity, priming, and polarization change. Our theory is dynamic in the sense that we expect shifts in the explanatory variables to have both direct and cumulative effects on political trust. Direct effects happen immediately. They occur when a change in one variable brings about an immediate change in another variable. Cumulative effects build over time. They are essentially a combination of direct effects and their residual effects that linger as time passes. It might be helpful to think about direct and cumulative effects in the context of a boxing match. A powerful punch will have an effect right after it is delivered. That is the direct effect. But its concussive aftershock will continue to affect its recipient, albeit to a diminishing degree, as rounds progress. The direct effect plus the effect of its aftershock represents the cumulative effect. Obviously, the cumulative effect will always be larger than its initial direct effect. To capture these dynamics, we estimate a time-series regression model.[13]

Theoretically, our model implies that both current (denoted with the subscript "t") and lagged values (denoted by the subscript "t-1") of the explanatory variables affect political trust. Because the lagged values of the explanatory variables (the five Ps) are measured *before* the dependent variable (political trust), we are able to use our time-series analysis to draw some causal inferences.[14]

Analysis and Results

The results of our model appear in table 3.3. The first data column reports
results that only account for the direct effects of each variable. The second
data column reports the results that also examine the conditional effect
of economic sentiment by including the hypothesized interaction between
economic sentiment and the proportion of the public that identifies the
economy as most important.

A quick inspection of the sign and significance of the estimated effects
in the first column reveals that our results comport well with theoretical expectations. Congressional approval is positively related to political
trust, while the effects of presidential approval are statistically negligible.
Consistent with previous research at both the individual and aggregate
levels, this result implies that political trust is more closely tied to public perceptions of Congress than to those of the president. As expected,
the results also show that political trust drops during periods of government scandal. Finally, consistent with performance-based explanations of
political trust, the results reveal a positive association between economic
sentiment and political trust.

Of central interest to us are the effects of the public's various national
importance judgments. To assess their impact, we turn to the results in
the second column, which take into account the fact that the effect of the
economy depends on the percentage of Americans who think the economy is an important problem. The results clearly suggest that political
trust responds to the issue areas the public thinks are most important.
The positive sign for the effect of *MIP International* means that political trust rises when international concerns are more salient. In addition,
the interaction between economic sentiment and *MIP Economy* is both
substantively and statistically significant, suggesting that the effects of
economic sentiment depend on the extent to which the public attaches
importance to economic issues. The positive sign here indicates that perceived economic performance exerts a greater impact on political trust
when the economy is more salient. Since the economy is more salient
when the economy is sour than when it is robust, this result supports the
hypothesized asymmetric effect in which political trust suffers more from
hard times than it benefits from good ones. Also central to our story is the
influence of partisan polarization. Its negative and statistically significant
coefficient suggests that when levels of polarization go up, levels of political trust go down.

TABLE 3.3 **Predictors of political trust**

	Political trust$_t$	Political trust$_t$	Immediate impact (%)	Cumulative impact (%)
	Parameter estimate (Standard error)	Parameter estimate (Standard error)	Parameter estimate (Standard error)	Parameter estimate (Standard error)
Political trust$_{t-1}$	0.40** (0.06)	0.38** (0.06)		
Congressional approval$_t$	0.41** (0.09)	0.46** (0.09)	16.6	28.1
Presidential approval$_t$	0.03 (0.05)	0.03 (0.05)	3.3	5.6
Partisan polarization$_t$	−0.09** (0.03)	−0.08** (0.03)	−5.0	−8.1
Government scandals$_t$	−0.03* (0.01)	−0.03* (0.01)	−3.0	−5.1
MIP International$_t$	0.14** (0.04)	0.12** (0.04)	5.2	8.8
MIP Economy$_t$	0.10** (0.03)	0.10** (0.03)		
Economic sentiment$_t$	0.29** (0.05)	0.28** (0.05)		
Economic sentiment$_t$ x MIP Economy$_t$	—	0.41* (0.21)		
Constant	0.23** (0.03)	0.25** (0.03)		
Economic sentiment				
High salience	—	—	26.0	41.9
Low salience	—	—	6.3	10.2
Durbin's H	1.92	1.36		
p-value	0.16	0.24		
Breusch-Godfrey	2.03	1.45		
p-value	0.15	0.23		
Portmanteau Q$_{(df = 40)}$	25.79	26.71		
p-value	0.96	0.95		
DF-GLS μ (trust)				
Number of cases	144	144		
Adjusted R^2	0.77	0.78		

Note: Entries in the first and second data columns are ordinary least squares (OLS) estimates with standard errors in parentheses. Data are quarterly and cover the period from 1976:1 to 2011:4. Durbin's H and Breusch-Godfrey test statistics indicate an absence of serial correlation in the residuals. Portmanteau Q tests fail to reject the null hypothesis that the residuals are white noise. The DF-GLSμ test rejects the null hypothesis that political trust contains a unit root at the 0.05 level. Entries in the third and fourth data columns report the percent change in political trust associated with a one-unit shock to each explanatory variable, while all other variables are at the mean values.

$*p < 0.05, **p < 0.01$

We turn now to consider the magnitude of these effects. Given the dynamic nature of our model, it is important to consider both the immediate and the cumulative effects of a given variable. Table 3.3 reports the effects of a one-unit change, holding all else constant, for each of our variables.[15] Consider first a one-unit change to *Congressional Approval*. The immediate impact of this shock on political trust would be an increase of nearly 16.6 percent, and the cumulative effect would be an increase of 28.1 percent.[16] When a scandal occurs, there is, on average, an immediate 3 percent reduction in political trust and a cumulative reduction of 5.1 percent. We can calculate the short-term and long-term effects of polarization similarly. A one-unit increase in partisan polarization has the immediate effect of reducing political trust by 5 percent. The effects of rising polarization accumulate over time. The cumulative effect of a one-unit increase in polarization is to reduce political trust by 8.1 percent.[17]

We can calculate the magnitude of the effects for national importance judgments in the same fashion. The immediate impact of a one-unit jump in *MIP International* on political trust is about 5.2 percent. After taking the rate of decay into account, the cumulative effect of this jump is an increase in political trust of nearly 9 percent. To illustrate the moderating influence of *MIP Economy* on economic sentiment, we compare the effect of a one-unit increase in economic sentiment when *MIP Economy* is at its minimum and maximum values. This reveals that, when the public does not consider economic matters to be important, the effect of economic perceptions is considerably smaller. Under such conditions, a one-unit increase in economic sentiment produces about a 5.8 percent increase in political trust immediately and about a 9.8 percent increase over time. When economic matters are most salient, however, the effects of economic sentiment are considerably larger. The same one-unit shock in economic sentiment increases political trust by roughly 26 percent immediately and by more than 44 percent over time. Simply put, the effects of economic sentiment on political trust are about four times larger when economic matters are most salient than when they are least salient.

This asymmetry helps explain why trust declines so much during periods of economic hardship but does not rise as rapidly during periods of economic strength. To illustrate this point, we conduct a simulation in which we use our model to recreate the economic worlds of 1998 and 2008, holding all other variables constant at their mean. The years 1998 and 2008 are particularly well suited for such a simulation because they are nearly mirror opposites in terms of economic conditions. In 1998, economic sentiment was quite positive, about 1.5 standard deviations above its mean. In 2008, economic sentiment was quite negative, about 1.5 standard deviations below its mean. Consistent with our theory, *MIP Economy* was approximately one standard deviation below its mean in 1998 and one standard deviation above in 2008. If we shocked both economic variables to their 1998 levels, our model predicts political trust would experience an immediate increase of approximately 4 percent. If we instead shocked the economic variables to their 2008 levels, however, our model predicts that political trust would decrease by about 17 percent, an effect roughly four times as large. In short, the moderating influence of *MIP Economy* means that negative economic perceptions erode trust much more than positive economic perceptions restore it.

Implications of Our Results

Quite understandably, scholars viewed post-1960s trust levels as atypical because they differed from those gathered in the late 1950s and the early 1960s when the trust questions made their survey debuts. The political events of the time, such as defeat in Vietnam, the Nixon resignation, and a decade of economic weakness, suggested that better performance over the long haul would return trust to bygone-era levels (Citrin and Green 1986). If variation in trust was only about performance, however, it should have achieved a level at least approaching those early readings at some point in the past thirty-five years. Yet, with the exception of a short-lived burst after 9/11, it has never come close.

Rather than the post-1960s period being atypical, our results suggest that it was the conditions and imperatives in post–World War II America that produced anomalously high levels of political trust. Through the 1950s and 1960s, economic performance was most often solid and sometimes spectacular. The threat from the outside world was always very high. This constellation of factors, which has yet to reoccur for any sustained period, combined to produce a rising tide of political trust.

Most periods in American history are not characterized by widespread fear of nuclear annihilation, however. As Americans started to think less about government in terms of external threat and more in terms of redistributive social programs (Jacoby 1994), trust in government went into a decline from which it has not recovered. The economy's asymmetric effect has kept trust relatively low. When the economy is performing badly, more people care about it, which increases its (negative) effect on trust. Since fewer people care about the economy when times are good, trust increases less in periods of prosperity than it decreases in periods of weakness. If economic performance is the engine that drives political trust, that engine needs to work about four times as hard for about four times as long to raise trust as it does to lower it. As a result, even the long, uninterrupted periods of economic success in the 1980s and 1990s could not return trust to its mid-1960s peak.

There is little to suggest that low to moderate levels of trust will go away in the future. Although terrorism has the capacity to unnerve the American public, analysts should not conclude that fears about terrorism are equivalent to those about the Soviet Union in the 1950s and 1960s. Accounting for the eighteen times the Gallup Organization asked its most important problem question during the 1950s, the median percentage of Americans choosing an international concern was fifty-three. Furthermore, in Gallup's fifteen surveys using the most important problem questions between May 1960 and October 1962, twelve recorded a percentage of international concerns greater than or equal to the 67 percent who cited terrorism and other international issues in the first poll taken after September 11, 2001. Whereas the post-9/11 percentage citing terrorism and foreign policy quickly receded into the forties, Americans in the late 1950s and early 1960s lived with 9/11 levels of anxiety about foreign threat for years.

The findings uncovered in this chapter have the potential to create two difficult challenges for effective governance. First, we have shown that political trust is quite sensitive to changes in issue salience. At the individual level, political psychologists have repeatedly shown that agenda setting and issue salience are subject to elite cues and elite manipulation. By selectively focusing individuals' attention on some issues rather than on others, partisan elites can indirectly manipulate levels of trust. When one set of partisan elites has political incentives to increase political trust while another set has reasons to depress it, the likely result is the polarization of political trust along partisan or ideological lines. Such polarization makes it difficult to forge consensus and govern. We begin to provide evidence for this proposition in the next chapter.

In addition, we have shown that the public is, in general, far less focused on international concerns now than it was in the 1950s and 1960s. At the outset of the Cold War in 1947, the chairman of the Senate Foreign Relations Committee, Senator Arthur Vandenberg (R-MI), famously asserted that "politics stops at the water's edge." The diminution of the persistent out-group threat that existed during the Cold War has, in some respects, diminished important opportunities for in-group solidarity. In short, the public is currently less focused on the types of issues that encourage bipartisan cooperation and compromise, both of which help grease the wheels of democratic governance.

Conclusion

The results in this chapter strongly suggest that political trust is a function of the issues on which the mass public is focused over time. Less concern about international issues has helped keep trust relatively low. In addition, the conditioning effect of national importance judgments on economic perceptions has inhibited often excellent economies from rescuing trust from its post–Great Society swoon.

The results also provide the first longitudinal look at the relationship between partisan polarization and political trust. Our analysis found that increases in polarization reduced levels of political trust. Given the nature of the analysis in this chapter (i.e., aggregate-level analysis), we cannot provide a precise account of the individual-level mechanisms that explain this relationship. In chapter 4, we will analyze individual-level panel data that will enable us to better explain how polarization erodes political trust.

Although our macrolevel design naturally limits our ability to draw individual-level inferences, the results suggest that individuals respond differently to economic and international threats. The root cause of such behavior likely lies not solely in elite rhetoric but rather in human nature itself. Social psychologists have long observed that out-group threats trigger various manifestations of in-group solidarity, including increases in patriotism and national identity. Since international dangers can pose a threat to a nation's political system, such dangers ought to increase support for that system. Economic problems, by contrast, tend to be more home-grown and are less likely to trigger such in-group/out-group thinking. In the next chapter, we begin to unpack some of the individual-level mechanisms that have created the polarization of trust that now characterizes our politics.

CHAPTER FOUR

How Political Trust Became Polarized

In chapter 3, we demonstrated that issue salience causes trust to fluctuate over time. We found that economic performance matters, but its effect depends on the salience of the economy. Since the economy tends to be more salient when times are bad, slumping economies drive trust down more than surging economies drive it up. We also found that trust tends to go up when international issues are prominent, something that has been significantly less common since the end of the Cold War than it was at the dawn of the survey era. In addition, we found that polarization also undermines political trust. Taking these factors together, we now better understand why trust today is about as low as it has ever been in the nearly sixty years scholars have been measuring it.

To reach these conclusions, we employed time-series analysis. Although time-series analysis has many strengths, especially as it relates to establishing causal order, it also has weaknesses. One weakness is that it does not allow researchers to account for the fact that different types of *individuals* might form opinions differently. In this chapter, we turn to the analysis of individual-level data. With individual-level data, the unit of our statistical analyses is no longer the year or the quarter but rather the individual American, which allows us to assess whether different types of people respond differently to the same political conditions. It is these data that allow us to reveal the polarization of political trust by party identification, which is, to us, a core explanation for today's governing crisis.

The downside to individual-level data analysis is that all the opinions that survey respondents provide are usually gathered at the same time, which makes establishing causal order more difficult than with time-series analysis. Fortunately, we often have available to us panel data, in which

interviewers ask the same individuals the same questions at different
points in time, allowing us to overcome some of the causality problems
inherent in most individual level data.

In this chapter, we discover two major causes of the polarization of political trust. The first is likely the foundation for the second. As we detailed
in chapter 2, partisans' feelings about the other political party have grown
much more negative over the last fifteen years. Indeed, we show that the
feelings partisans have about the other party are as negative today as the
feelings Americans had about fringe groups like the John Birch Society in
the 1970s. These feelings are directly linked to how much trust people express. Frigid feelings about the governing party lead to low levels of trust
in the government it leads.

In addition to contributing directly to polarized trust, we suspect these
icy feelings toward political opponents cause partisans to perceive relevant conditions increasingly differently depending on whether their party
is in power. This is true of even seemingly objective matters like the state
of the economy (Bartels 2002). In addition to perceiving conditions differently, we find that when their party is in power, partisans employ criteria
favorable to their side when asked to evaluate the government, causing
them to express more trust. When their party is out of power, however,
partisans employ criteria that are unfavorable to their political opponents,
causing them to express less trust. Taken together, these regularities have
combined to produce the polarization of political trust.

Explaining the Recent Polarization of Political Trust

In chapter 1, we established that the early 2000s witnessed an unprecedented polarization of political trust along partisan lines that, we believe,
is fundamentally important to understanding the dysfunctional politics
of the period. Whereas Republicans and Democrats rarely differed by
much in their levels of political trust between the 1950s and the 1990s
(see Hetherington 2008), things changed dramatically in the early 2000s.
Indeed, in the last years of the Bush administration and in the middle two
years of Barack Obama's first term, fewer than 10 percent of partisans
who identified with the party opposite the president reported trusting the
government at least "most of the time." Oftentimes, about 95 percent of
these out-party partisans said they trusted government either "only some
of the time" or "never."

Having identified this important trend, we turn to establishing its causes and its timing. We bring to bear several different data collections to help us answer these questions. None perfectly suit our purposes, but, taken together, all provide us with some leverage. Our first cut relies on panel data gathered during the period when polarization first took root, 2000–2004. To ensure the political world has, indeed, changed as we suspect, we replicate the panel analysis, using panel data gathered from 1992 to 1996. We augment the panel analysis with an analysis of cross-sectional data collected in 2010 and 2012, allowing us to examine whether Republicans behaved the same way that Democrats did when faced with a president of the opposite party as was the case for Democrats from 2000 to 2004.

Frosty Feelings about the Other Party

Our explanation for polarization has two components. The first is very straightforward, almost obvious. A key explanation for polarized trust is partisans' increasing dislike of the other party. Recall from chapter 2 that ordinary Republicans and Democrats of the 1980s and 1990s didn't strongly dislike the opposing political party. The average feeling thermometer scores that partisans provided the other party were not far below the neutral point of fifty degrees on the American National Election Study (ANES)'s feeling thermometer scale. In contrast, the 2010s have seen partisans' average temperatures for the other party fall into the twenties. In 2011, specifically, the average score that Democrats gave the Republican Party was about twenty-three degrees, roughly the same average score Republicans gave the Democratic Party.[1] In 2012, the averages increased a bit, but not above freezing.

Such temperatures are frigid not just in an absolute sense but also in a relative one. Over the many decades that the ANES has asked Americans to rate dozens of groups, we calculate the average score for every feeling thermometer that appears in the ANES Cumulative Data File. Of the thirty-eight groups that fit these criteria, only four produced mean scores of forty degrees or below: "gays and lesbians" (forty degrees), "illegal aliens" (thirty-eight degrees), "radical students" (twenty-five degrees), and "black militants" (twenty-three degrees). Put another way, it is only groups like these that induce feelings as negative as those that partisans now hold for each other.

By bringing to bear all the biennial ANES studies, not just the ANES Cumulative File, including a wider array of groups, we can paint an even

TABLE 4.1 **Average feeling thermometer toward disliked groups, 1968–2011**

Polarizing group	Negative feelings thermometer score
1968	
Vietnam protestors	30°
1970	
Ministers leading protest marches	32°
People who go to rock festivals	26°
John Birch Society	24°
Radical students	15°
Black militants	15°
People using marijuana	12°
People who riot in cities	10°
1972	
Radical students	26°
Marijuana users	21°
Black militants	17°
Urban rioters	12°
1974	
Radical students	24°
Marijuana users	20°
Black militants	16°
1976	
Marijuana users	32°
Radical students	30°
Black militants	24°
1980	
Radical students	30°
Black militants	30°
1984	
Black militants	32°
Homosexuals	30°
1986	
Black militants	28°
1988	
Illegal aliens	36°
Homosexuals	29°
1994	
Gays and lesbians	36°
Illegal immigrants	33°
2011	
Democrats about the Republican Party	23°
Republicans about the Democratic Party	23°

Source: American National Election Study, 1968–2008, 2011, YouGov survey.

more vivid picture of just how much today's partisans dislike their opponents. The results in table 4.1 take a finer-grained look at which groups
have generated such negative feelings and when, specifically, those negative feelings occurred. In the table, we include only groups for which the
average score in a given year is below forty degrees. The first thing to note

is that, of the groups the ANES has asked about, very few generate such negative feelings. Of those that do, most occupy the fringe of American political life, at least at the time the specific ANES survey turned up such negative feelings.

Although Americans in 1968 did not like "Vietnam protesters" much (thirty degrees), they still liked them a bit more than partisans liked the other party in 2011. In 1970, "ministers leading protest marches" (thirty-two degrees) and "people who go to rock festivals" (thirty degrees) were also somewhat more warmly evaluated than our comparison groups. With the ANES asking about a much more colorful set of groups in 1970 than they do today, the survey turned up four groups for whom feelings were more negative than partisans' feelings about the other party today. These four fall into two categories. The first set includes explicit lawbreakers—namely, "people who riot in cities" (ten degrees) and "people using marijuana" (twelve degrees). The other set includes groups that explicitly rebelled against existing norms—namely, "radical students" (fifteen degrees) and "black militants" (fifteen degrees). Tellingly, perhaps, feelings about the "John Birch Society" in 1970 (twenty-four degrees) were about the same as those that partisans today have about their political opponents. It is also noteworthy that by 1976, feelings about "marijuana users" (thirty-two degrees) had become warmer than partisans' feelings about their opponents today.

By the 1980s, the ANES had stopped asking thermometer questions about fringe groups, so we uncovered many fewer groups with average scores below forty degrees. The only exceptions were "illegal aliens" and "gays and lesbians." Moreover, the average score for "gays and lesbians" moved from the high twenties in the late 1980s toward fifty degrees by the 2000s. All this is to suggest that partisans' feelings about their counterparts today are extraordinarily negative when viewed relative to feelings about other groups. When Republicans think about the Democratic Party and Democrats think about the Republican Party, it is akin to Americans thinking about John Birchers and pot smokers in the 1970s or gays and lesbians during the height of the AIDS scare in the 1980s. These are terribly negative feelings indeed.

We suspect that the remarkably low thermometer scores that partisans give the other party helps explain the near absence of trust in government expressed by partisans who do not identify with the president's party. It is rare in life when people trust those whom they dislike. People are more likely to view members of their own social groups as more trustworthy than nongroup members because they are perceived to be like them (Uslaner 2012). Although such findings have dealt primarily with trust in other people, we see no reason to believe that the same reasoning would not hold for *political* trust. A political climate that has wrought the level of hostility toward political adversaries that we are experiencing today ought to be a key reason why partisans express so little trust in government when government is run by the other party.

Motivated Reasoning

There is more to our story than frigid feelings toward the other party, although we do suspect that the second component of our explanation for polarization is related to it. The second mechanism that we identify for the polarization of political trust is somewhat more complicated and requires more explanation. Scholars know well that perceived performance by the government causes change in political trust, with the economy being particularly important. The research to date, however, suggests that poor performance ought to drive down trust for all people, at least to the extent that everyone perceives roughly the same performance. We provide evidence below that suggests Americans, in fact, perceive increasingly different economic and foreign policy performance depending on their party identification. We also find that they weight these perceptions differently when they decide, in turn, how much they trust the government.

Our hypothesis starts with theories of what scholars call "motivated reasoning" (Kunda 1990; Lodge and Taber 2000, 2013; Redlawsk 2002; Rudolph 2006; Taber and Lodge 2006). Scholars have shown that motivated reasoning leads people to process information or evidence in a biased manner to allow them to reach a preferred judgment or conclusion. In other words, people tend to see things the way they are predisposed to see them, regardless of whether their perceptions are fully grounded in reality. Partisans evaluate things more favorably when their party is in power and more negatively when the other party holds the reins. Republicans and Democrats might be experiencing the same economy, for example, but they are prone to evaluate it much differently based on political context (Bartels 2002; Gerber and Huber 2010). With political elites more polarized now than before and negative feelings about the other side growing more acute, we suspect this tendency toward motivated reasoning has grown sharper of late.

We also extend the application of motivated reasoning. We believe that different political elites have incentives to make different *forms* of performance salient to their issue publics. Hence different components of perceived performance might come to be weighted differently by partisans of different stripes. For example, consider a situation in which the economy has been flagging, but foreign policy has been a success. Elites of the president's party would want to avoid talking about economic failures and instead focus on foreign policy triumphs. Out-party elites would want to do the reverse because they have incentives to focus their followers on the president's frailties. As a result, partisans who identify with the president's party ought to be more likely to update how much they trust the government based on evaluations of foreign policy, while partisans who do not identify with the president's party ought to be more likely to update based on evaluations of economic performance.

In that sense, our thinking moves motivated reasoning from why people evaluate things as they do to what consequences such evaluations have. Specifically, we posit that motivated reasoning can also lead people to place greater *emphasis* on evaluative criteria that benefit their political friends and harm their political foes. Put another way, we argue that partisans act as biased information processors by selectively focusing on information that favors their political allies or disfavors their political adversaries. Some evidence for such a process already exists. When making judgments about gubernatorial responsibility for states' negative fiscal conditions, for example, Democrats place less weight on information that ought to increase perceptions of responsibility for a Democratic governor (Rudolph 2006). Republicans, by contrast, place less weight on information that could be used to decrease perceptions of responsibility for a Democratic governor. Political elites facilitate such partisan bias in information processing by focusing on their side's advantages and the other's liabilities. That is the first lesson in Campaigning 101: encourage voters to consider the election in terms of criteria favorable to you and unfavorable to your opponent.

Theories of motivating reasoning, then, generate two sets of expectations. First, based on the original understanding of motivated reasoning, people from different partisan groups will provide quite different evaluations of political conditions. Moreover, the divergence ought to be greater in the 2000s than in decades past because political elites have polarized, which has increased the motivation partisans have to perceive the world in a way that favors their side. Second, based on our extension of motivated reasoning, people from different partisan groups will place differential weight on those evaluations when they express how much they trust the government. As a result, when Democrats are in power, they will not only evaluate various conditions better than Republicans will but also weight the most unambiguously favorable evaluations more heavily in expressing levels of trust. Republicans will, of course, do the reverse. Combined with more negative feelings about the other party, we show that these processes have produced a polarization in political trust.

Before moving forward with testing our thinking, a note about terminology is order. As strongly as we embrace the tenets of partisan-motivated reasoning, we fear the term sounds like academic jargon to many. This could become particularly problematic if we tried to extend the term to describe the secondary effects of motivated reasoning, specifically the different weights that partisans place on different criteria. Hence we introduce two terms here that we believe are sufficiently descriptive of the processes we hope to describe while, at the same time, less daunting than the specific terms: "partisan-motivated reasoning" and "second-order partisan-motivated reasoning." When we use the term "partisan assessment," we have in mind the traditional understanding of partisan-motivated reasoning. When we use the term "partisan weighting," we have in mind our extension of the traditional theory.

Testing the Hypotheses

The period between 2000 and 2004 provides excellent conditions to test our hypotheses. We are fortunate that the ANES fielded a panel survey in three waves (2000, 2002, and 2004), allowing us to track the same survey respondents' political trust scores at three points in time. In all three waves, the ANES asked all four of the trust-in-government items.[2] Unlike in the previous chapter where data limitations forced us to use a single item to measure trust, we have in this case a more comprehensive, and hence more reliable, measure. Moreover, the panel component allows us to see how the same people with specific characteristics changed their trust scores and what criteria they based those changes on. Our focus here is on different performance criteria.

To that end, the ANES asked Americans to assess performance in both the economic *and* foreign policy domains. This allows us to compare whether Republicans and Democrats evaluated conditions differently and weighted those evaluations differently when they were asked the trust-in-government questions. Much literature suggests that retrospective *economic* evaluations cause changes in political trust (e.g., Weatherford 1984; Citrin and Green 1986). Questions about the economy appear in a wide range of surveys. Only the ANES regularly asks people to assess whether the United States' position in the world has grown stronger, weaker, or remained the same over the past year, which allows us to tap performance in the foreign policy domain as well.

Evidence of Partisan Assessments

In the population as a whole, political trust increased substantially between 2000 and 2002 and then dropped a bit between 2002 and 2004. The surge in political trust likely had its roots in the general surge in positive feelings about most things in American life after 9/11 (Hetherington and Nelson 2003). In addition, the results in chapter 3 suggest that the increased salience of the parts of government that handle foreign policy was important. Since people like the parts of government that handle foreign policy more than the parts that handle domestic policy, trust rises when those that handle foreign policy capture headlines.

Examining change in trust for the whole population obscures some important group differences, however. We begin to examine those in figure 4.1. Here we have placed trust on a (0,1) interval, so differences can be interpreted as percentage differences between groups. In 2000, the difference between Republicans and Democrats in their political trust was a statistically insignificant 2.5 percentage points. In 2002, the difference grew to a statistically meaningful 8 percentage points. Between 2002 and 2004, the difference nearly doubled to 15 percentage points. The average trust score for Republicans shot up by 13 percentage points between 2000 and 2002. For Democrats, the increase was less than 3 percentage points, not even a statistically significant change. In contrast, trust did not drop significantly for Republican identifiers between 2002 and 2004, but it dropped by a lot (9 percentage points) among Democrats. Over the four year period, trust increased significantly for Republicans and decreased significantly among Democrats. These results make clear that partisans responded differently to the same world.

Evaluations of performance ought to help explain these changes in trust. In figure 4.2, we see a pattern in retrospective assessments of the economy that strongly suggests partisan assessment. Objectively speaking, economic conditions in 2002 were not particularly strong. After the

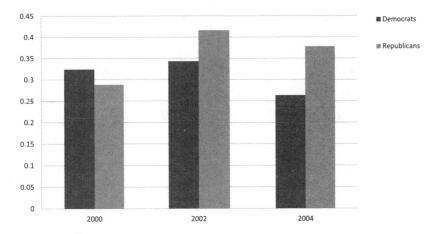

FIGURE 4.1. Political trust by party identification, 2000, 2002, and 2004

Source: American National Election Study, 2000–2004, panel study.

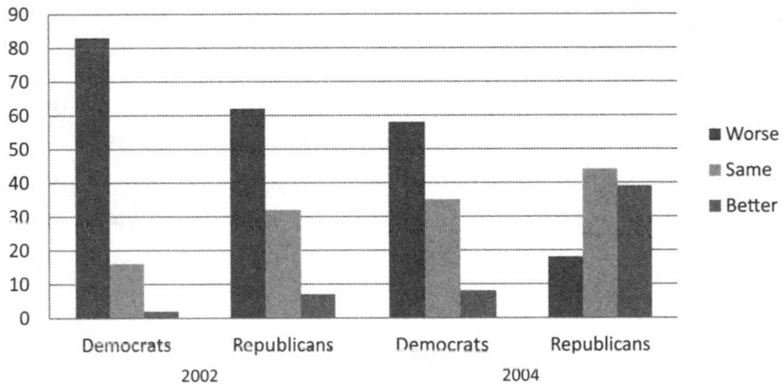

FIGURE 4.2. Perceptions of economic performance, 2002 and 2004

Source: American National Election Study, 2000–2004, panel study.

dot-com boom of the late 1990s faded, the economy became mired in recession. Gross domestic product (GDP) growth dropped below 2 percent in late 2002. Although inflation remained relatively steady, unemployment jumped to nearly 6 percent. Growth in real income was also poor, dropping by 1.1 percent compared with 2001. Add to those numbers several high-profile scandals involving major corporations, such as Enron and World-Com, and it is clear that the economic picture had darkened considerably since the end of the Clinton presidency. In 2002, Republicans perceived a deteriorating economy, but Democrats' assessments were gloomier still.

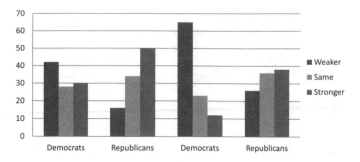

FIGURE 4.3. Perceptions of foreign policy performance by party, 2002 and 2004

Source: American National Election Study, 2000–2004, panel study.

More precisely, 83 percent of Democrats thought the economy had gotten "somewhat" or "much" worse, while only 62 percent of Republicans did. More than 30 percent of Republicans thought the economy was about the same, whereas half that percentage of Democrats did.

By 2004, signs of economic recovery were evident, although the economy was not exactly roaring. The employment situation had improved with the unemployment rate dropping to 5.5 percent after it had topped out at 6.3 percent in 2003. Growth remained somewhat slow by historical standards, but it was better than the several previous years, with GDP increasing at a nearly 3 percent clip. Republicans were much more likely than Democrats to recognize the recovery, such as it was. Thirty-nine percent of them thought the economy had gotten better, with only 18 percent saying it had gotten worse. Democrats perceived things much differently (and incorrectly), with only 8 percent saying the economy had gotten better and 58 percent saying it had gotten worse. These substantial gaps in perceptions provide clear evidence of partisan assessment, people's tendency to perceive conditions the way they want to perceive them.

We see the reverse pattern on foreign affairs. In figure 4.3, we chart how Americans assessed America's changing position in the world. In 2002, with the United States building a "coalition of the willing" and achieving a quick military victory in Afghanistan, 39 percent of Americans thought that America's place in the world had grown stronger over the past year. Consistent with partisan assessment, Republicans were more likely to see it that way with a Republican president in the White House. In 2002, 50 percent of them saw the United States' position as stronger, while only 30 percent of Democrats did. Indeed, the most common response for Republicans was "stronger," while the most common response for Democrats was "weaker." In 2004, that tendency to assess America's fortunes abroad in different terms was even sharper. With the wars in Iraq and Afghanistan bogging down, about 65 percent of Democrats viewed the nation's stature on the world stage as weakening. Only 25 percent of Republicans saw it that way. For Republicans, the most common assessment remained "getting stronger."

For our purposes, it is also useful to compare the distributions in figures 4.1 and 4.2. Republicans' assessments of foreign affairs were much more favorable than were their assessments of the economy; the pattern was the opposite among Democrats. As a result, we expect that Republicans will be more inclined to use their assessments of foreign policy performance than of economic performance to update how much trust in government they express during the time frame. In contrast, Democrats ought to weight their economic assessments more heavily when they update their trust evaluations.

Evidence of Partisan Weighting, 2000–2002

To test this hypothesis, we estimate a regression model, which allows us to take into account multiple potential causes of a phenomenon at the same time. Specifically, our dependent variable is political trust measured in 2002.[3] To estimate change in political trust, we include political trust measured in 2000 as an independent variable. This set up allows us to assess change in political trust between the two years. Our panel data allow us to include lagged values of two assessments that are commonly used to explain political trust, presidential approval, and congressional approval. By using a lagged value, we can be more certain that these assessments are causes, not consequences, of political trust. In addition, we include lagged measures of the party feeling thermometers that we referenced at the beginning of the chapter. The increased tendency of out-party partisans to assess the in-party negatively should be centrally important in explaining trust. To increase confidence in our estimates, we also include a set of demographics in our model—namely, race, age, gender, and education. Finally, we include our two measures of performance from 2002: retrospective economic evaluations and evaluations of the United States' relative strength in the world.

The results from our statistical model appear in table 4.2. Since we expect Democrats and Republicans to weight different evaluations differently,

TABLE 4.2 **Change in political trust as a function of partisan assessment and other variables, 2000–2002**

	Democrats	Republicans
	Parameter estimate (Standard error)	Parameter estimate (Standard error)
Political trust$_{2000}$	0.599* (0.048)	0.481* (0.058)
Foreign policy evaluations$_{2002}$	0.038 (0.028)	0.082* (0.034)
Economic evaluations$_{2002}$	0.180* (0.059)	−0.044 (0.062)
Feeling thermometer: Democratic Party$_{2000}$	0.044 (0.056)	−0.009 (0.075)
Feeling thermometer: Republican Party$_{2000}$	0.132* (0.054)	0.146* (0.081)
Presidential approval$_{2000}$	−0.082* (0.036)	0.002 (0.030)
Congressional approval$_{2000}$	0.026 (0.024)	0.038 (0.028)
Race (African American)	−0.050 (0.033)	−0.406 (0.282)
Gender (female)	0.006 (0.022)	0.044* (0.026)
Education (some college)	0.023 (0.027)	−0.045 (0.032)
Education (college)	0.012 (0.033)	−0.003 (0.036)
Education (graduate school)	0.030 (0.048)	−0.058 (0.042)
Age	0.000 (0.001)	0.001 (0.001)
Constant	0.076 (0.059)	0.065 (0.081)
Number of cases	296	266
Adjusted R^2	0.42	0.28

*$p < 0.05$, one-tailed test
Source: American National Election Study, 2000–2004, panel study.

we divide our sample by party. Because leaning partisans tend to behave similarly to weak partisans (Keith et al. 1986), we include leaners in our partisan categories.[4] This leaves a sample of pure independents too small to make any confident inferences about, so we discard them from the analysis. In the first column of table 4.2, we display the results for the Democrats. They follow the expected pattern. Among the opinions and evaluations of central interest to us, first note the effect of national retrospective economic evaluations among Democrats. In updating how much they trust in government between 2000 and 2002, Democrats relied on what were, on average, their very poor assessments of the economy. These results suggest that, not only was there evidence of partisan assessment, but there was also strong evidence of partisan weighting. In contrast, the effect of Democrats' assessments of the United States' strength in the world is less than half the size of that of their economic assessments and fails to reach conventional levels of statistical significance. In short, when given the choice to evaluate the Republican-led government on criteria helpful or harmful to the GOP, Democratic partisans chose the latter. As a result, the 9/11-induced rally in trust did not continue into late 2002 among Democrats.

We next turn to the results for Republican identifiers, which we display in the second column of table 4.2. Here we often find the reverse pattern of results, which, combined with the results for Democratic partisans, helps us understand why political trust has become polarized by party. Not only did Republicans overwhelmingly think that things had improved on the world stage for the United States in 2002, but its effect on changing trust was large and statistically significant. In contrast, retrospective economic evaluations, which were quite poor among Republicans (although not as poor as they were among Democrats), had no discernable effect on trust. Republicans, then, were using performance criteria that drove trust up for them, while Democrats were using performance criteria that drove trust down for them.[5]

The Effects of Feelings about the Parties

Also critical to our story is the effect of feelings about the political parties (as measured in 2000). Feelings about the Republican Party, specifically, produce statistically significant effects among both Democrats and Republicans, although feelings about the Democratic Party do not affect either set of partisans. That people would update how much they trust the government based on how they feel about the Republican Party but not the Democratic Party makes sense, insofar as the government was in Republican hands in 2002.

The reason these effects for feelings about the Republican Party produce greater polarization in trust requires a little explanation and, extrapolating past 2002, a few assumptions. First, because we only have panel data from 2000 to 2004, we must assume that the *effect* of feelings about the Republican Party is the same in this time period as in 2006 or 2008, when panel data are not available. We do not believe this is a controversial assumption. In fact, it is probably a conservative one given how much more important political parties have become for people in evaluating the political world as the twenty-first century has progressed. The effect of feelings about the Republican Party is likely increasing with time, which would make our results even more dramatic if true, but data limitations do not allow us to test this directly.

We can, however, use this estimated effect of the Republican Party feeling thermometer on trust and how feelings about the party have changed over time to get a rough sense of its impact. Between 2000 and 2004, Republican Party identifiers' feelings about the Republican Party increased from seventy-four degrees to seventy-seven degrees. During this same period, Democratic Party identifiers' feelings about the Republican Party dropped from forty-one degrees to thirty-six degrees. These changes in average thermometer scores combined with the regression results in table 4.2 suggest that the slight increase in positive affect among Republicans toward the GOP during the period increased trust for them. For Democrats, however, the increasingly negative affect they expressed toward the GOP during the period depressed trust for them.

Of course, it is also critical to note that this was only the beginning of a process that would grow much starker with time. It seems clear that increasingly negative feelings about the other party are a central cause of the polarization of trust. We have already detailed that Democrats' feelings grew much more negative as the Bush presidency progressed. By 2008, the average feeling thermometer score that Democrats gave the Republican Party fell to thirty degrees, which, according to our model, would drive Democrats' trust in government down further still. It is worth noting that the steepness of these over-time changes in feelings about the other party are quite remarkable in survey data. Those thermometer scores had moved only a few degrees downward over the twenty-year period between the start of the Reagan presidency and the end of the Clinton presidency. That the Republican thermometer plummeted by ten degrees among Democrats in the space of just eight years is stunning.

A Fluke? Evidence of Partisan Weighting, 2002–4

We replicate the analysis above, this time moving to the 2002–4 component of the panel. Unfortunately, the ANES did not ask panel respondents about their feelings about the parties in either 2002 or 2004.[6] Hence we must drop the party thermometers from the analysis.

The first column in table 4.3 displays the estimates for Democratic identifiers. As in the 2000–2002 period, the effect of retrospective economic evaluations on changes in political trust is statistically significant. Since most Democrats continued to perceive a deteriorating economy during the previous year (despite the fact that it was improving), relying on these evaluations served to hold their trust in government down between 2002 and 2004. Although most Democrats also thought the US position in the world had deteriorated during the past year, they apparently did not rely on these evaluations to update their trust in government, which is evidenced by the fact that this evaluation fails to achieve statistical significance. We suspect this is because Democratic presidential candidate John Kerry and other Democratic elites tried to focus the electorate during the campaign on what they described as a jobless, soft economic recovery more than on conditions abroad.[7]

Among Republicans, we again find the same basic tendency to update trust evaluations in a manner systematically different from the way Democrats updated theirs. The results for Republicans appear in the second column of table 4.3. In contrast to Democrats, foreign policy evaluations have a large and statistically significant effect. Since Republicans generally saw the country's strength on the world stage as improving, relying on these evaluations kept their trust in government relatively high. Republicans did not rely on their economic evaluations to update how much trust in government they expressed between 2002 and 2004. Although economic evaluations were much better among GOPers in 2004 than they were in 2002, we suspect the reason they were not influential in 2004 is twofold: First, the economy, while better, was not exactly roaring. Hence many Republicans might have believed, rightly, that the economy was at least the same as it was in 2003, if not better, without believing the economy was particularly good. Second, reflecting the first reason, Republican elites worked hard to frame the presidential election around foreign policy, sending a message to Republicans in the electorate that evaluating the political system on these grounds was the proper thing to do.[8]

Is This Pattern of Findings Different from the Past?

Perhaps Republicans and Democrats have always relied on different criteria when asked to evaluate the government. If true, it would cast doubt on

TABLE 4.3 **Change in political trust as a function of partisan weighting and
other variables, 2002–4**

	Democrats	Republicans
	Parameter estimate (Standard error)	Parameter estimate (Standard error)
Political trust$_{2000}$	0.577* (0.042)	0.556* (0.047)
Foreign policy evaluations$_{2004}$	−0.042 (0.030)	0.088* (0.028)
Economic evaluations$_{2004}$	0.118* (0.046)	0.049 (0.051)
Presidential approval$_{2002}$	0.015 (0.021)	0.088* (0.051)
Congressional approval$_{2002}$	0.015 (0.020)	0.061* (0.025)
Race (African American)	0.038 (0.027)	−0.188* (0.064)
Gender (female)	0.034* (0.019)	−0.043* (0.022)
Education (some college)	0.027 (0.023)	−0.006 (0.026)
Education (college)	0.038 (0.029)	−0.009 (0.030)
Education (graduate school)	0.058 (0.041)	0.049 (0.037)
Age	0.002* (0.001)	−0.001 (0.001)
Constant	−0.125 (0.040)	0.017 (0.064)
Number of cases	307	330
Adjusted R^2	0.48	0.42

*$p < 0.05$, one-tailed test
Source: American National Election Study, 2000–2004, panel study.

our explanation for the recent emergence of the polarization in political trust. If partisans behaved the same way when trust was not so polarized by party as they did when trust started to polarize by party, our explanation could not provide much purchase on what we have identified as a new phenomenon. To test this possibility, we turn to panel data that were collected between 1992 and 1996—before any significant polarization of political trust had occurred.

First, we compare the degree of partisan assessment in the early to mid-1990s with what we found in the early 2000s. As we demonstrated in the previous section, partisans' assessments of economic and foreign policy conditions differed by a lot during the George W. Bush years. The average amount of optimism that Republicans expressed about the economy was 13 percentage points higher than it was for Democrats in 2002 and 23 percentage points higher in 2004. The differences in foreign policy evaluations were even larger: 22 percentage points in 2002 and a remarkable 33 percentage points in 2004.

We find that partisan assessment was present in the earlier time period, but it was much weaker. With Bill Clinton in the White House, economic evaluations of Republicans and Democrats differed by a mere 5 percentage points in 1994 and only 10 percentage points in 1996, a fraction of the 13 and 23 percentage-point differences we found in the Bush years. Although differences in foreign policy evaluations were larger than those in economic evaluations during the Clinton years—at 17 and 22 percentage points, respectively, in 1994 and 1996—they were still far less than the peak of 33 percentage points achieved in 2004. Taken together, the results from the Clinton years suggest that lower levels of partisan assessment would produce less polarization in political trust, insofar as partisans of different stripes in the 1990s evaluated the world more similarly than they did in the 2000s.

We can also evaluate whether Republicans and Democrats updated their trust in government using partisan weighting. Since the ANES asked exactly the same questions in the 1990s panel as the one from the 2000s, we can estimate a near perfect replica of the models we estimated for the 2000–2004 period. The only difference is that the ANES asked the party feeling thermometer questions in all waves of the panel, which allows us to include their lagged readings in both the 1992–94 model and the 1994–96 model. The results appear in table 4.4. We find little to no evidence of partisan weighting here. The effect of foreign policy evaluations is about the same for both Republicans and Democrats in both waves. In the 1992–94 wave, its effect was not statistically significant for either Democrats or Republicans. Foreign policy evaluations did exert a significant effect in the 1994–96 wave of the panel, but its effect was about the same for both partisan groups.

The effect of economic evaluations was significantly larger for Democrats in the 1992–94 wave than for Republicans and vice versa in the 1994–96 wave. But given that both groups perceived the economy to be about the same, it doesn't appear that people had strong motivations to weight these evaluations differently. In fact, because Democrats' evaluations of the economy were more favorable in 1996 than in 1994, it seems

TABLE 4.4 **Change in political trust as a function of partisan weighting and other variables, 1992–96**

	1992–94		1994–96	
	Democrats	Republicans	Democrats	Republicans
	Parameter estimate (Standard error)	Parameter estimate (Standard error)	Parameter estimate (Standard error)	Parameter estimate (Standard error)
Political trust$_{t-1}$	0.253* (0.052)	0.259* (0.044)	0.483* (0.060)	0.382* (0.074)
Foreign policy evaluations$_t$	0.025 (0.037)	0.048 (0.032)	0.068* (0.036)	0.075* (0.032)
Economic evaluations$_t$	0.105* (0.054)	0.026 (0.047)	0.061 (0.059)	0.115* (0.047)
Feeling thermometer: Democratic Party$_{t-1}$	0.077 (0.067)	0.021 (0.061)	−0.029 (0.081)	0.166* (0.082)
Feeling thermometer: Republican Party$_{t-1}$	0.022 (0.062)	−0.077 (0.066)	0.052 (0.066)	0.116 (0.079)
Presidential approval$_{t-1}$	0.116* (0.036)	0.028 (0.026)	0.114* (0.033)	0.063* (0.036)
Congressional approval$_{t-1}$	0.025 (0.027)	0.050* (0.029)	0.065* (0.028)	0.069* (0.034)
Race (African American)	0.001 (0.031)	0.138* (0.073)	−0.072* (0.033)	−0.067 (0.086)
Gender (female)	−0.024 (0.025)	−0.055* (0.023)	0.019 (0.026)	−0.017 (0.027)
Education (some college)	−0.043 (0.029)	−0.020 (0.029)	−0.039 (0.032)	0.036 (0.035)
Education (college)	−0.026 (0.035)	−0.007 (0.029)	0.032 (0.037)	0.046 (0.036)
Education (graduate school)	−0.024 (0.044)	0.020 (0.039)	0.017 (0.047)	0.024 (0.043)
Age	0.001 (0.001)	0.002* (0.001)	0.000 (0.001)	0.001 (0.001)
Constant	0.008 (0.071)	0.021 (0.064)	−0.035 (0.083)	−0.171 (0.080)
Number of cases	275	266	223	194
Adjusted R^2	0.183	0.210	0.359	0.315

Source: American National Election Study, 1992–96, panel study.

they would have had more motivation to update their political trust based on the economy in the second part of the panel than the first. We found the reverse to be true.

Because partisan assessment was weaker and partisan weighting non-existent in the 1990s, both continue to be attractive explanations for why

trust began to polarize in the early 2000s. Partisans' perceptions of economic and foreign policy conditions were much larger in the later panel
than in the earlier one. In addition, we found strong evidence that Republicans and Democrats used different evaluative criteria in deciding how
much they trusted the government in the 2000–2004 panel but little evidence of it in the 1992–96 panel. We suspect that both these phenomena
might be the result of the increasingly negative view that partisans have
developed about the other party—a trend that began to accelerate in the
2000s, not the 1990s.

Confronting One Last Concern Using Data from 2010 and 2012

After the end of the 2004 ANES panel study, the polarization of political trust continued to deepen in the electorate. The best evidence that
we can patch together from other surveys suggests that party differences
in trust reached a maximum in 2010 or 2011. Ideally, the ANES would
have completed a panel survey during the 2008–10 or 2011 periods that
included the same items we used in the analyses above.[9] Of particular
concern to us, one alternative explanation for the pattern of findings we
have presented thus far still exists. Perhaps Republicans these days simply
use foreign policy considerations and Democrats use economic considerations to update their trust judgments because those are the issue areas
most important to them. If we were to find that economic evaluations and
trust in government were unrelated among Republicans in 2010 with a
Democratic president, a Democratic Congress, and a flagging economy,
it would undermine our interpretation of why trust polarized when it did.
Certainly Republicans would be motivated to evaluate the Democratic
government based on a poor economy.

   We can get at least some leverage using the 2010 Cooperative Congressional Election Study (CCES) and the 2012 ANES. We included on
the CCES the first of the four items that the ANES has used to measure
trust in government. The one difference between the CCES item and the
ANES item is that we included a fourth response option allowing people
to say that they "never" trust the government in Washington to do what is
right. In the ANES, respondents can volunteer "never," but they are not
prompted with "never" as a response option. Based on this measure, trust
in government in our CCES sample was very low. With only 15 percent
of respondents saying that they trusted the government in Washington
almost always or most of the time, it represents the lowest percentage of

trustful responses relative to any reading taken by the NES, which has been asking the question since 1958.

In addition to the trust item, the CCES included the same five-point scale item that the ANES uses to measure people's economic evaluations. It did not, however, ask respondents to evaluate America's strength on the world stage. Although this makes the survey less than ideal, it does at least allow us to test whether Republicans in the twenty-first century do not evaluate the government based on how well the economy has been doing. Of course, we found that they used foreign policy—not economic policy— criteria in our analysis of the panel data gathered during George W. Bush's first term. If, in fact, trust and economic evaluations are unrelated all the time for Republicans, then the correlation between our measures of trust and economic evaluations in 2010 ought to be near zero. This would be terrible news for our theory. If, however, partisan weighting is at work as we suspect, the correlation between trust and economic evaluations should be especially strong for Republicans because the economy was barely emerging from the depths of the Great Recession and was still quite poor. Republicans should want to evaluate the government based on these negative perceptions. It would also follow that the correlation between trust and economic evaluations for Democrats should be weaker in 2010 than in the earlier period. With the economy a weak point for Democrats in government, it should have motivated Democrats to ignore it as best they could.

The results from these 2010 data strongly support the presence of both partisan assessment and partisan weighting. Even with the economy continuing to struggle, Democrats were reasonably positive about its performance. Forty percent of them said the economy was either somewhat better or much better than the previous year. Fewer than 5 percent of Republicans shared that view. In contrast, only 25 percent of Democrats thought the economy had gotten somewhat worse or much worse. Seventy-four percent of Republicans saw it that way. Comparing the average evaluations of Republicans and Democrats between 2004 and 2010, we find that Republicans were more than 20 percentage points more optimistic about the economy in 2004 than Democrats were, while Democrats were more than 30 percentage points more optimistic about the economy than Republicans were in 2010. In short, partisans were even more strongly motivated to see what they wanted to see in the economy in 2010 than in 2004.

But how do these economic evaluations translate into people's trust in government? With neither panel data nor several of the explanatory variables from the regression models we presented above, it is probably safest to compare the correlations between political trust and economic evaluations in the two time periods to provide a rough sense of whether and, if so, how relationships changed. According to the 2004 panel data, the correlation between retrospective economic evaluations and political trust among Republicans was statistically insignificant and even carried an unexpected negative sign (−0.05). That is why, in our regression model, economic evaluations exerted no effect on trust. Among Democrats in 2004, however, the correlation between economic evaluations and trust was a very strong 0.42.

The story is mostly reversed in 2010. Among Republicans, the correlation between political trust and economic evaluations was 0.41, almost precisely the same as it was for Democratic identifiers when George W. Bush and the Republicans were presiding over a sluggish economy. Among Democratic respondents in 2010, the correlation was not zero, as it was for Republicans in 2004, but it was much weaker (0.25) than it had been in 2004. Although 0.25 is a moderately strong correlation, perhaps it exists because the GOP was successful in making the economy unambiguously the main issue of the 2010 midterm elections, whereas the message was more divided between American strength abroad and the economy in 2004. Regardless, the partisan weighting part of our story holds. Republicans in 2010 not only saw a gloomier economy than Democrats did but expressed less trust in government based on these gloomy perceptions.

It is possible that the 2010 CCES data are problematic because (1) they were gathered using an online opt-in sampling frame or (2) only one of the four items the ANES uses to tap trust in government was available.[10] Just to be absolutely certain of the robustness of our finding, we perform one last test using the 2012 ANES.

As expected, the results here follow the hypothesized pattern. As it relates to perceptions of the economy, 47 percent of Democrats (rightly) saw the economy over the past year as improving, compared with only 12 percent of Republicans. In contrast, 50 percent of Republicans (wrongly) perceived that the economy had gotten worse in the year leading up to the 2012 election, while only 18 percent of Democrats thought that. Again, we find massive differences in economic perceptions, indicating strong partisan assessment. Equally important for our purposes, the correlation between these assessments and political trust was 0.27 for Republicans and only 0.13 for Democrats, indicating evidence for partisan weighting as well. Taken together, the results from 2010 and 2012 suggest that Republicans think about the economy when they are evaluating how trustworthy they think the government is, at least when they are motivated to do so.

Conclusion

Exploiting the analytical advantages of individual-level panel data, this chapter has informed our understanding of political trust in several important ways. First, our analysis represents the first scholarly attempt to document the polarization of political trust by party. Partisans are now much less likely to trust government when the president belongs to the other political party. Conversely, partisans are much more likely to trust government when the president is a member of their political party. Second, using two different sets of panel data, we were able to identify the period of time in which the polarization of political trust really got under way. Our analysis revealed that even though political trust was not particularly polarized as late as 1992–96, it had become quite polarized by 2000–2004.

Most significantly, though, this chapter provides theoretical and empirical evidence to explain *why* trust became polarized by party. We attribute the polarization of trust to the constellation of three interrelated factors. The first concerns the increasingly cold feelings that partisans now feel toward members of the opposing party. The level of warmth that contemporary partisans feel toward those who belong to the other party rivals that felt by Americans toward some of the most unpopular social groups of the 1970s. The second factor is based on the observation that partisan assessment is now stronger than before. When Republicans control government, for example, Democrats are much more likely to perceive the nation's economic performance as more negative than are Republicans. Finally, and perhaps most importantly, such performance judgments, once formed, appear to be selectively used by partisans when they are evaluating government. Partisans increasingly base government evaluations (such as political trust) on the performance criteria that are most favorable to their preferred party and least favorable to their nonpreferred party. The combination of these three factors, we believe, is responsible for the polarization of political trust in contemporary American politics.

This analysis mostly ends our efforts to pinpoint how, why, and in what pattern trust changes over time. In the next several chapters, we examine trust's *consequences* on other political attitudes. First, we establish just how potentially broad political trust's effects might be, spanning all manner of domestic and foreign policy preferences. Second, we place particular emphasis on providing evidence for our main claim—namely, that polarized trust is an impediment to consensus formation.

CHAPTER FIVE

How Priming Changes the Consequences of Political Trust

The conventional approach to the study of public opinion is to use only the most stable attitudes to explain other opinions. If an attitude remains mostly constant over time, it suggests that it is a strongly held belief. In other words, attitude stability is often thought to imply attitude centrality. In contrast, attitudes that change a lot over time are thought not to be firmly rooted enough to guide other opinions. For most attitudes about politics, such reasoning makes sense. But, as it relates to trust in government, we challenge the conventional approach. Both this chapter and chapter 6 explain why.

We not only go against convention in embracing trust as an explanatory variable, but we go as far as to argue that the range of opinions that political trust plausibly affects is much wider than scholars have demonstrated to date. Our thinking is rooted in the sources of trust that we uncovered in chapters 3 and 4. Chapter 3 provided aggregate-level evidence that issue salience guides Americans' trust judgments. Chapter 4 provided individual-level evidence that partisans are motivated to use different criteria to arrive at their just judgments. These results do not necessarily suggest that aggregate- and individual-level instability in trust ought to relegate it to the periphery of Americans' political belief systems. Instead, they may suggest that people have several different—yet still meaningful—understandings of the government in Washington, which they express at different times depending on political context.

We believe that trust judgments are context dependent and are thus susceptible to change over time. If so, rather than undermining the explanatory power of political trust, the effects of political trust may be even wider than scholars have suggested. Although the existing evidence implies that trust is primarily of value to liberals who want to use government to redistribute wealth (e.g., Hetherington 2005; but see Rudolph 2009; Rudolph and Popp 2009), we argue that it can benefit a wide range of political actors. Exactly *who* and *how* are the result of the issues that become salient. If, for example, people are thinking about the government in terms of foreign policy, trust can be a commodity that leaders can tap to generate support in this realm. If, however, people are thinking about the government in terms of health care or a host of other domestic policy concerns, then trust can be a commodity that leaders can tap to generate support in these realms.

This is so, we contend, because when people are asked to evaluate the "government in Washington," they do not construct an image of the entire government and provide what amounts to an average evaluation of all its components. Instead, they carry in their heads potentially different evaluations of the different parts of government, with the evaluation of "the government in Washington" that they express driven by what part they have been thinking about lately. Those who think government is trustworthy in the foreign realm but not the domestic realm (or vice versa) ought to express more or less trust when one or the other domain becomes salient. Indeed, this is what the results in chapter 3 firmly suggest.

This understanding of trust in government ought to have downstream consequences. Salience, in turn, ought to affect the influence that trust exerts on other political opinions and behaviors. Since neither the military nor the Department of Defense governs policy about race and redistribution, for example, it makes little sense to think that political trust derived with foreign policy actors in mind would affect preferences for spending to assist African Americans or government-run health care. Such trust evaluations should, instead, affect preferences in the defense domain. Similarly, when evaluations of government trustworthiness are measured when people have race and redistribution on their minds, trust ought to affect preferences for government action in the domain of race, not defense. In short, trust's effect on preferences about an issue domain ought to depend on that domain being salient.

Our reasoning is actually consistent with the pattern of scholarly findings on trust, although the literature does not acknowledge the pattern. In the late 1980s and 1990s, when race-targeted and redistributive programs represented the dominant party cleavage (Carmines and Stimson

1989), trust affected preferences in this policy domain (Hetherington and Globetti 2002). When health care reform became salient in 1994, political trust affected preferences in this domain (Hetherington 2005, chapter 7). When Social Security reform became salient, trust affected preferences for privatization (Rudolph and Popp 2009). When the protection of civil liberties became an issue after 9/11, political trust affected whether people were willing to trade civil liberties for enhanced safety and security (Davis and Silver 2004).

To begin to provide evidence that salience is the specific mechanism that underlies these findings, we turn to a different type of data. Rather than observational survey data of the entire US population, we employ an experiment that manipulates issue attention and allows us to examine the consequences of political trust depending on what we have encouraged, or "primed," our participants to think about. By conducting the study ourselves, we can carefully control what individuals are thinking about immediately prior to being asked how much they trust the government. More important, the experimental design allows us to examine the downstream effects of this priming by testing whether our manipulation influences the consequences of the trust judgments offered by the participants in our experiment when we next ask them about their preferences on a set of different policies. To foreshadow a bit, we find that the effects of political trust on support for different policies are most pronounced among those whose thoughts we focused on government action in that specific policy domain at the time they expressed their level of political trust. Trust, after such priming, has no effect on preferences in areas different from those in which we did not focus our participants' thoughts.

In the next section, we further explore theories about establishing causal order with individual-level data and explain why trust in government ought not to fit the conventional approach. Next, we review the concept of priming and the psychological assumptions on which it rests. We propose an extension of priming theory in which priming is expected to influence not only the sources of political trust, which we showed in chapter 3, but also its consequences. After developing our theoretical expectations, we describe our research design and our experimental manipulation of issue attention. We then report the results of an empirical analysis in which we explore the effects of priming and political trust on individuals' policy preferences. We conclude this chapter by discussing the theoretical and empirical implications of our findings.

Attitude Instability and Causation

In chapter 4, we used panel data to explore the factors that cause trust to change. Our very approach demonstrates our belief that, to some degree, trust lacks stability at the individual level. This might not seem like much of a revelation, but it is in survey research. Opinions or predispositions that exhibit significant individual-level variation over time are rarely considered causes of other political opinions. This practice is relevant for us because the latter chapters of our book employ political trust as a central cause of other opinions, particularly policy attitudes. This requires us to go into some detail to support our seemingly unconventional approach.

The reason that the stability of an attitude or opinion is important is that it is critical in helping researchers impose causal order on cross-sectional survey data, by far the most common type of data used in survey research. Because all the data are gathered at once, it is not always possible to say with certainty that variable x causes variable y. But if one knows that a variable tends to remain the same over a long period of time, one can surmise that it was probably in place well before the survey was administered. This allows for a theoretical temporal ordering. For example, one is on pretty solid footing in making an inference from cross-sectional data that being a woman influences voting for Democratic presidential candidates rather voting for Democratic presidential candidates influencing a person to be a woman. Women were women long before they decided for whom they would vote.

That same general idea holds for political attitudes, although they are obviously subject to more change than demographic characteristics. To provide some order to all the potential chaos in the analysis of cross-sectional data, Converse (1964) introduced the notion of centrality in political belief systems. People use central attitudes all the time; hence they are well established in the brain. Conceptually speaking, centrality suggests that an attitude is *meaningful* to a person. It is these central attitudes that guide other opinions and behaviors. Peripheral attitudes, in contrast, are fleeting. They are far from fixed and hence appear to change almost willy-nilly from survey to survey. In Converse's reckoning, central attitudes can be discerned from the peripheral ones by testing how stable they are over time. Although the specific practice is somewhat problematic (Luskin 1987), the most common method of testing stability is to examine the correlation between panel respondents' answers to the same question at two different points in time. To the extent that the correlation between the respondents' opinions at the first and second asking approaches 1.0, the opinion is viewed as very stable and hence a central belief. The lower the correlation, the more peripheral the opinion is considered to be. Central parts of the belief systems are thought to develop early in life and tend to be used a lot, which encourages people to continue to use them as guides in future encounters with politics (Fazio 1986).

The authors of the *American Voter* (Campbell et al. 1960) identified party identification as the most important causal force in the study of mass behavior, in part, because it exhibited more stability in their panel data than any other opinion or predisposition. If people were Republicans one year, for example, they tended to be Republicans two or four years later. This fact is critical to survey research because it allows scholars to argue that party identification was in place long before, say, voter choice in a specific election, even if all they have is cross-sectional data in which party identification and voter choice are gathered at the same time. Because people were Republicans long before they decided to vote for Nixon in 1960, one could conclude that their party identification *caused* their voting behavior rather than their voting behavior causing their party identification.

We have no quarrel with this way of thinking. It is important to keep in mind, however, that the centrality of an opinion in one's belief system and stability in one's survey responses over time are not the same thing. The latter (stability) is merely a measure of the former (centrality). It is a good measure most of the time, but it has limitations. Its limitations are especially pronounced when people have ambivalent feelings about something. This is particularly important to our thinking because Americans' feelings about government are surely ambivalent. Many people like some parts of government but not others. For example, we demonstrated in chapter 4 that the military is much more popular than the parts of government that redistribute resources. The Supreme Court is more popular than Congress. We also demonstrated these differences matter for how much political trust a person or the population expresses. When political actors make foreign affairs more salient, people express more political trust because the parts of government that handle foreign affairs are relatively popular. When political actors make redistributive policy more salient, people express less trust in government because the parts of government that handle it are controversial and hence relatively unpopular. In this respect, political trust is context dependent. Such context dependency all but ensures that trust will vary over time. It is this lack of over-time stability that would reflexively scare many survey researchers away from using political trust as an explanation for other political opinions.

But does the lack of stability in trust necessarily indicate a lack of centrality of feelings about government to someone's political belief system? We do not believe that it does. Instability in trust can also be generated by its context dependency. Recall from chapter 3 that people think about political trust differently depending on whether they are focused on international or domestic concerns. The key point here is that both evaluations—those that people have about government in the foreign arena and those people have about government in the domestic arena—are real and meaningful (in other words, *central*), not tenuously held or peripheral to how they think about politics. It is just that they are based on different stimuli, which causes people to offer different trust evaluations when asked about government at different times. As a result, a certain amount of individual-level instability in response to the trust in government survey items is inevitable because political context is often changing. In addition, as we have seen in chapter 4, individual partisans respond differently to these stimuli. Although this apparent instability might discourage researchers from thinking about political trust as a cause of other opinions and behaviors, we argue that it should not.

Reintroducing the Steve Sax analogy might be helpful to explain our reasoning. Recall Sax was the Dodgers second baseman with excellent offensive skills but awful defensive skills. Consider a situation in which a sample of baseball fans is asked how much they "trust Sax to do what is right" on a baseball field, much the same way that we ask Americans how much they trust the government to do what is right. A fan's overall trust in Sax ought to differ depending on whether those in the sample are thinking about him on offense or defense. To test this notion, let's say a randomly selected group of fans was asked to provide their trust evaluation of Sax after watching him single to right, steal a base, and score on a single by a teammate. The trust they express in Sax is likely to be quite high because they have been primed to think about Sax's offensive prowess. In contrast, let's say a second randomly selected group of fans was asked to share how much they trusted Sax after watching him toss a routine throw into the fourth row of seats behind first base. Their trust in Sax is likely to be a lot lower than the first group's because the second group was primed to think about Sax's defensive liabilities. Individuals did not arrive at these evaluations of Sax at random. Both are meaningful evaluations based on different stimuli. The instability in trust in Sax is a function of people thinking about two different parts of his game when asked to provide an overall evaluation of him. Trust in Sax, like trust in government, is context dependent.

This observation has important implications for the downstream effects that trust might exert on other opinions. In the Sax example, we might theorize that trust in Sax ought to affect whether people support or oppose the manager keeping him in a baseball game or taking him out for a replacement. The overall evaluation that fans made of Sax after seeing him hit should inform their preferences for whether or not the manager should pinch hit for him; however, the trust evaluations gathered when his offense was salient ought to have much less bearing on whether he should be removed for a defensive replacement. The same holds for the overall evaluations gathered after seeing Sax play defense. They should be most relevant to whether the fans thought the manager should remove him for a defensive replacement but not whether the manager should pinch hit for him. In both cases, the part of Sax's game that fans were thinking about likely leaves an enduring imprint on their degree of trust in Sax, an imprint that later affects the influence of trust in Sax on fans' judgments about whether he should be removed from a game.

The fact that survey researchers tend to be concerned by attitude instability has at least one unfortunate consequence: it limits what individual-level data analysts can tell us about real world politics. Real world politics is dynamic. Things change over time. If our explanations for other opinions and behaviors, such as party identification and ideology, are attractive because of their *stability*, those variables, almost by definition, cannot tell us much about political change.[1] A constant cannot explain a variable. Explaining change usually requires us to turn to things that change over time, but, of course, opinions that change over time are objects of concern for survey analysts because change is thought to indicate that an opinion is peripheral, not central, to people's political belief systems. As we have tried to make clear, though, attitude instability, if generated by context dependency rather than the absence of meaningful beliefs, can provide great analytical leverage in trying to explain what causes political change.

More on Priming

Theories of priming are commonly premised on two fundamental psychological assumptions. First, individuals are assumed to have limited cognitive capacity and, as a result, to behave as "cognitive misers" (Fiske and Taylor 1984). Under this perspective, people seldom use all available information when making judgments because they lack either the ability or the motivation to do so. Second, when making judgments about the world around them, individuals rely on heuristics or cognitive shortcuts in order to simplify their decision-making process (Tversky and Kahneman 1974). One heuristic that is particularly relevant to the theory of priming is the accessibility heuristic. Accessibility refers to the ease with which stored information comes to mind during the decision-making process. Accessible information, psychologists inform us, is more easily brought to mind and thus more likely to be used in making judgments (Higgins 1996; Higgins and King 1981).

Recall from our discussion in chapter 3 that priming occurs when a stimulus, such as media coverage, influences the weight that people assign to particular criteria when they make political judgments. Priming is typically viewed as an extension of agenda setting; "[b]y making some issues more salient in people's minds (agenda setting), mass media can also shape the criteria that people take into account when making judgments about political candidates or issues (priming)" (Scheufele and Tewksbury 2007, 11). Through its selective emphasis on certain issues or considerations, the media can focus public attention on them and temporarily increase their accessibility. Issues with heightened accessibility are more easily activated and thus more likely to be used during subsequent political evaluations. Under this accessibility-based account of agenda setting and priming, "it is not information about the issue that has the effect; it is the fact that the issue has received a certain amount of processing time and attention that carries the effect" (Scheufele and Tewksbury 2007, 14).

The theory of media priming enjoys empirical support across a wide variety of studies. Experimental analyses have shown, for example, that exposure to stories about a particular issue problem (e.g., energy, defense, inflation) strengthens the relationship between domain-specific presidential performance ratings and overall presidential performance ratings (Iyengar and Kinder 1987; Iyengar et al. 1984). Using a quasi-experimental design, Krosnick and Kinder (1990) used survey data collected immediately before and after the disclosure of the Iran-Contra affair to show that news coverage of the scandal altered the determinants of support for presidential approval. While foreign affairs attitudes were only weakly connected to presidential approval prior to Iran-Contra revelations, they were strongly connected to it afterward. Similarly, Krosnick and Brannon (1993) used panel data from the 1990–91 American National Election

Study (ANES) to show that the impact of domain-specific evaluations on overall evaluations of President Bush changed in line with changing news coverage. In particular, the effect of Bush's Gulf crisis approval on his overall job approval was much stronger after the media's months-long focus on the war than before it. Content analyses of campaign coverage have shown that media priming can also affect the ingredients of voter choice in elections (Druckman 2004; Mendelsohn 1996). As we demonstrated earlier in chapter 3, the ingredients used in the public's political trust judgments are partly determined by the issues on which the public is most focused at the time. When the public is focused on concerns about the economy, for example, economic perceptions are weighted more heavily in trust judgments.

Downstream Consequences of Priming

In conventional priming studies, political scientists examine the effects that a prime or stimulus has on political evaluations. A priming effect is said to occur when exposure to a prime influences the sources of subsequent political evaluations. We believe that priming may also influence the consequences of those evaluations. In chapter 3 we showed that public attention to certain issues influences the weight attached to those issues during the formation of trust judgments. In this chapter, we use an experiment to explore whether priming influences the consequences of political trust on individuals' policy preferences.

A recurring theme of this book has been that political trust is shaped by what people are thinking about at the time they render their judgment. We submit that trust judgments are influenced by the particular issues and the particular parts of government that people are thinking about when they express their level of trust. When people are primed to think about particular issue domains or particular institutions of government, considerations concerning those issues or institutions (e.g., perceptions of domain-specific government performance) should receive special weight during the formation of trust judgments. When these trust judgments are then encoded and stored in individuals' memories, they should still be imbued with those domain-specific considerations. If our line of reasoning is correct, then the strength of the relationship between political trust and individuals' subsequent policy preferences should be regulated by the degree of congruence between the domain-specific nature of the prime that individuals received and their domain-specific policy preferences.

Overview of Expectations

Our general expectation is that the effects of political trust on policy preferences will depend on what individuals are thinking about at the time that they render their trust judgments. More specifically, we expect that the effects of political trust on support for a given policy will be most pronounced among individuals whose thoughts were focused on government action in that policy domain when they expressed how much they trusted the government. The effects of political trust on support for health care reform, for example, should be greatest among those who were primed to think about government action in the context of health care prior to expressing their level of political trust. Similarly, political trust should most influence support on cap and trade among people who were primed to think about government action in the environmental context prior to expressing their level of trust. Finally, the effects of political trust on support for potential military action in Yemen should be largest among those whom we primed to think about government action in the context of the military.

Experimental Design

Participants and Procedures

The data analyzed in this chapter are taken from a survey experiment conducted at the University of Illinois at Urbana-Champaign during the fall 2011 semester. Two hundred one students enrolled in an introductory political science course participated in this study as an opportunity to earn extra credit. The study consisted of a between-subjects experiment in which each subject was randomly assigned to one of four experimental conditions (health care, environment, foreign policy, or control). Three of these conditions were designed to prime subjects to think about particular government agencies and policies prior to expressing their trust in government. Priming occurred by having subjects read a carefully constructed news story, the content of which was based on their assigned condition. We present the precise wording for these news stories in table 5.1. We based the stories on actual news stories that appeared during the month prior to the experiment. By doing so, we helped increase the external validity of the experimental treatment (Cook and Campbell 1979). Subjects in the control condition did not read a news story.

Immediately after reading the news article assigned to their experimental condition, all subjects were queried about their level of trust in government. Specifically, we asked subjects to answer the familiar "do what is right" trust question commonly used by the ANES with the addition of the "never" option. The close proximity of the trust instrument to the experimental manipulations was designed to influence what the subjects were thinking about immediately prior to rendering their trust judgments. After the trust question, we asked all subjects to express their preferences on three policy issues. Political trust was, by design, measured after the salience treatment. This allowed us to test whether the salience treatment affected *levels* of trust and whether the salience treatment *moderated* the effects of trust.

Experimental Manipulations

Table 5.1 shows the specific treatments. We assigned subjects in the health care condition to read an article about the constitutionality of the health care law enacted by Congress in 2010. The article is balanced in that it mentions reasons why some might support the law (e.g., it provides health insurance to people who could not afford it) as well as reasons why others might oppose it (e.g., it requires people to purchase health insurance even if they don't want to). The article also notes that lower courts have been

TABLE 5.1 **Description of experimental treatments**

Experimental condition	Specific wording of news stories
Health care	**Decision on Health Care Law Means Supreme Court Will Likely Determine Constitutionality Next Summer**
	The constitutionality of the 2010 health care law could be determined by the Supreme Court this term, with a decision coming next summer in the thick of the 2012 presidential campaign. Under the new law, tens of millions of Americans who have not had health insurance in the past will be covered. For those who were not covered before because they could not afford health insurance, the law says that the government will provide subsidies to help them pay for it. For those who did not have coverage before because they did not want to pay for it, the new law requires them to buy insurance coverage.
	Appeals courts that have considered the law are split, particularly about the provision that requires all people to have a health insurance policy.
	In June, a divided panel of the US Court of Appeals for the 6th Circuit in Cincinnati upheld the health care law.

TABLE 5.1 (*continued*)

Experimental condition	Specific wording of news stories
	In August, however, a split 11th Circuit Court in Atlanta returned a strong ruling against the mandate that all individuals have health insurance.
	A Supreme Court decision either way—that the law is a valid exercise of Congress's power or an unconstitutional overreach—could have political effects neither side can predict. (Barnes 2011)
Environment	**New US Fuel Rules Delayed**
	The Environmental Protection Agency (EPA) has decided to delay releasing new fuel economy rules until November. These new rules are designed to reduce carbon emissions into the atmosphere. Carbon emissions are what scientists believe causes climate change.
	Under a deal between the federal government and American car makers reached several months ago, the average fuel economy of an automaker's cars and light trucks would need to reach 54.5 miles per gallon by 2025. This roughly doubles the current standard. Critics argue that the jump is too dramatic and will require car manufacturers to produce cars that are lacking in power and safety.
	The new rule on fuel economy standards was supposed to be released by government agencies at the end of September. But the agencies now say they need more time to iron out the final language. The EPA said in a statement Wednesday that "given the historic nature of this rule, it was recently determined that additional time was needed."
	The agency now plans to have a proposed rule by mid-November. (Kessler 2011)
Foreign policy	**Two-Year Manhunt Led to Killing of Awlaki in Yemen**
	Anwar al-Awlaki, the radical American-born cleric who was a leading figure in Al Qaeda's Yemen affiliate and was considered its most dangerous English-speaking propagandist, was killed in an American drone strike that deliberately targeted his vehicle on Friday. The strike was controversial because it killed two Americans: Mr. Awlaki, as well as an American colleague traveling with him.
	One American official said that Mr. Awlaki, whom the United States had been hunting in Yemen for more than two years, was killed with a Hellfire missile fired from a drone operated by the Central Intelligence Agency (CIA). The official said it was the first CIA strike in Yemen since 2002. This was the second high-profile killing of an Al Qaeda leader in the past five months. American commandos killed Osama bin Laden in Pakistan last May.
	American officials called the strike a significant success in the campaign to weaken Al Qaeda in the Arabian Peninsula Critics expressed concern that such drone strikes could signal a wider conflict with Yemen. (Mazzetti, Schmitt, and Worth 2011)
Control	**No newspaper article**

Note: Each story represents a modified version of an actual newspaper article that was published within one month prior to the study.

split on the question of whether the law is a valid exercise of congressional power or an unconstitutional overreach. By virtue of its substantive content, the article primes subjects to think about government action in the domain of health care.

We assigned subjects in the environment condition to read an article about government regulations concerning fuel efficiency. The article discusses a decision by the Environmental Protection Agency to delay the announcement of new, more stringent fuel economy standards. The article is balanced in that it mentions arguments in favor of stricter standards (e.g., protecting the environment by reducing carbon emissions) and arguments against them (e.g., potential reduction in automotive power and safety). The purpose of assigning subjects to read this article was to prime them to think about government action in the context of environmental regulation.

Last, we assigned subjects in the foreign policy condition to read an article about the targeted killing of Anwar al-Awlaki, an American-born leading figure in Al Qaeda's Yemen affiliate. The article describes how Mr. Awlaki was killed by a drone operated by the Central Intelligence Agency. It takes a balanced view by characterizing the CIA's action as both a success (e.g., it weakens Al Qaeda) and a cause for concern (e.g., it might trigger a wider conflict in Yemen). Assignment to this condition primed subjects to think about government action in the context of foreign policy.

Dependent Variables

We asked all subjects, regardless of experimental assignment, to express their level of support or opposition for three policy issues. We present the question wording for these three instruments in table 5.2. Specifically, we asked them about the extent to which they supported or opposed a health care reform act that included an individual mandate to purchase health insurance and that would raise taxes on those making more than \$280,000 per year; whether they supported or opposed a "cap-and-trade" proposal that would regulate the amount of greenhouse gases that companies could produce; and, finally, whether they would support or oppose additional military strikes in Yemen to reduce future threats from terrorist attacks.

Responses to these three policy questions will serve as the primary dependent variables in the analyses to follow. The results presented in table 5.3 demonstrate considerable variation in the level of support for each of the proposed policies. More than one-half of the subjects expressed at

TABLE 5.2 **Measures of issue attitudes**

Policy issue	Question wording
Health care reform	Congress considered many important bills over the past several years. Tell us whether you support or oppose the legislation in principle. The Comprehensive Health Reform Act. It requires all Americans to obtain health insurance. Allows people to keep current provider. And increases taxes on those making more than $280,000 a year (strongly support, support somewhat, neither support nor oppose, oppose somewhat, strongly oppose).
Cap and trade	There's a proposal system called "cap and trade" that some say would lower the pollution levels that lead to global warming. With Cap and Trade, the government would issue permits limiting the amount of greenhouse gases companies can put out. Companies that did not use all their permits could sell them to other companies. The idea is that many companies would find ways to put out less greenhouse gases, because that would be cheaper than buying permits. Would you support or oppose this system? (strongly support, support somewhat, neither support nor oppose, oppose somewhat, strongly oppose).
Yemen strike	The U.S. government believes that a new Al Qaeda cell based in Yemen may be planning future terrorist attacks against the United States, and the military has been considering stepped up drone attacks in the country. Opponents of this type of military action argue against it because we are not at war with Yemen and such attacks might provoke a wider war. How about you? Would you support or oppose the United States taking military action to remove this potential threat? (strongly support, support somewhat, neither support nor oppose, oppose somewhat, strongly oppose).

TABLE 5.3 **Distribution of policy preferences**

	Health care reform (%)	Cap and trade (%)	Yemen strike (%)
Strongly oppose	10.9	5.5	13.9
Oppose somewhat	20.4	15.9	38.8
Neither support nor oppose	14.4	16.9	15.4
Support somewhat	38.8	48.3	23.4
Strongly support	15.4	13.4	8.5
Number of cases	201	201	201

Note: Table entries are the percentage of subjects expressing the specified level of support or opposition to each policy. Percentages may not sum to one hundred due to rounding.

least some support for health care reform (54.4 percent). Roughly one-third of subjects opposed it (31.3 percent), while the remaining subjects expressed neither support nor opposition (14.4 percent). A majority of subjects also supported cap and trade (61.7 percent), while more than one-fifth of the sample (21.4 percent) opposed it, and the remainder of subjects reported neither support nor opposition (16.9 percent). Less than one-third of subjects supported military action in Yemen (31.9 percent). About one-half subjects opposed it (52.7 percent), and the rest expressed no clear preference (15.4 percent).

Results

Before testing whether the salience treatments moderate the effects of political trust on policy preferences, we first test whether the salience treatments affect levels of political trust.

We find that levels of trust in the control group are not statistically different from those in the health care condition ($M = 2.40$ vs. $M = 2.41$, $t = 0.18$, $p > 0.18$), the environmental condition ($M = 2.40$ vs. $M = 2.54$, $t = 1.17$, $p > 0.24$), or the foreign policy condition ($M = 2.40$ vs. $M = 2.53$, $t = 0.99$, $p > 0.32$). These null results confirm that across all three issue domains, the salience treatments do not influence levels of trust.[2]

Earlier we argued that the effects of political trust on individuals' policy preferences will depend on what those individuals were primed to think about prior to rendering their trust judgments. Before turning to the results of our fully specified model, it is instructive to first look at the simple bivariate correlations between trust and policy preferences by experimental condition. If our expectations are correct, the size of the correlation between trust and policy preferences should depend on the experimental treatment.

The results appear in figure 5.1. As expected, the correlation between trust and health care preferences is largest in the health care condition ($r = 0.34$). In fact, the correlation between trust and health care preferences is not significant in the environmental ($r = 0.03$), foreign policy ($r = -0.07$), or control conditions ($r = -0.13$). Similarly, the correlation between trust and environmental preferences is greatest in the environmental condition ($r = 0.30$) but insignificant in the health care ($r = 0.01$), foreign policy ($r = 0.02$), and control conditions ($r = -0.08$). Finally, and also consistent with expectations, the correlation between trust and foreign policy preferences is greatest in the foreign policy condition ($r = 0.43$) but fails to reach significance in the health care ($r = -0.05$), environmental ($r = 0.09$), and control conditions ($r = -0.18$). In short, the effects of trust on policy preferences depend greatly on the experimental treatment.

To increase certainty that these effects are not the result of some other

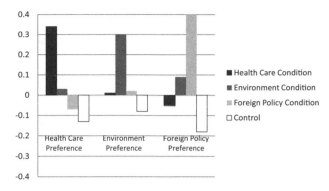

FIGURE 5.1. Effect of trust priming on policy preferences

cause, we estimated three similarly specified, ordered probit models—one for each of the three dependent variables. Specifically, we model support for each policy as a function of political trust, which experimental condition the subject was in, and, importantly, a series of interactions between political trust and experimental assignment. In addition, we include ideological self-identification as a control variable. The results of these three models appear in table 5.4.

We begin by examining what determines support for health care reform. The first data column of table 5.4 displays the results. The coefficient denoting liberals is positively signed and statistically significant. This means that liberals are more supportive of health care reform than are moderates (the excluded ideological category). The coefficient representing conservatives, by contrast, is negatively signed and statistically significant, which indicates that conservatives are less supportive of health care reform than are moderates. Although neither of these results is at all surprising, they increase confidence that the model is working as it should.

Of central interest in our analysis are the effects of political trust and whether they depend on the experimental condition that the subjects received. Starting with the health care reform analysis, the coefficient for political trust is statistically insignificant. This null finding means that political trust has no impact on health care attitudes among those who were assigned to the control condition (the excluded experimental category). In other words, if they received no issue prime at all, their trust judgments have no effect on preferences for health care policy. Our first hypothesis was that the effects of political trust on support for health care reform should be greatest among those who were primed to think about

TABLE 5.4 **Determinants of policy preferences by experimental condition**

	Health care reform	Cap and trade	Yemen strike
Control condition	—	—	—
Health condition	−1.85**	−0.30	−0.83
	(0.83)	(0.79)	(0.78)
Environment condition	−0.85	−2.24**	−1.35
	(0.99)	(0.98)	(0.98)
Foreign policy condition	−0.71	−0.79	−1.78**
	(0.86)	(0.86)	(0.87)
Political trust	−0.05	−0.14	−0.29
	(0.25)	(0.32)	(0.24)
Political trust ×	0.71**	0.14	0.32
Health care	(0.33)	(0.32)	(0.32)
Political trust ×	0.21	0.76**	0.52
Environment	(0.39)	(0.38)	(0.39)
Political trust ×	0.25	0.17	0.83**
Foreign policy	(0.34)	(0.33)	(0.34)
Liberal	0.40**	0.34*	−0.16
	(0.19)	(0.19)	(0.19)
Conservative	−1.29***	−0.44**	0.82***
	(0.22)	(0.21)	(0.21)
τ_1	−2.08	−2.20	−1.70
	(0.65)	(0.64)	(0.63)
τ_2	−1.03	−1.33	−0.44
	(0.63)	(0.63)	(0.62)
τ_3	−0.51	−0.79	0.02
	(0.63)	(0.63)	(0.62)
τ_4	0.84	0.74	1.08
	(0.64)	(0.63)	(0.63)
Log likelihood	−258.3	−261.4	−275.6
Number of cases	201	201	201

Note: Table entries are ordered probit estimates of the dependent variables with standard errors in parentheses. The control condition is the omitted experimental category.
*$p < 0.10$, **$p < 0.05$, ***$p < 0.01$

government in the context of health care prior to rendering a trust judgment. If this is true, we should observe a positively signed and statistically significant interaction between political trust and assignment to the health care condition. That is precisely what we see in the first column of table 5.4. Substantively, this interaction means that political trust increases support for health care reform more among subjects in the health care condition than it does among subjects in the control condition. Table 5.4 also shows that, in the health care model, there are no significant interactions between political trust and assignment to the environment or foreign policy conditions. This means that the effects of trust among subjects in these two conditions are statistically indistinguishable from the effects of trust among those in the control condition, which, recall, was zero.

In addition to observing whether the effects of political trust vary across experimental conditions, we are also interested in determining the overall effect of political trust within each condition. To establish the effect of political trust within each of the experimental conditions, we performed a series of joint hypothesis tests (Wald tests). Specifically, we tested the null hypothesis that $\beta_{trust} + \beta_{trust \, x \, [experimental \, condition]} = 0$. As expected, the overall effect of political trust in the health care condition $(\beta_{trust} + \beta_{trust \, x \, health \, care \, condition})$ is positive and significant $(\chi^2_{1df} = 8.16, p < 0.01)$. Political trust does not exert any influence on attitudes toward health care reform among those in the environment $(\chi^2_{1df} = 0.30, p > 0.58)$ or foreign policy conditions $(\chi^2_{1df} = 0.84, p > 0.35)$. Collectively, these results provide strong support for the hypothesized priming effect. Consistent with expectations, political trust exerts its greatest influence on health care attitudes among those primed to think about government in the context of health care.

We turn next to an analysis of the sources of support for cap and trade. As shown in the second data column of table 5.4, ideological identification once again has its anticipated impact on policy support. Liberals are more likely to support cap and trade, whereas conservatives are more likely to oppose it. As before, we are primarily interested in the effects of political trust and whether those effects vary across experimental conditions. As was the case with the health care model, the coefficient for trust alone is indistinguishable from zero, indicating that trust has no impact on support for cap and trade among those in the control condition. If our second hypothesis holds, we should see a positive and significant interaction between political trust and assignment to the environment condition. Indeed, we do. This confirms that political trust has more influence on cap-and-trade attitudes among those in the environment condition than among those in the control condition. The interactions between political trust and assignment to the health care or foreign policy conditions, though positively signed, are statistically insignificant. In other words, the effects of trust in these two conditions are not reliably different from those in the control condition, which is what we expected.

To assess the overall effects of political trust on attitudes toward cap and trade within each condition, we again performed a series of joint hypothesis tests. Political trust has no appreciable impact on support for cap and trade among those who were primed to think about government in the context of health care $(\chi^2_{1df} = 0.00, p > 0.99)$. Similarly, trust fails to shape attitudes toward cap and trade for those assigned to the foreign policy condition ($\chi^2_{1df} = 0.02$, $p > 0.89$). Among those in the environment condition, however, political trust has a positive and statistically reliable impact on support for the proposed cap-and-trade policy ($\chi^2_{1df} = 4.27$, $p < 0.04$). Consistent with expectations, we find that the effects of trust on cap-and-trade preferences are most pronounced among those primed to think about government in terms of the environment.

We continue our analysis by considering the determinants of support for increased military action in Yemen. The results in the third data column of table 5.4 show that support is greater among conservatives than it is among moderates or liberals. Liberals are slightly less supportive of military action than moderates, although this difference is not significant in a statistical sense. As in the two previous tests, the coefficient for political trust alone is not statistically significant, which means that trust has no influence on attitudes toward military strikes among those assigned to the control condition. The interactions between trust and assignment to the health care or environment conditions are also insignificant, indicating that trust's impact in these two conditions cannot be distinguished from its impact in the control condition. Finally, and most importantly, consistent with expectations, the interaction between trust and assignment to the foreign policy condition is both positive and significant. Simply put, trust has a larger impact on foreign policy preferences among those in the foreign policy condition than it does among those in the control condition.

Next we assess the net impact of political trust on support for military action in Yemen within each experimental condition. Our joint hypothesis tests reveal that trust has no discernible influence on support for military action in Yemen for those in the health care condition ($\chi^2_{1df} = 0.02$, $p > 0.89$) or for those in the environment condition ($\chi^2_{1df} = 0.59$, $p > 0.44$). Only among those assigned to the foreign policy condition does political trust increase support for heightened military strikes in Yemen ($\chi^2_{1df} = 5.44$, $p < 0.02$). As predicted, trust's greatest influence occurs among those who were primed to think about government in the context of foreign policy.

Implications of the Results

The preceding analyses have established that the effects of political trust on policy preferences are strongly conditioned by what people are primed

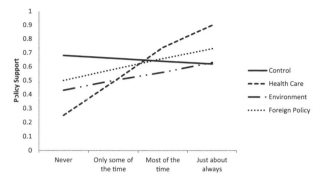

FIGURE 5.2. Effects of political trust on support for health care reform by experimental condition

Note: This figure shows the predicted probabilities of support for health care reform across levels of political trust and across experimental conditions.

to think about prior to forming their trust judgments. To better assess the magnitude of these priming effects, we calculated the predicted probabilities of policy support for each issue so that we could observe the relative size of trust's impact across experimental conditions. These predicted probabilities are depicted graphically in figures 5.2, 5.3, and 5.4.

Figure 5.2 displays the predicted probabilities of support for health care reform by level of political trust and by experimental condition. For those in the control condition, the slope for political trust is essentially flat. A one-unit increase in political trust, which we define as the difference between trusting government "only some of the time" and trusting government "most of the time," reduces the probability of support for health care reform by a mere 2 percentage points. Among individuals in the environment or foreign policy conditions, the slope for political trust is positive but substantively modest. The same one-unit increase in political trust raises the probability of support by only 6 or 8 percentage points, respectively. Among those in the health care condition, however, the slope for political trust is steep. Here a similarly sized increase in trust increases the probability of support for health care reform by 25 percentage points, a substantively large effect.

Figure 5.3 shows the predicted probabilities of support for cap and trade by level of political trust and by experimental condition. Among those assigned to the control condition, the slope for political trust is slightly negative. A one-unit increase in trust lowers the likelihood of

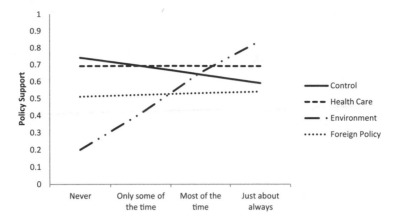

FIGURE 5.3. Effects of political trust on support for cap and trade by experimental condition

Note: This figure shows the predicted probabilities of support for cap and trade across levels of political trust and across experimental conditions.

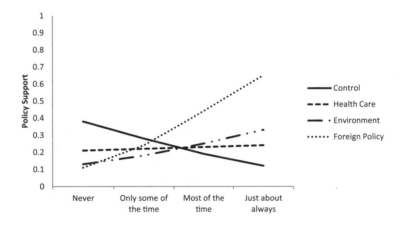

FIGURE 5.4. Effects of political trust on support for Yemen strike by experimental condition

Note: This figure shows the predicted probabilities of support for a Yemen strike across levels of political trust and across experimental conditions.

support for cap and trade by 5 percentage points. In the health care and foreign policy conditions, the slope for political trust is unmistakably flat. The same one-unit shock to trust raises the probability of policy support by 0 and 1 percentage points, respectively. For those who were primed to think about government in the context of the environment, though, the slope for political trust is positive and steep. Here we see that a one-unit change in trust increases the probability of supporting cap and trade by the sizable amount of 24 percentage points.

Finally, figure 5.4 presents the predicted probabilities of support for military action in Yemen by political trust and by experimental condition. Once again, the slope for political trust in the control condition is negative but not particularly steep. A one-unit increase in political trust dampens support for military action in Yemen by 9 percentage points. For those in the health care or environment conditions, the slope for trust is positive but modest in magnitude. Trusting government "most of the time" instead of "only some of the time" increases support for military action in Yemen by 1 and 7 percentage points, respectively. Trust's greatest impact occurs among those primed to think about government in terms of foreign policy. Among such individuals, the same increase in political trust raises policy support by 20 percentage points.

Conclusion

The results of chapter 5 provide important new insights about the relationship between trust and priming at the individual level. First, using a simple survey experiment, we showed how individuals' issue attention can be selectively focused on a particular issue at a particular moment in time. Second, we found that priming people to think about government action in a given issue domain can activate the importance of political trust in informing individuals' policy preferences in that domain.

The fact that issue priming has such a strong impact on the consequences of political trust has important political implications. The experiments reported in this chapter show how easily even passive issue frames can direct individuals to focus their attention on a particular issue. This suggests that it would not be difficult for partisan elites to strategically manipulate or prime issue attention during the course of a political campaign. Why does this matter? By guiding the public to focus its attention on a particular set of issues, elites can, in essence, strengthen or weaken the effects of political trust on citizens' policy preferences. This could, for example, enable elites to minimize the negative effects of a distrustful public on policy preferences or, under different circumstances, to maximize the positive effects of a trustful public on policy preferences. In either scenario, our results suggest that elites have the ability to shape the climate of public opinion in meaningful ways. Given the extent to which lawmakers are responsive to public opinion (Stimson, MacKuen, and Erickson 1995; Erikson, MacKuen, and Stimson 2002), our results imply that elites can influence policy outcomes by manipulating the consequences of trust through issue priming.

CHAPTER SIX

Political Trust Can Help Conservatives, Too

The results from chapter 5 suggest that scholars may have underestimated the range of opinions that political trust affects. It is not that the list was short before, but scholars in the past have primarily focused on trust's effect on support for liberal "big government" initiatives (e.g., Hetherington and Globetti 2002; Chanley, Rudolph, and Rahn 2000; Hetherington 2005; Rudolph and Evans 2005). In an experiment using college students, however, we were able to change the policy preferences that trust in government affected simply by priming different issue areas in advance of asking people how much they trusted the government. The strong correlations that our priming experiment produced between trust and support for an environmental program and for a military intervention, respectively, are two areas in which scholars have not typically found effects for trust.

That we could derive such results in a lab is important. This suggests that the hypothesized relationship is possible. But to be more certain that the effect is generalizable to the population as a whole, we next attempt to match the pattern of results produced in the previous chapter with results that use survey data gathered from a representative sample of Americans. In this chapter, we focus on foreign policy preferences expressed during the George W. Bush administration. During the early Bush years, in particular, foreign policy was on the minds of most Americans. The tragedy that occurred on September 11, 2001, placed terrorism on the agenda like never before, and the United States subsequently went to war in Afghanistan and Iraq. As a consequence, people ought to have been evaluating how trustworthy they thought government was with foreign policies in mind. Our theory suggests that political trust would, in turn, affect preferences in the foreign policy realm, not the domestic policy realm, as is usually the case.

That trust in government might affect foreign policy preferences makes theoretical sense. If people need to trust the government to support more government intervention (Hetherington 2005), as is true on the domestic policy side, the same should be true for foreign affairs. More military spending and a more aggressive foreign policy require increased government intervention, just as more investment in the social safety net does. Hence when foreign issues are salient, trust in government has the potential to serve conservative foreign policy ambitions, just as it serves liberal domestic policy ambitions. In fact, political trust might even provide a deeper reservoir of support for foreign policy than it does for domestic policy because as we have shown in chapter 3, political trust tends to be higher when international issues are salient.

In this chapter, we demonstrate that differences in salience have a concrete effect on the actual opinion environment as opposed to just the lab setting. Our demonstration occurs in two parts. First, using panel and cross-sectional data, we show how critical trust in government was to George W. Bush in pursuing foreign policy ambitions early in his presidency. With trust high, most Americans supported his administration's policies. We also provide a glimpse of how Iraq became the most partisan military engagement of the survey era (see Jacobson 2006). Recall from chapter 4 that trust in government among those on the left dropped as the Bush presidency progressed. This change would have profound implications for foreign policy support because liberals were the ones asked to make an ideological sacrifice to support Bush's aggressive policies, and therefore it was liberals for whom trust would be most critical. As liberals' trust dipped, so did their support for the wars in Afghanistan and Iraq as well as other war-related policies.

Second, we merge data from media content analyses with American National Election Study (ANES) data collected between 1980 and 2004 to show that trust's effect on both racial policy and foreign policy domains depends on how much attention the media provide these issue domains. When race and redistribution receives more coverage, as in the late 1980s and 1990s, trust's effect on racial policy preferences is large. When defense and foreign policy receives more coverage, as in the mid-1980s and in 2004, trust's effect on defense preferences is large. Its effect on preferences in these domains diminishes as media coverage diminishes.

How and When Political Trust Matters

Much of the book so far has been devoted to what causes movement in trust. Now we are transitioning to what preferences trust ought to affect and why it ought to affect them. Our reasoning about why trust ought to affect a range of things starts from a simple observation. The inner-workings of government are opaque to most, and developing constrained belief systems is too taxing for many (e.g., Converse 1964). In that context, political trust provides people a useful decision rule. If they trust government—the entity that produces and administers public policies— they ought to be more likely to support more government involvement; if not, they ought to be less likely.

We suspect that when national security becomes salient, the effect of trust on defense and foreign policy preferences ought to be particularly strong and wide-ranging. Because most Americans have neither much personal experience with nor much information about the world abroad (Delli Carpini and Keeter 1996), their preferences tend to be more uncertain than they are for other issues (Hurwitz and Peffley 1987, Lavine et al. 1996). Trust can help overcome uncertainty (see Yamagishi, Cook, and Watabe 1998). Moreover, the media often cannot present interpretations of international events beyond what the government shares with them because most information is available only from the executive branch (Baker and Oneal 2001; Bennett and Paletz 1994). Unlike domestic concerns, such as the economy, very few Americans have access to the information necessary to make an independent assessment of conditions in remote locations like Iraq or Afghanistan. How people judge whether the costs of military intervention were worth the benefits must be, in part, a function of whether they trust the government to have portrayed conditions truthfully. As a result, trust may also affect people's evaluations of government performance in foreign affairs in addition to their preferences for future government action.

Testing Our Thinking

We again turn to the ANES 2000–2004 panel data, which allow us to explore whether trust causes policy preferences or the reverse. After we establish that trust is a cause of, as opposed to a consequence of, policy preferences, we turn to the 2004 ANES cross section because it contains a wide range of foreign and defense policy preferences to study. This analysis also allows us to demonstrate the importance of the polarization of political trust during this time frame in creating increasingly polarized foreign policy preferences as the Bush years progressed.

To increase our confidence that trust has an independent effect on foreign policy preferences, we must build statistical models to account for all competing factors. Although scholars once suggested that foreign policy attitudes were not firmly held and ostensibly arrived at randomly (see, for example, Almond 1950; Converse 1964; Gamson and Modigliani 1966), later research suggests that these opinions are reasonably stable over time (Achen 1975) and are structured in predictable ways (Hurwitz and Peffley 1987). Political predispositions and general postures toward force tend to carry the most weight in explaining foreign policy preferences (Berinsky 2009). As political predispositions, we use ideology and partisanship, expecting that conservatives and Republicans will be most supportive during this period. To tap attitudes about force, we use authoritarianism (Altemeyer 1996; Merolla and Zechmeister 2009; Hetherington and Weiler 2009) and isolationism (e.g., McClosky 1958; Hurwitz and Peffley 1987). Those who score higher in authoritarianism ought to be more hawkish, while those who express isolationist attitudes ought to be less hawkish.

Core values, including patriotism (e.g., Rokeach 1973; Hurwitz and Peffley 1990) and moral traditionalism (Peffley and Hurwitz 1992), are important as well. For both, those scoring higher ought to provide more hawkish responses. Herrmann, Tetlock, and Visser (1999) find that people differ in their willingness to support the use of force under different circumstances, suggesting that context matters (see also Peffley and Hurwitz 1992). Since context is difficult to measure with cross-sectional data, we rely on people's perceptions of that context.[1]

Finally, scholars have found that some demographic variables affect foreign policy preferences. Those with more formal education tend to be less supportive of interventionism and military spending under most, but not all, circumstances (Gamson and Modigliani 1966; Bartels 1994). Women tend to be less supportive of the use of force than men (e.g., Shapiro and Mahajan 1986). In addition to these variables, we also include measures for race (being African American), age, and being a resident of the South.

Results

We must first demonstrate that trust affects foreign policy preferences and evaluations rather than vice versa. Since the ANES surveyed the same respondents in 2000, 2002, and 2004, we can estimate models in which the dependent variables are measured in 2004 and the independent variables are measured in 2002 (or 2000 if they are unavailable in 2002). Unfortunately, the ANES asked a full complement of panel respondents only two foreign policy questions—namely, whether the Afghan and Iraq wars, respectively, were worth the cost. If political trust measured in 2002 affects these evaluations measured in 2004, and the evaluations of Afghanistan and Iraq measured in 2002 do not affect trust measured in 2004, then our study suggests that political trust causes foreign policy preferences.

To estimate the Afghan and Iraq war models, we use the variables described above as explanatory variables, employing lagged measures to impose temporal order when possible. To estimate the panel model for political trust, we replicate as closely as possible the model estimated by Hetherington (1998), also using lagged independent variables when possible. Because the Afghan War had begun by the time respondents were interviewed in 2002, the same question was asked both years, allowing for the estimation of a traditional cross-lagged model. Since the Iraq War had not yet begun in 2002, however, people were not asked whether they thought the war was worth the cost. Here we must substitute their preference about whether the United States should go to war, which was asked in 2002, as a lagged approximation of the dependent variable.

The results of the first half of the panel analyses appear in table 6.1 and conform to expectations. Political trust, as measured in 2002, had a significant effect on whether people thought the Afghan and Iraq wars were worth the cost in 2004, suggesting that political trust shapes foreign policy preferences. Although encouraging, it is possible that the relationship is more complicated. If the war preferences measured in 2002 are also significant in explaining political trust in 2004, it would suggest simultaneity. The results in table 6.2, however, suggest that simultaneity is not a problem. Neither a preference for going to war in Iraq in 2002 nor a belief that the Afghan war was worth the cost in 2002 approaches statistical significance in explaining political trust in 2004. Based on these results, we can be fairly confident that trust causes foreign policy preferences and

TABLE 6.1 **Foreign policy preferences as a function of lagged political trust and other variables, 2000–2004**

	Model 1 Parameter estimate (Standard error) Iraq worth cost, 2004	Model 2 Parameter estimate (Standard error) Afghanistan worth cost, 2004
Iraq War preference$_{2002}$	1.513*** (0.263)	— (—)
Afghanistan War worth cost$_{2002}$	— (—)	1.315*** (0.260)
Political trust$_{2002}$	0.814* (0.435)	0.744* (0.422)
Party identification$_{2002}$	3.024*** (0.379)	1.828*** (0.359)
Authoritarianism$_{2000}$	0.482 (0.414)	0.465 (0.407)
Conservatism$_{2002}$	1.559** (0.565)	0.425 (0.530)
African American	0.328 (0.487)	−0.246 (0.385)
Age	−0.486 (0.548)	−0.244 (0.498)
Female	0.036 (0.215)	−1.089*** (0.215)
Education	−0.268 (0.414)	1.353*** (0.413)
Moral traditionalism$_{2000}$	1.623** (0.582)	1.422** (0.573)
Isolationism$_{2002}$	−0.527* (0.281)	−1.192*** (0.233)
Patriotism$_{2002}$	0.800* (0.383)	0.112 (0.358)
South	0.485* (0.226)	0.009 (0.217)
Constant	−5.592*** (0.734)	−2.346*** (0.613)
Number of cases	682	702
Pseudo R^2	0.546	0.408

Note: Logistic regression.
*$p < 0.05$, **$p < 0.01$, ***$p < 0.001$, one-tailed tests
Source: American National Election Study, 2000–2004, panel study.

TABLE 6.2 **Political trust as a function of lagged foreign policy preferences and other variables, 2000–2004**

	Model 1 Parameter estimate (Standard error)	Model 2 Parameter estimate (Standard error)
Political trust$_{2002}$	0.571*** (0.031)	0.579*** (0.032)
Iraq War preference$_{2002}$	0.005 (0.018)	— (—)
Afghanistan War worth cost$_{2002}$	— (—)	0.017 (0.020)
Thermometer: Bush$_{2002}$	0.077* (0.039)	−0.006 (0.037)
Thermometer: Congress$_{2002}$	0.060 (0.049)	0.096* (0.048)
Thermometer: Democrats$_{2002}$	0.015 (0.032)	−0.035 (0.032)
Thermometer: Republicans$_{2002}$	0.053 (0.038)	0.108** (0.039)
Moral traditionalism$_{2000}$	−0.006 (0.035)	0.023 (0.037)
Retrospective economic evaluation$_{2002}$	−0.103** (0.035)	−0.115** (0.036)
Education	0.058* (0.025)	0.068** (0.025)
Age	0.026 (0.037)	0.071* (0.036)
African American	−0.006 (0.029)	0.011 (0.028)
Female	−0.003 (0.014)	0.004 (0.014)
Constant	0.018 (0.054)	0.001 (0.056)
Number of cases	706	683
Adjusted R^2	0.460	0.451

Note: Ordinary least squares (OLS) regression. Dependent variable is political trust in 2004.
*$p < 0.05$, **$p < 0.01$, ***$p < 0.001$, one-tailed tests
Source: American National Election Study, 2000–2004, panel study.

not vice versa, allowing us to investigate a wider range of foreign policy opinions that appear in the 2004 ANES cross-sectional survey but not in the panel survey.[2]

Cross-Sectional Models

Each column in table 6.3 contains the results from a model for one of six foreign policy preferences or evaluations that we expect political trust will affect. Specifically, the survey asked respondents whether the wars in Iraq and Afghanistan, respectively, were worth the cost; the degree to which they thought the war in Iraq reduced the threat from terrorism; whether spending on the war on terror ought to be increased, decreased, or kept about the same; and the importance of a strong military. Finally, the ANES asked people to place themselves on a seven-point defense spending scale.[3]

Again, the results conform to expectations. Political trust has a consistently positive effect on support for the government's position on these foreign policies.[4] The results from many of the statistical models here are more complicated to interpret than those we have used before. Hence we have to employ simulations to evaluate the magnitude of political trust's effect. We do this by first fixing the variables other than trust at politically relevant values and allowing trust to vary across its range.[5] When we fix trust at its minimum, the predicted probability that our "typical" respondent thinks Iraq was worth the cost is only 0.33; we would classify him or her as not believing that Iraq was worth the cost because that probability is well below 0.50. If we increase political trust to its maximum, however, the predicted probability more than doubles to 0.72, a 39 percentage-point increase. Not only is this change large; it is substantively important, too. With trust at its maximum, our "typical" respondent believes Iraq was worth the cost, whereas with trust at its minimum, our "typical" respondent does not.

Trust's effect is also impressive in relative terms. We can replicate the simulation we just did, this time fixing trust at its mean and allowing other variables to vary across their respective ranges. Partisanship's effect is the largest by far. Moving from its minimum (strongly Democratic) to its maximum (strongly Republican), the probability of seeing Iraq as worth the cost increases from 0.20 to 0.90. The effect of political trust, however, compares favorably with all the other variables. The effects for moral traditionalism, education, and isolationism across their ranges are 0.33, 0.31, and 0.29, respectively—about the same as political trust's.

TABLE 6.3 **Foreign policy preferences as a function of contemporaneous political trust and other variables, 2004**

Dependent variable	Was the war in Iraq worth the cost? Model 1 Parameter estimate (Standard error) 0–1	Did the war in Iraq reduce terrorism? Model 2 Parameter estimate (Standard error) 1–3	Is it important to have a strong military? Model 3 Parameter estimate (Standard error) 1–4	Should spending on the War on Terror increase? Model 4 Parameter estimate (Standard error) 1–3	Should spending on defense increase? Model 5 Parameter estimate (Standard error) 1–7	Was the war in Afghanistan worth the cost? Model 6 Parameter estimate (Standard error) 0–1
Political trust	1.681*** (0.397)	0.816*** (0.172)	0.566** (0.183)	0.609*** (0.172)	0.346* (0.184)	0.615 (0.394)
Party identification	4.240*** (0.412)	1.195*** (0.169)	0.299* (0.180)	0.387* (0.171)	0.846*** (0.184)	2.534*** (0.393)
Conservatism	0.906 (0.646)	0.884** (0.272)	0.478* (0.287)	–0.102 (0.271)	0.072 (0.289)	–1.066* (0.626)
Authoritarianism	0.105 (0.354)	0.281 (0.152)	0.371* (0.158)	0.179 (0.151)	0.008 (0.159)	0.007 (0.343)
Education	–1.553*** (0.443)	–0.449* (0.181)	–0.387* (0.187)	–0.442* (0.180)	–0.900*** (0.193)	1.354** (0.422)
South	0.200 (0.196)	0.058 (0.083)	0.056 (0.089)	0.032 (0.083)	0.178* (0.090)	0.436* (0.204)
Age	–0.774 (0.407)	–0.150 (0.169)	–0.128 (0.174)	0.923*** (0.168)	0.165 (0.182)	0.166 (0.464)
Female	–0.179 (0.183)	–0.055 (0.078)	–0.181* (0.082)	–0.291*** (0.078)	–0.283*** (0.082)	–1.237*** (0.183)

continues

TABLE 6.3 (*continued*)

Dependent variable	Was the war in Iraq worth the cost? 0–1 — Model 1 Parameter estimate (Standard error)	Did the war in Iraq reduce terrorism? 1–3 — Model 2 Parameter estimate (Standard error)	Is it important to have a strong military? 1–4 — Model 3 Parameter estimate (Standard error)	Should spending on the War on Terror increase? 1–3 — Model 4 Parameter estimate (Standard error)	Should spending on defense increase? 1–7 — Model 5 Parameter estimate (Standard error)	Was the war in Afghanistan worth the cost? 0–1 — Model 6 Parameter estimate (Standard error)
African American	-0.123 (0.294)	-0.005 (0.123)	0.040 (0.126)	-0.040 (0.121)	-0.071 (0.135)	-1.059*** (0.244)
Patriotism	0.783 (0.631)	0.387 (0.255)	1.670*** (0.248)	1.238*** (0.246)	2.084*** (0.268)	1.858*** (0.544)
Moral traditionalism	1.867** (0.650)	0.512 (0.273)	1.309*** (0.283)	0.419 (0.268)	1.115*** (0.290)	1.118 (0.603)
Importance of defense spending	1.081* (0.520)	-0.036 (0.214)	0.890*** (0.225)	0.752*** (0.214)	1.561*** (0.235)	-0.610 (0.470)
Isolationism	-1.450*** (0.268)	-0.166 (0.102)	-0.041 (0.105)	-0.264** (0.101)	-0.264* (0.113)	-0.963*** (0.209)
Constant/cut 1	-5.308*** (0.724)	1.580*** (0.290)	0.341 (0.320)	1.173*** (0.286)	0.877** (0.311)	-1.625* (0.635)
Cut 2	—	2.707*** (0.297)	1.888*** (0.296)	2.453*** (0.292)	—	—
Cut 3	—	—	3.205*** (0.306)	—	—	—
Number of cases	950	963	967	962	870	962
Adjusted or Pseudo R^2	0.378	0.136	0.151	0.109	0.124	0.252

Note: Logistic regression: Models 1 and 6. Ordered probit regression: Models 2–4. OLS regression: Model 5.
*$p < 0.05$, **$p < 0.01$, ***$p < 0.001$, one-tailed tests
Source: American National Election Study, 2004.

The effect of political trust is also substantively very large in understanding how people thought the Iraq war affected the threat of terrorism.
Replicating the simulation we did above, we find that, with trust fixed at
its minimum, the predicted probability of falling into the "increased" category is 0.47, the "stayed the same" category is 0.38, and the "decreased"
category is only 0.15. This suggests that a very politically distrustful person would think that Iraq increased the threat from terrorism because
the predicted probability of falling into this category is highest. But if
someone scored at the trust maximum, the predicted probability of falling
into the "increased" category is just 0.19, while the probability of falling
into both the "stayed the same" and "decreased" categories is 0.41. Put
another way, the predicted probability that our typical person sees the
war in Iraq as a net harm decreases by 28 percentage points (from 0.47 to
0.19), while the predicted probability that people see Iraq as a net benefit
increases by 26 percentage points (from 0.15 to 0.41) when we increase
trust from its minimum to maximum.

To put trust's effect into perspective, consider the effect of ideology. If
we fix ideology at "extremely liberal," the predicted probability that our
"typical" person would say Iraq caused an increase in the risk of terrorism is 0.58 compared with 0.33 that the threat remained the same and 0.09
that the threat decreased. If we fix ideology at "extremely conservative,"
the respective probabilities move to 0.25, 0.42, and 0.33. In other words,
extreme conservatives were 34 percentage points less likely than extreme
liberals to see Iraq as harming the nation's efforts to combat terrorism and
about 24 percentage points more likely to think that it helped. The effect
of ideology is roughly the same as the effect of political trust.

Trust also exerts a strong effect on preferences for spending on the war
on terrorism. When we replicate the above simulations and fix trust at its
minimum, the predicted probability of thinking that such spending ought
to be decreased is 0.14, the predicted probability of thinking that it ought
to remain about the same is 0.44, and the predicted probability of thinking that it ought to increase is 0.42. If we increase trust to its maximum,
while holding all else constant, the predicted probability of thinking that
spending ought to be decreased drops to 0.05, the predicted probability
of thinking that it ought to remain the same decreases to 0.30, and the
predicted probability of thinking that it ought to increase surges to 0.66.
Increasing political trust from its minimum to its maximum increases the
probability of wanting to increase spending on the war on terrorism by
more than 20 percentage points. In this case, the effect of political trust is
about the same as the effect of partisanship.

Taken together, these results make clear that more trust in the Bush years than was typical helped the administration to pursue its favored policies. Of course, the results also suggest that as trust dropped and polarized during Bush's middle and later years, support for muscular foreign policies may have dropped and polarized, too. We turn to this question in the next section.

The Role of Ideological Sacrifice

The preceding results demonstrate the importance of political trust in shaping individuals' foreign policy preferences. Simply put, trustful citizens are more likely than distrustful ones to endorse the government's position on foreign policy matters. The decision to endorse an expansion of military action, however, does not impose equal ideological costs on liberals and conservatives. Supporting an expansion of the war on terror, for example, requires a greater ideological sacrifice from liberals than it does from conservatives. As a result, our theory anticipates, the effects of trust on support for such policies should be greater among liberals than among conservatives.

To explore whether political trust does, in fact, exert more influence on liberals' support for conservative foreign policy initiatives, we use the 2004 ANES data to cross-tabulate the relationship between trust and foreign policy preferences by ideology. We report the results in table 6.4. The effects of political trust on policy support are greater among liberals than among conservatives across all six policy issues. Approximately 58 percent of low-trust conservatives felt that the war in Iraq was worth the cost, while about 70 percent of high-trust conservatives felt it was worth it, an effect of roughly 12 percentage points. The corresponding effect of trust among liberals was comparatively larger at about 17 percentage points. Indeed, high-trust liberals were about four times more likely to say that the war in Iraq was worth the cost than were low-trust liberals.

On the question of whether it is important to have a strong military, the effect of trust among conservatives is quite modest at roughly 2 percent. Among liberals, by contrast, the effect of trust is much larger at nearly 17 percent. A similar pattern emerges across the other issues. The asymmetric effects of trust on support for increased spending on the war on terror are particularly interesting. High-trust conservatives are no more likely to favor greater spending on the war on terror than are low-trust conservatives. Among liberals, trust increases support for such spending

TABLE 6.4 **Foreign policy preferences by political trust and ideology**

Conservatives	Low trust	High trust	Effect
War in Iraq was worth cost	57.9	70.2	+12.3
War in Iraq decreased terror threat	39.8	42.1	+2.3
Important to have strong military	95.1	96.9	+1.8
Increase spending for war on terror	40.9	38.4	−2.5
Increase spending for defense	66.1	74.9	+8.8
War in Afghanistan was worth cost	82.6	86.7	+4.1
Mean effect of trust			+4.5

Liberals	Low trust	High trust	Effect
War in Iraq was worth cost	6.3	23.1	+16.8
War in Iraq decreased terror threat	4.8	10.6	+5.8
Important to have strong military	69.8	86.4	+16.6
Increase spending for war on terror	48.6	56.9	+8.3
Increase spending for defense	24.5	37.3	+12.8
War in Afghanistan was worth cost	64.1	73.8	+9.6
Mean effect of trust			+11.7

Note: Table entries are the percentage of participants that agree with the specified (row) statement.
Source: American National Election Study, 2004.

by more than 8 percentage points. From a policy standpoint, this increase is substantively important because it means that a majority of high-trust liberals actually favored greater spending on the war on terror.

This asymmetric effect of trust across ideological groups has proven to be politically consequential—namely, it has served to produce polarization on the early twenty-first century wars. The Iraq war has the ignominious distinction of being the most polarized in the history of survey-era wars in terms of public opinion (Jacobson 2006). The pattern of results in table 6.4 explains why.

Relative to Iraq, conservative support remained high, and liberal support collapsed. Our survey work through 2004, presented here, captures a moment when trust was still quite high among conservatives but was dropping to some degree among liberals. Hence the increasingly different levels of political trust by ideology are probably part of the reason for the polarization concerning the Iraq war at this point. However, trust eventually diminishes among both liberals and conservatives, yet conservative support for the war remained stout through the end of the Bush years. For example, in November 2007, a Virginia Commonwealth University poll of the United States found that only 13 percent of liberals and 17 percent of conservatives said they trusted the government in Washington to do what was right either most or all of the time. It would seem that support for the war should have plummeted among conservatives as well, but it did not, with 70 percent or more typically supporting it through the end of the Bush presidency.

The asymmetric effect of political trust helps answer this puzzle. Even though political trust declined among conservatives in the late Bush years, our results suggest that conservatives' diminished trust ought to have relatively little impact on their foreign policy preferences because supporting these initiatives does not require an ideological sacrifice of them. In contrast, the fact that trust plummeted among liberals did serve to undermine public support for Bush's foreign policy agenda because this group needed to trust government to make the ideological sacrifice necessary to support it.

A More Direct Test of the Salience Hypothesis: Defense Spending

Although we believe that an increase in the salience of defense issues after 9/11 explains why trust affected foreign policy preferences in 2004, we have not provided direct evidence yet. As preliminary evidence, contrast the strong relationship that we have reported between defense preferences and trust in 2004 with their relationship in 2000, a period of low foreign policy salience. Trust's correlation with the seven-point defense spending scale, the only one of the six dependent variables from our 2004 analysis that is also available in the 2000 ANES data, is 0.01. In other words, there is no relationship between political trust and defense spending preferences in 2000. Also consistent with the issue salience hypothesis, trust's usually strong relationship with preferences in the race and redistribution domain disappeared in 2004. After 9/11 pushed other issues off the public agenda, the strongest relationship between trust and any of the four racial policy preferences included in the 2004 ANES was a paltry 0.06.[6] Such small correlations suggest that there is no meaningful relationship at all.

To provide a more systematic treatment of how salience helps determine the influence that political trust has, we use the ANES Cumulative File. We augment these data with media content analysis data that allow us to measure issue salience directly. If trust's effect on foreign policy preferences is larger when foreign policy is more salient in the media, it would provide firmer evidence for the salience hypothesis. Unfortunately, the potential dependent variables available to test our hypotheses are few;

the ANES has asked only the seven-point defense spending scale question over a long period of years. It has appeared in almost every survey between 1980 and 2004.

To measure the salience of defense and foreign affairs over time, we relied on media content analysis from Baumgartner and Jones's Policy Agendas Project (PAP), which is available at www.policyagendas.org. The PAP includes a database of more than thirty-seven thousand news stories randomly sampled from the *New York Times* News Index from 1946 to 2005. Since the ANES defense spending scale runs from 1980 to 2004, we use these years from the PAP. The PAP classifies each article as one of twenty-seven policy domains with coding decisions cross-checked by three coders. Among the domains, two are germane to foreign policy: "defense" and "international affairs." We calculate the percentage of stories in specific domains each year by dividing the number of mentions in that domain by the total number of stories coded that year.[7]

The results of the content analysis follow the expected pattern. The defense and international issue domain was particularly salient both in the mid-1980s and especially after 9/11 but was much less salient in the 1990s and 2000. The maximum percentage of national defense stories (31 percent) occurred in 2004, and the percentage was also very substantial in 1986 (29 percent) and 1984 (28 percent) with Cold War tensions running high. In contrast, the percentage of national defense stories between 1994 and 2000 never exceeded 17.5 percent, with the minimum occurring in 2000 (14 percent).

To test whether the effect of political trust is conditional on the salience of defense, we merge the yearly results of the content analysis into the ANES Cumulative File. Each respondent in a given year receives a score for national defense salience that corresponds to the proportion of stories written in the domain for that year. For example, since 31 percent of stories in 2004 were in this domain, each 2004 respondent receives a score of 0.31 for defense salience. Next we create an interaction between defense salience and political trust. The effect of the interaction should carry a positive sign, indicating that the difference between the most and least trustful in their support for defense spending increases as the salience of national defense increases.

To test our hypothesis, we replicate the defense spending model from above, adding the trust × defense salience interaction and the base variable effect for defense salience. Of the twelve right-hand-side variables in the 2004 model, all are available in the ANES Cumulative File except for perceived importance of defense spending, authoritarianism, and patriotism. Fortunately, the effect of authoritarianism was not large in our 2004 analysis, so its absence should not affect the results much.[8] Moreover, the salience of defense spending, as measured by our media content analysis in the over-time analysis, actually better measures context than the importance of defense spending, which we used in the 2004 cross section. Patriotism's effect was substantial in 2004, but unfortunately, data limitations force us to proceed without it. Because moral traditionalism and isolationism appear in most but not all of the years that the dependent variable does, we estimate a model that includes only the independent variables available in all years as well as two additional models that include moral traditionalism and isolationism. In all three models, we employ clustered standard errors on defense salience to account for the limited variation in the contextual data.[9]

The results of the defense spending analysis appear across three columns in table 6.5. The first column includes the results of the reduced-form model. The second column includes moral traditionalism, which was missing from the 1980, 1982, and 1984 studies, and the third column includes both moral traditionalism and isolationism. Regardless of specification, the results follow the same pattern. The interaction between trust and defense salience carries a positive sign and is statistically significant. The sign on political trust is negative, which might seem anomalous at first but is, in fact, meaningless because this coefficient reflects the effect of trust when defense salience equals zero, which never occurs in practice. The main effect for the salience of national defense is positive, which is consistent with previous scholarship (Herrmann, Tetlock, and Visser 1999) but not statistically significant.

Since the model in column one produces estimates that are substantively the same as the others but with more years included, we interpret the conditional effect of trust based on it. When the salience of defense issues is high, as it was in 2004, the estimated effect of political trust on defense spending is substantial, $-0.806 + 5.521(0.31) = 0.906$ with a standard error of 0.167 ($t = 5.43, p < 0.05$). Our model also suggests that the effect of political trust on defense spending was large in the mid-1980s when the percentage of defense mentions was also high. In 1984, for example, trust's estimated effect was $-0.806 + 5.521(0.28) = 0.746$ with a standard error of 0.130 ($t = 5.74, p < 0.05$). But when salience of defense was low, as was the case for most of the 1990s, the effect of political trust was statistically indistinguishable from zero. In 1996 and 1998, for example, trust's estimated effects were 0.114 with a standard error of 0.206 ($t = 0.52, p > 0.05$) and 0.156 with a standard error of 0.224 ($t = 0.25, p > 0.05$),

TABLE 6.5 **Defense spending preferences as a function of political trust conditional on foreign policy salience, 1980–2004**

	Model 1 Parameter estimate (Standard error)	Model 2 Parameter estimate (Standard error)	Model 3 Parameter estimate (Standard error)
Political trust	0.806 (0.529)	−0.212 (0.366)	−0.275 (0.380)
Defense salience	1.063 (2.774)	1.488 (2.439)	2.317 (2.349)
Trust × defense salience	5.521* (2.066)	3.873* (1.498)	3.697* (1.625)
Conservatism	0.211*** (0.010)	0.170*** (0.017)	0.156*** (0.015)
Party identification	0.631*** (0.077)	0.603*** (0.067)	0.619*** (0.073)
Female	−0.142** (0.044)	−0.155** (0.038)	−0.164** (0.037)
Education	−0.202*** (0.030)	−0.170*** (0.024)	−0.200*** (0.021)
Age	0.003 (0.002)	0.003* (0.001)	0.003 (0.001)
South	0.317*** (0.039)	0.356*** (0.028)	0.333*** (0.027)
African American	−0.103* (0.053)	−0.032 (0.034)	−0.026 (0.036)
Moral traditionalism	— —	0.558*** (0.099)	0.640*** (0.074)
Isolationism	— —	— —	0.239** (0.045)
Constant	3.344** (0.818)	2.353** (0.515)	1.906** (0.501)
Number of cases	16,086	10,451	9,046
Adjusted R^2	0.1064	0.1325	0.1485

Note: OLS regression. Standard errors clustered on year in parentheses.
*$p < 0.05$, **$p < 0.01$, ***$p < 0.001$, one-tailed tests
Source: American National Election Study, 1948–2004, cumulative data file.

respectively. In short, trust's effect on defense spending is statistically significant when the salience of national defense is high, but not when it is low.[10]

A Second Test of the Salience Hypothesis: Aid to African Americans

We attempt to replicate this result for the race and redistribution domain. Unfortunately, the PAP content analysis is not as helpful in measuring salience in this domain. Of the twenty-seven categories that the PAP coded, only two capture race and redistribution directly: "social welfare" and "civil rights." The percentage of stories coded into these two categories, however, fails to reflect the actual importance of this domain. The maximum percentage of such stories in a given year is only 8.8 percent, and most years the percentage is under five. If we expand the PAP codes to include fewer explicitly racial categories, such as crime, housing, and community development, the percentage remains very low, suggesting the PAP data do not allow us to tap the salience of the race domain with enough precision.[11]

We, therefore, carried out an original content analysis, using Lexis-Nexis to analyze articles published in the *New York Times* between January 1 and December 31 of federal election years starting in 1980, the first full year Lexis-Nexis contains holdings, and ending in 2004. We limited the analysis to articles that appeared in Section A from the National Desk so that we could capture articles that centered primarily on the United States. We counted articles across several issue domains—namely, defense, the economy, race and redistribution, morality, the environment, aging, and education. Following Gilens (1999), we used "welfare," "food stamps," "big government," "homeless," "urban poor," "public assistance," "public housing," "Medicaid," and "civil rights" to tap the salience of the race and redistribution domain. We derived our measure of salience for the race and redistribution domain by dividing the number of articles containing the key words related to this domain by the total number of articles in all domains.[12]

The salience of race and redistribution follows the opposite pattern of defense but with less year-to-year variation. Race and redistribution stories were particularly salient in the mid-1990s with welfare reform atop the agenda. In 1994, for example, one-quarter of stories included one of our search terms, and 22 percent of stories fell into the race and redistribution domain in 1996. In 2004, with terrorism front and center, only 12 percent did. As above, we merged these data into the ANES Cumulative File with each respondent each year receiving a score for the proportion of stories that met the search criteria for race and redistribution for that year. For example, all 1994 respondents received a race and redistribution salience score of 0.25, and so forth. We then created an interaction between political trust and race and redistribution salience.

As for dependent variables, the ANES has consistently asked only one question from this issue domain since 1980, the aid to African Americans seven-point scale.[13] We reverse the ANES's coding, such that the conservative response is coded one and the liberal response is coded seven. A positive sign on the interaction would suggest that the difference in preferences between the most and least trustful is largest when the salience of racial issues is highest.

Since only non–African Americans pay the costs for these programs and do not receive direct benefits, we use only non–African American respondents in our analysis (see also Hetherington and Globetti 2002; Hetherington 2005).[14] We include as many of the right-hand-side variables as possible from Hetherington's (2005) model and make substitutes when possible. Unfortunately, neither support for equality nor racial resentment appears in the ANES Cumulative File, although both have large

TABLE 6.6 **Effect of political trust on aid to African Americans: preferences conditional on racial issue salience, nonblack respondents, 1980–2004**

	Parameter estimate (Standard error)
Political trust	−0.592 (0.541)
Race salience	−0.858 (1.259)
Trust × race salience	6.465* (2.905)
Conservatism	−0.223*** (0.016)
Party identification	−0.600*** (0.054)
Female	0.031 (0.022)
Education	0.176*** (0.026)
Age	−0.001 (0.001)
South	−0.232*** (0.042)
Income	−0.100*** (0.020)
Retrospective economic evaluation	−0.021 (0.023)
African Americans thermometer	0.015*** (0.001)
Constant	3.694*** (0.293)
Number of cases	13,124
Adjusted R^2	0.1393

Note: OLS regression. Standard errors clustered on year in parentheses.
*$p < 0.05$, **$p < 0.01$, ***$p < 0.001$, one-tailed tests
Source: American National Election Study, 1948–2004, cumulative data file.

effects on racial policy preferences. Finding a suitable proxy for support for equality proved impossible, but we used people's feeling thermometer scores for African Americans in place of racial resentment. Of course, the differences between our model and those from previous scholarship suggest that we must be careful not to overinterpret the estimates. Still, if we find the same pattern of results here as we found for the salience of defense issues above, we contend that it would represent strong corroborating evidence for the salience hypothesis.

The results appear in table 6.6. Again, they follow the expected pattern. The interaction between the salience of racial issues and political trust carries a positive sign and is statistically significant. In 2004, when the percentage of stories about race was at its minimum, the effect of political trust is $-0.592 + 6.465(0.12) = 0.184$ with a standard error of 0.190 ($t = 0.97$ $p > 0.05$), which is not statistically distinguishable from zero. But when the salience of race and redistribution is high, as it was in 1996, the effect of political trust is large: $-0.592 + 6.465(0.23) = 0.895$ with a standard error of 0.140 ($t = 6.39$, $p < 0.05$). Using a second issue domain, we have found evidence that issue salience conditions the effect of political trust.

Conclusion

We have shown that political trust affects the public's preferences and evaluations in the foreign policy domain, suggesting that trust influences public opinion in more areas than previously known. However, we have also found that trust's effects are more contingent than previously known. Specifically, trust's effects depend on issue salience. When defense issues become salient, people are primed to evaluate government trustworthiness with defense-based considerations in mind, which, in turn, causes trust to affect preferences in this domain. When the domain of race and redistribution becomes salient, people are primed to evaluate government trustworthiness with welfare state considerations in mind, which, in turn, causes trust to affect preferences in that domain. Our results imply that political trust is not only a resource for domestic policy liberals; it can provide a reservoir of public support for foreign policy conservatives as well. These results provide a nice replication of those in chapter 5, this time using a nationally representative survey rather than a group of college students.

In fact, political trust may provide a particularly deep reservoir for foreign policy ambitions. With the country on the brink of war with Iraq in late 2002, the ANES found that trust was higher than it was at any time since the 1960s. By disposition, liberals would be the group most likely to put a brake on war policies, yet fewer than half expressed outright opposition to the war, according to the ANES data. Although liberals' trust in government usually drops after a Republican replaces a Democrat in the White House, liberals among ANES panel respondents expressed, on average, the same amount of trust in 2002 as they did in 2000, despite the onset of the Bush presidency, an economy sliding into recession, and a bevy of corporate scandals. Relatively high trust among liberals appears to have been of consequence. Liberals whose political trust increased between 2000 and 2002 expressed 21 percentage points more support for the war in Iraq than liberals whose trust in government remained constant or dropped. Consistent with our priming theory, liberals whose trust increased between 2000 and 2002 also rated "the military" on the ANES's feeling thermometer score substantially more positively (mean = 69.54) than liberals whose trust in government remained constant or dropped (mean = 62.75).

We can also use these data to understand why attitudes about the war in Iraq, in particular, became polarized later in the Bush years. It is during this time that trust in government polarized, with trust in government plummeting among liberals and Democrats and while holding relatively steady among conservatives and Republicans. Liberals needed to make ideological sacrifices to continue to back Bush's policies. Whereas many were willing to make such ideological sacrifices in the year or two after 9/11, precious few were as accommodating later in the Bush presidency. As their trust dropped, so did their support for Iraq, in particular.

There are more general implications for these results. Republicans tend to talk about foreign policy because they "own" it while Democrats tend to talk about social welfare policy because they "own" it (Petrocik 1996). This might explain why political trust has generally been higher during Republican administrations than Democratic ones (Pew Research Center for the People and the Press 2010). When domestic issues are salient, trust will be both lower and connected to preferences in this domain, making it harder for liberals to generate public support for their favored initiatives. In contrast, trust will be both higher and connected to foreign policy preferences when foreign policy issues are salient, making it relatively easier for conservatives to generate public support for their favored initiatives.

We next turn our attention to the role that low and polarized political trust played during Barack Obama's first term. It was during this time that political trust reached its lowest level ever and trust among Republicans and conservatives disappeared almost entirely. We demonstrate the impact that the trust environment had for economic stimulus and health care reform, specifically, although we expect the story is similar for much of the Obama agenda. Low and, especially, polarized trust makes policy making difficult because it renders public opinion incapable of overcoming polarization in Washington.

CHAPTER SEVEN

The Gordian Knot

A Bad Economy, Low Trust, and the Need for More Spending

The waning months of 2008 were an economic disaster. Panic gripped the financial sector in September. The combination of a rapidly deflating housing bubble, the weight of a slew of risky subprime mortgages, the unraveling of complicated financial instruments, a liquidity crunch at major world banks, insufficient regulation of the banking industry, and myriad other factors ultimately led to the failure of one of the "big five" American investment banks, Lehman Brothers. In addition, American International Group (AIG), the insurance behemoth that underwrote many of these toxic financial instruments, went bankrupt under the weight of the crisis. Although the US government bailed out AIG, the uncertainty about what might come next sent economies around the world into free fall.

The ensuing economic downturn had devastating effects in the United States. Gross Domestic Product began to contract in the third quarter of 2008 and did not return to positive territory for more than a year (Swann 2014). Whereas unemployment was below 5 percent before Lehman's collapse, it spiked to 10 percent a year after it; the number of unemployed Americans jumped from about 7 million to greater than 15 million (US Bureau of Labor Statistics 2014). With the housing bubble inflating in the mid-2000s, many Americans used their rapidly rising home values as an ATM, refinancing their mortgages and taking out equity to fund all manner of things. After home values started to tank, ultimately falling by 30 percent relative to their 2006 peak, people stopped spending. Worse, they could no longer refinance their mortgages because they owed more on their houses than their houses were now worth. As rates on adjustable mortgages spiked, home foreclosures skyrocketed from fewer than one hundred thousand in May 2006 to almost three hundred seventy thousand in March 2010 (RealtyTrac 2011).

Stock prices plummeted. Major stock indexes dropped by nearly 50 percent between July 2008 and March 2009, which translated into a loss of $7.4 trillion in stock wealth.[1] Median real income dropped by more than $3,000 from the year before the crash to the year after. The lower and middle classes were particularly hard hit, with their share of the country's overall wealth dropping by 15 percent. By 2010, the percentage of people living under the poverty line had jumped to 15.1 percent, a level not seen in the United States since Lyndon Johnson declared a "war on poverty" in the 1960s (Snyder 2013).

The financial crisis helped Democrats win the White House and increase their House and Senate majorities in 2008. Polls taken just before the collapse of Lehman Brothers showed Barack Obama and John McCain in a statistical dead heat, but the numbers trended strongly toward Obama thereafter. During bad economic times, voters typically punish the president's party (Key 1966; Fiorina 1981).[2] Steps taken in the last days of the Bush presidency averted a complete meltdown of the financial sector, but the economic ramifications of the crisis proved to be both sustained and painful, lasting well into Obama's presidency. Job one for the new president would necessarily be to take steps to resuscitate the battered economy. During such times, a large store of political trust would come in handy. When trust is high, public support for government solutions to political problems increases (Hetherington 2005). As we demonstrated in chapter 3, however, bad economies cause people to lose trust in government, so high trust was not a luxury policy makers enjoyed in early 2009.

In this chapter, we demonstrate how the trust environment undermined public support for many of the best policy prescriptions available to treat an ailing economy. It was, in part, low and polarized levels of political trust that explain the watered-down economic stimulus that limped out of Congress in February 2009. Specifically, we find that low trust in government reduces public support for Keynesianism—running deficits and increasing government spending, which are both essential components of fiscal stimulus. Following a theme developed throughout the book, we also find that the effects of trust are particularly profound on conservatives, those who needed to make an ideological sacrifice to follow such a policy course. That so little trust in government existed among conservatives during this period is a key reason policy consensus in the electorate failed to emerge. As a result, conservative members of Congress could provide the president little to no support for stimulus without worrying about alienating conservative constituents.

A number of other interesting findings emerge from our analysis as well. We also find that political trust is unrelated to public support for using tax cuts as fiscal stimulus. Hence when trust drops, as it typically does during a downturn, it does not undermine support for conservatives' favored policy prescription: tax cuts. But it does undermine support for liberals' favorite prescription: spending increases. This pattern of results explains why, despite the presence of a Democrat in the White House and sizable Democratic majorities in Congress, a stimulus barely half as large as originally proposed, nearly half of which was composed of Republican-backed tax cuts, was ultimately enacted.

These results are particularly troubling from a normative perspective. In the case of dealing with an economic collapse like the one experienced in late 2008 and early 2009, no real debate exists among economic policy experts about whether governments need to run deficits and increase spending to stimulate the economy. As Paul Krugman noted in the *New York Times*, thirty-six out of thirty-seven economists surveyed from all ideological stripes and backgrounds agreed that the 2009 stimulus package had a salutary effect (Krugman 2014). More stimulus would almost certainly have been a good thing for the economy. In that sense, low and polarized trust was quite clearly an impediment to implementing economic policies that would best serve the public interest. Indeed, low and polarized trust seems to have led policy makers to suboptimal policies with far-reaching consequences for ordinary Americans.

The Choices for Policy Makers

When the economy teeters on the brink of disaster because of a worldwide banking panic, no magic lasso exists to pull it back. Recovering from even garden-variety downturns takes, on average, about ten and a half months. At eighteen months, the 2007–9 recession was the longest of the ten recessions that have occurred in the postwar period (Federal Reserve Bank of Minneapolis 2007). Policy makers can try to stimulate the economy. Unfortunately, some attractive means were not available in 2008–9.

Conservative economists in the mold of Milton Friedman believe that if policy makers must intervene in the economy, monetary policy provides the most effective stimulus. Specifically, the Federal Reserve can take steps to increase the money supply to encourage people and businesses to spend more money. Given that poor economic performance undermines political trust, monetary policy is an especially attractive lever. Because the Fed is an independent agency whose members do not have to face voters, it need not concern itself much with public opinion. This is helpful because bad economies spawn low trust, which undermines public support for government action. Unfortunately, short-term interest rates, the lever the Fed uses to influence the money supply, were already near zero when the worst of the economic slump hit in late 2008. Although the Fed took less conventional steps to lower long-term rates in an effort to increase people's willingness to spend, monetary policy could not play as central a role as it might have otherwise.

With the monetary policy option mostly blocked, elected representatives needed to play a central role in providing economic stimulus. Specifically, the president and members of Congress can use fiscal policy, in the form of either increasing government spending or cutting taxes, to stimulate the economy. Followers of the economist John Maynard Keynes think the most effective means of fiscal stimulus is to increase government spending. For example, major road and bridge projects cost tens and sometimes hundreds of millions of dollars and are usually paid for with government resources. Keynesian stimulus would, in the short run, increase the amount of money government spends on such projects. The theory holds that businesses would, in turn, not lay off workers but rather employ more to meet the demand created by increased government spending. These workers would, as a result, have more money in their pockets to stimulate other parts of the economy. Because elected leaders have to pay close attention to public opinion, however, fiscal policy brings low and polarized trust in government into play.

To the extent that government directs spending toward ordinary people, Keynesians advocate targeting those who are less well off. For government stimulus to be successful, it must be pumped directly into the economy. Those with fewer means have fewer options in terms of what they will do with the benefits they receive from government stimulus, needing to spend it to meet their basic needs. Better-off people might spend stimulus money, too, but they also have the luxury of saving it, which will not have the same impact on economic growth. By increasing government spending and targeting the less well off, it follows that Keynesians tend to be liberals.

If conservatives decide fiscal policy is necessary, they are more inclined to favor tax cuts to businesses and citizens rather than increasing government spending. One conservative worry is that once government spending is increased, even if it is only supposed to be a short-term fix, policy makers will be reluctant to turn the spigot off later. In addition, tax cuts put money in the hands of people who, conservatives believe, will make the best decisions about how stimulus should be invested, ultimately providing more bang for the buck months or years in the future.

The problem with tax cuts, from a Keynesian perspective, is that the stimulus might not be pumped quickly into the economy. Upper-income people could pocket their tax savings rather than spend or invest it. Behavioral economists show that such concerns are warranted during bad times (see, for example, Ariely 2008 for a particularly readable treatment). Fearing what the future holds, people become more conservative in their spending habits during bad times than good. Moreover, Keynesians are suspicious that the better off will invest tax savings in ways that will be more productive than pumping it directly into the economy, as government spending on things like construction projects, unemployment benefits, and food stamps do. Benefits to the economy from investment will most often be realized later, whereas the threat to the economy and to ordinary people's well-being is immediate during an economic crisis.

In practice, the history of fiscal policy during hard times in the United States has been to use a combination of spending increases and tax cuts. The question is what mix policy makers agree on. The stimulus package passed in 2009 had a 45 percent to 37 percent split of spending increases to tax cuts.[3] This breakdown is more heavily tilted toward tax cuts than one might expect from a Democratic president and two houses of Congress with reasonably large Democratic majorities. It is certainly the case that Obama's initial plan asked for both a larger amount of government stimulus ($1.2 trillion) than was ultimately approved ($787 billion) and a higher percentage of spending increases relative to tax cuts. But congressional Republicans successfully negotiated a smaller stimulus package that included a more substantial percentage of tax cuts.

One reason the GOP had success negotiating its side of the deal was that public opinion was squarely on its side. When the CBS News/*New York Times* polling unit asked Americans in February 2009 "which will do more to protect or create jobs: increased government spending on infrastructure, health care, education and other fields, or tax cuts that would put more money in the hands of individuals and businesses," tax cuts won by about 10 percentage points (Zeleny and Thee-Brenan 2009).[4] That the public would like tax cuts more than government spending increases makes sense on two levels. First, Americans have an aversion to taxes. They even favor cutting or eliminating taxes that do not directly affect them. For example, support for eliminating the estate tax, a levy that a vanishingly small percentage of Americans pays, is incredibly high even among those who are not well off (Bartels 2008). Second, the notion of *increasing* spending when times are bad simply doesn't sound right. When times are tough for a household, the solution is never to spend more but rather to tighten one's belt. Although any introductory economics text would suggest the need for more public spending to make up for lagging private-sector demand, most ordinary people do not appreciate such nuances.

This is where the need for political trust comes in. To go along with increased government spending would appear to require a fair amount of trust, particularly from people who are not ideologically disposed to follow such a policy course. Hence we suspect that a low and polarized trust environment is critical to understanding why congressional Republicans owned a key advantage from the start.

The Economic Downturn and Political Trust

A bedrock finding in the study of political trust, highlighted in chapter 3, is that people trust the government less when they perceive the economy to be doing poorly. The late Bush and early Obama years were no exception. During the last two years of the Bush presidency, when the deflating housing bubble began to wreak havoc, economic pessimism ran high and political trust ran low.

In February 2007, for example, a CBS News poll revealed that only 15 percent of Americans thought the economy was getting better, 34 percent thought it was getting worse, and 49 percent thought it was staying about the same (Roberts 2007). These turned out to be the salad days of economic optimism for the late Bush years. By late September 2007, the percentage of Americans saying the economy was getting better had dipped to the single digits and the percentage saying it was getting worse hovered around 50 percent. Even worse days were to come. In March 2008, the investment bank Bear Stearns failed. The Fed forced Bear to merge with J. P. Morgan, another of the country's largest investment banks, with

Morgan acquiring Bear for pennies on the dollar (Onaran 2008). Bear's collapse, along with more general liquidity problems throughout the banking system, rattled Wall Street. Indeed, the Standard and Poor's 500 gave away more than 10 percent of its value between the start of 2008 and mid-March. As this process played out, CBS News again asked Americans about the state of the economy. Only 2 percent thought the economy was getting better, 75 percent thought it was getting worse, and 21 percent thought it was about the same (CBS News 2008).

Over this period, political trust dropped precipitously, just as social scientists would have predicted. At the beginning of 2006, before the housing bubble started to deflate, a Pew survey found that 34 percent of Americans trusted the government to do what was right either "just about always" or "most of the time" (Pew Research Center for the People and the Press 2006). That percentage dropped to 27 percent when the CBS News/*New York Times* polling unit surveyed Americans in September 2007. In the summer of 2008, after Bear's failure but before Lehman's, both Pew and CBS News/*New York Times* polls found that only about a quarter of Americans trusted the government, low by historical standards. In October 2008, after Lehman's collapse, the percentage fell to 17, where it remained until the 2008 election. These trust readings are lower than any that we are aware of taken before 2008 (Montopoli 2008).

This relationship creates a Gordian knot of sorts for policy makers. Bad economies cause trust to drop. But fixing an ailing economy requires increased government action, and that requires people to trust government. Specifically, political trust ought to increase people's willingness for the government to (1) run deficits during hard times and (2) have the government spend more money to stimulate the economy. Because most people are not well-versed in Keynesian economic theory, it must take a real leap of faith for people to embrace a policy course in which the government purposefully spends more than it is taking in and at a greater rate than usual at the same time that circumstances are forcing ordinary Americans to spend less. Harder still, many Americans believe government spending usually benefits those who are "undeserving" of assistance (Gilens 1999). Increasing such spending would only serve to increase the amount of assistance the "undeserving" will receive. Supporting such a policy course requires trust in government, particularly for conservatives for whom more spending requires an ideological sacrifice.

Fiscal stimulus through tax cuts is different. We suspect that having political trust is not necessary for Americans to support them. In the past fifty years at least, policy makers have targeted tax cuts broadly. Although people with higher incomes tend to benefit more because they tend to pay more taxes to begin with, people with lower incomes still tend to support tax reduction packages because they receive part of the pie (Bartels 2008). Trust is unnecessary for people to support a policy when they perceive themselves to be its beneficiaries (Hetherington 2005). Taken together, a low political trust environment should make it harder to generate support for spending increases but should not affect support for cutting taxes at all. The political implications of this asymmetry are clear. When trust is low, spending increases will be harder to sell the public on than tax cuts.

Data

In October 2012, we had the opportunity to field several survey questions that queried Americans about how best to combat slow economic growth.[5] By 2012, policy makers were no longer grappling with the worst of the Great Recession, but we have no reason to believe that the pattern of relationships among opinions in this period would be any different from early 2009 had we been able to field a survey then. Moreover, during the period in which we had our survey in the field, policy makers were discussing the merits of a second stimulus package, finding it to be a political nonstarter. As a result, our questions about fiscal stimulus in 2012 appeared in much the same context as in 2009.

Specifically, we first asked people whether they thought it was better to "run a budget deficit" or "balance the budget" during tough economic times. We then asked two separate questions about two forms of stimulus. Both forms would increase the deficit, despite what supply-side economists might argue. Specifically, we asked people (1) whether they favored or opposed tax cuts and (2) whether they favored or opposed increased government spending. Of these three questions, the deficit question always came first. We randomized the order of the tax cut and spending increase questions such that half the sample received the tax-cut question first and the other half received the spending increase question first. People could express support for both forms of stimulus, just one, or neither.

Starting with the budget item, we found Americans were 24 percentage points more likely to want to balance the budget (62 percent) than run a budget deficit (38 percent) during hard times. As a practical matter, such budget balancing would require spending cuts if the economy were bad because tax revenues shrink as incomes and profits contract. This apparent desire in the public to cut government spending below usual levels at the exact time that a flagging private sector requires government to do more and definitely not less may suggest why conservative politicians in Europe were able to sell austerity to the public despite the lack of evidence for its utility.

As for the two specific approaches to stimulus, the public is keen on one but not the other. In our survey, 65 percent of Americans said that they favored tax cuts with only 35 percent opposed. Not surprisingly, we find much more resistance to spending increases as economic stimulus. In fact, the distribution of opinion is an exact mirror image of the one for tax cuts, with only 35 percent in our sample supporting more spending and 65 percent opposing it.

In table 7.1, we drill more deeply into these numbers because the three distributions, taken together, produce such irrational results. Recall that, in answering the budget deficit versus budget balancing question, only 38 percent of Americans thought that running a budget deficit was a good idea during a downturn, which is obviously far less than the 65 percent who supported tax cuts that would do just that. This makes clear that a large percentage of Americans do not believe (or would rather not consider) that tax cuts increase the budget deficit. In fact, among the 62 percent of Americans who said that they favored balanced budgets over deficits in hard times, more than three-quarters (77 percent) simultaneously favored tax cuts as stimulus. Indeed, only 20 percent of those who said they favored balancing the budget favored neither tax cuts nor spending increases. Although this remarkable lack of understanding about deficit spending is dismaying, it is not altogether surprising. Many Americans are notoriously poor at recognizing what should be obvious tradeoffs (Converse 1964), particularly when they do not want to recognize them (Gaines et al. 2007).[6]

The results in table 7.1 also reveal that the 38 percent of Americans who supported the government running deficits were not as excited about tax cuts, with only 46 percent supporting them. Nearly 70 percent of those in the deficit spending group favored increased government spending. A little more than a quarter thought that both tax cuts and spending increases were worth implementing, with only about one in ten favoring neither. We suspect that low levels of trust in government help explain this opinion environment and, in turn, help us understand the final stimulus bill passed by Congress.[7]

TABLE 7.1 **Support for forms of economic stimulus by disposition toward budget deficits**

	Percent supporting
Deficit spending	38
Tax cuts	46
Spending increases	69
Both	27
Neither	11
Balancing budget	62
Tax cuts	77
Spending increases	14
Both	11
Neither	20

Source: Cooperative Campaign Analysis Project, 2012.

Political Trust and Support for Stimulus

To test whether a relationship between political trust and support for fiscal policy exists, we first break down support for our three economic stimulus items (running deficits, cutting taxes, and increasing spending) by political trust. To simplify presentation, we collapse those who said they trust the government either "just about always" or "most of the time" into one category (trusters) and those who said they trust the government "only some of the time" or "never" into another (distrusters). The results, which appear in figure 7.1, follow the expected pattern.

First, consider the apparent influence of trust on support for running deficits. We noted above that running a budget deficit is not popular with the public, but it is particularly unpopular among those who lack trust in government. Among the distrusters, only about a third (34 percent) supported running deficits over balancing budgets during hard times. Among the small percentage of trusters in our sample, however, a majority (55 percent) supported deficit spending. Had trust been high rather than low, these results suggest there would have been much more support for running deficits.

The relationship between trust and support for the two approaches to fiscal stimulus also follows expectations. Trust in government has no effect on support for tax cuts. Among trusters, 65 percent supported tax cuts to stimulate economic growth, and, among distrusters, nearly the same percentage (68 percent) did. In other words, trust makes no difference in

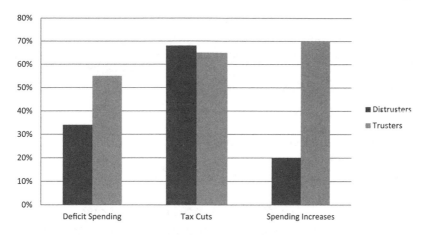

FIGURE 7.1. Support for economic stimulus plans by political trust

Source: Cooperative Campaign Analysis Project, 2012, Bartels module.

support levels. In a low trust environment, such results are great news for tax cut advocates. High trust is unnecessary for public support.

In contrast, trust appears to play a central role in structuring support for spending increases. Among trusters, nearly 70 percent expressed support for more government spending to stimulate the economy. Among distrusters, only about 20 percent did. Put another way, political trust had a nearly 50 percentage-point effect on support for increasing government spending as a stimulus measure— enormous by any standard. Again, the implication is clear. In Lyndon Johnson's day, when nearly everyone trusted government, policy makers would have had a much stronger hand in gaining support for more government spending as fiscal policy. The situation was much harder for Barack Obama.

Although we are using these data to speak to circumstances in 2009, they also make clear why there was never a second stimulus package late in Obama's first term. Compared with early 2009, trust levels in late 2012 were even lower and more polarized. In our late 2012 survey, only 3 percent of Americans reported trusting the government in Washington to do what is right "just about always" and another 15 percent expressed trust in government "most of the time." Put another way, about 18 percent provided trusting responses. Over the fifty years the American National Election Study (ANES), specifically, has asked the trust-in-government question, the percentage of trusting responses never fell below twenty.

Particularly problematic was the near absence of trust in government among self-identified conservatives. Among this group, only 9 percent said that they trusted the government either "just about always" or "most of the time." In other words, fewer than one in ten respondents were in the mood to make ideological sacrifices by late 2012.

Accounting for Alternative Explanations

We turn next to a set of regression models that allows us to account for other potential causes of stimulus preferences. If trust continues to exert large effects after we apply statistical controls, we can be more confident that trust in government is central to understanding opinions on stimulus and that our findings are not an artifact of partisanship or ideology. Recall from previous chapters that regression allows us to assess the independent effect of potential causes of an opinion while controlling for the effects of a range of other potential causes. Given that the analysis above revealed no relationship between political trust and support for tax cuts, we estimate a regression model only for running deficits and increasing spending. For both models, we employ the same explanatory variables with one exception: if people possess any "logical constraint" at all, then support for deficit spending should cause support for government spending increases. So we also include support for deficit spending as an explanatory factor in the increased spending model.

For both models, the most important explanatory factor is political trust; it should have a positive effect on respondents' willingness to run a deficit and their willingness to increase government spending as a stimulus measure. We also include party identification and ideology. Their inclusion is particularly important insofar as we have repeatedly shown that trust has polarized by party, a finding also confirmed by the 2012 Cooperative Campaign Analysis Project (CCAP).[8] If we do not control for party and ideology in our statistical models, we cannot be certain that political trust has an effect independent of them. To this end, we include two sets of two dummy variables, one each for identifying oneself as a Democrat or a Republican and one each for classifying oneself as a liberal or a conservative. The reference category is independents for party identification and either moderate or not sure for ideology.

We also include in our models two measures of perceived economic performance. Specifically, the 2012 CCAP asked whether people thought the economy was getting better, getting worse, or staying about the same, which we use as our measure of national economic conditions. Such "sociotropic" evaluations are often important in informing political choices (Kinder and Kiewiet 1979, 1981). The survey also asked whether people's personal financial situation had gotten better, gotten worse, or stayed the same over the past year. We use this as a measure of "pocketbook" evaluations (Fiorina 1978). Our thinking is that how people evaluate their own economic situation ought to affect the steps people think are necessary to stimulate the national economy. Finally, we include a range of demographic controls as well, accounting for education, race, ethnicity, and gender.

Since the dependent variables both have two categories (support or oppose), we use logistic regression to estimate the models. If people say they support running deficits over balanced budgets, we code those responses as one. We code support for balanced budgets as zero. If people support spending increases, we code those responses as one; if they express opposition, we code them as zero. A positive sign on a coefficient indicates that increases or decreases in the explanatory factor increase or decrease support for running deficits and spending increases, respectively. A negative sign means that an increase in the explanatory factor decreases support for these fiscal policies.

Results

The results of these regressions appear in table 7.2. We start with support for deficit spending. These results appear in the first column of the table. Even with the wide range of controls in place, trust exerts a large and statistically significant effect on preferences for deficit spending, with its estimated effect more than five times its standard error. By and large, the other variables perform as expected. Being a Democrat or liberal, respectively, increases one's support relative to being an independent or moderate, respectively. Similarly, being a Republican or conservative reduces support. Women are less supportive of deficit spending than men. Lower levels of education are also related to less support for deficit spending. Economic evaluations play an interesting role, but the relationships sometimes suggest difficulties for Keynesian policy makers. When people perceive their own financial situations as having improved, they are less supportive of deficit spending, which makes sense. But problematically, when people perceive that the national economy is getting worse, they are less supportive of deficit spending, a point we return to in some detail below.

The second column of table 7.2 reveals that political trust is also a determinant of support for increasing government spending. Indeed, trust's effect appears even larger than in the previous analysis, as its parameter estimate is nearly twice the size of the one in the first column. Not surprisingly, party identification and ideology also have significant effects in the expected directions. Republicans and conservatives are less supportive

TABLE 7.2 **Support for deficits and increased spending as a function of political trust and other variables**

	Support for deficit spending	Support for increased government spending
Trust in government	1.244***	2.207***
	(0.223)	(0.266)
Liberal	0.842***	0.455***
	(0.114)	(0.128)
Conservative	−1.201***	−1.216***
	(0.132)	(0.165)
Support for deficit spending	—	1.820***
		(0.112)
Democrat	0.488***	0.814***
	(0.112)	(0.125)
Republican	−0.657***	−0.179
	(0.156)	(0.195)
Personal financial assessment	−0.448**	−0.003
	(0.157)	(0.181)
National economic assessment	1.100***	0.674***
	(0.151)	(0.172)
African American	−0.270	0.621***
	(0.143)	(0.161)
Latino	−0.113	0.395*
	(0.156)	(0.171)
Female	−0.226*	−0.203
	(0.094)	(0.110)
High school or less	−0.674***	−0.275
	(0.171)	(0.196)
Some college	−0.503**	−0.255
	(0.175)	(0.200)
Four-year college	−0.245	0.004
	(0.189)	(0.216)
Constant	−0.589**	−2.562***
	(0.196)	(0.244)
Number of cases	2,942	2,919
Pseudo R^2	0.288	0.406

Note: Standard errors in parentheses.
*$p < 0.10$, **$p < 0.05$, ***$p < 0.01$, two-tailed tests
Source: Cooperative Campaign Analysis Project, 2012.

of increased spending than independents and moderates. Democrats and liberals are more supportive. Both African Americans and Latinos are more supportive than whites of using spending increases as economic stimulus. And, as in the previous model, the effect of evaluations of the national economy is perverse. Those who perceive a deteriorating national economy are less likely to support increased government spending than those who think the economy is getting better.

Logistic regression coefficients are not readily interpretable, so, as in previous chapters, we use a simulation to demonstrate what the substantive effects of these factors are. To do so, we fix each at theoretically interesting values and allow the value for political trust to vary.[9] We find that the effect of trust is large in both absolute and relative terms. We start with preferences for running deficits. The predicted probability of supporting deficit spending if our simulated respondent said he never trusted the government to do what is right is 0.341. That probability increases to 0.438 if he reports trusting the government only some of the time. If the respondent falls into the more common of the trusting categories (trusting the government most of the time), the probability jumps to 0.544. And in the few cases in which respondents say they trust the government almost always, the predicted probability of supporting deficit spending is 0.642. Put another way, the effect of trust in government across its full range affects support for deficit spending by about 30 percentage points (from 0.341 to 0.642).

This change in predicted probabilities is not only large but substantively important. We can use these predicted probabilities to classify whether or not we would expect a respondent to support or oppose deficits depending on his or her level of political trust. The convention is to classify a person as a supporter if the predicted probability is above 0.5. If the probability is below 0.5, we would classify the person as opposing. For our simulated respondent above, then, we would predict opposition when trust is low (trusting the government either never or only some of the time), but we would predict support for deficits when trust is high (trusting the government either most of the time or just about always). In short, possessing a higher level of trust has the potential to change people's opinions on deficit spending.[10]

The effect of people's assessments of the national economy is also large. But as we noted above, its direction is perverse from the standpoint of what most economists think is necessary during a financial crisis. Fixing all the other variables as described above and perceptions of the economy at "getting worse," the predicted probability of supporting deficit spending is only 0.287. In other words, when a respondent perceives a sour economy, he or she will likely oppose a Keynesian approach to economic stimulus. But, oddly and unhelpfully, support for deficit spending actually grows a great deal as his or her assessment of the national economy grows more positive. If our simulated respondent perceives the economy to be "getting better," the predicted probability of support for deficit spending rises to 0.603; we would expect this person to support Keynesianism. In other words, people are most likely to support running deficits when the government least needs to run them—during times of plenty. But people are least likely to support running deficits when the government most needs to run them—when times are tough.

Such a result provides further evidence that people think of government spending the same way they think about household spending. When ordinary people are flush with cash, they can let the good times roll. The accumulation of debt during recent boom times suggests people will engage in deficit spending of their own when they believe they can "make it up" in the next paycheck or two. When resources are scarce, however, they naturally tighten their belts. Although such behaviors make good financial sense for a household, they are the antitheses of good fiscal policy for a government. Governments must run deficits to provide stimulus when private sector supply dries up.

We next turn to a similar simulation, this time assessing the effects of our explanatory factors on support for increasing government spending. The effect of political trust is even larger in this case. When we fix all variables as we did above and fix preferences for budget deficits at support, we find that the effect of trust in government is dramatic. Among those who express no trust at all, the predicted probability of their supporting increased government spending is only 0.322. Since the predicted probability is well below 0.5, we would classify these respondents as opposing more government spending. But if we increase trust in government to almost always, the predicted probability is 0.872, a 55 percentage-point increase. With the predicted probability well above 0.5, we would be very confident that these same people, only this time possessing high trust in government, would support increased spending as a stimulus measure.

In sum, these results suggest just how important widespread political distrust was in thwarting what Keynesians believe is the best policy course to stimulate the economy. Low trust had a profound negative effect on support for running deficits and increasing government spending during a downturn.

Accounting for Ideological Sacrifice

We have shown that trust in government is critical to understanding preferences for policy to combat the Great Recession. But our theory regarding political trust and perceived sacrifice requires that we refine our model a bit. To this point, we have shown what the *average* effect of political trust is across *all* respondents in our survey. That probably underestimates the effect of trust for some and overestimates it for others. Specifically, trust ought not to be important in informing policy preferences when people do not perceive that they need to make sacrifices, but it ought to be especially important when people do. Ideological sacrifices seem particularly germane in this case, given that identifying those who need to make a material sacrifice to run deficits and increase spending is not at all clear. In contrast, conservatives are clearly being asked to make significant ideological sacrifices to support such things.

The near complete absence of political trust among those needing to make such ideological sacrifices (i.e., conservatives) is the problem of greatest consequence from our perspective. If a fair number of conservatives trusted the government as they did in the 1950s and 1960s, then the president might have been able to encourage them to pressure their elected representatives to support more stimulus. This, theoretically, might have had a particularly big impact on conservative lawmakers because conservative citizens are a central part of conservative lawmakers' reelection constituencies. Our data demonstrate just how few conservative constituents in 2012 differed in their preferences from conservative elites. In our survey, only 8 percent of conservatives said they supported the government increasing spending during a downturn. We think it is not a coincidence that only 9 percent of conservatives said they trusted the government to do what was right at least most of the time in the same survey.[11]

To test whether the effect of trust depends on ideological sacrifice, we make a couple minor adjustments to the models we estimated above. Specifically, we include interactions between political trust and (1) being a conservative and (2) being a liberal. The effect of political trust among moderates can be deduced from the estimated effect for political trust in the table that follows. Since we expect the effect of trust to be largest among conservatives, the interaction between political trust and being a conservative ought to carry a positive sign, which would indicate that the effect of trust is larger among conservatives than moderates. And since liberals do not have to make an ideological sacrifice to support deficits or spending increases, the sign on the interaction between political trust and being a liberal ought to be negative, which would indicate that liberals require trust less than moderates do to support these things.

The results of this analysis appear in table 7.3. Since the effects for the controls we used are about the same as they were in table 7.2, we only include the interactions and their component parts in the table. The model for supporting deficit spending appears in the first column. It shows that the effect of political trust among moderates is positive and is statistically significant, which means that moderates need to trust government to support running a deficit during bad times. This makes sense given how heterodox it seems to spend beyond one's budget during bad times. The positive effect of trust's interaction with being a self-identified conservative suggests that trust's effect is even larger among conservatives than it is among moderates. The magnitude of the effect, however, falls just short of statistical significance, which means that we are somewhat less confident that the effect exists. Finally, the negative and significant effect of the interaction between political trust and being a liberal indicates that trust has a much smaller effect among liberals than among moderates; in fact, it turns out that trust has no effect at all among liberals.

To estimate how profound trust's effect is among those with different ideologies, we return to the simulation that we performed above.[12] We

TABLE 7.3 **Support for deficits and increased spending conditional on ideological sacrifice**

	Support for deficit spending	Support for increased government spending
Trust in government	1.368***	2.003***
	(0.296)	(0.352)
Liberal	1.291***	1.013***
	(0.229)	(0.262)
Conservative	−1.481***	−2.485***
	(0.239)	(0.347)
Trust in government* Liberal	−1.118*	−1.404*
	(0.501)	(0.579)
Trust in government* Conservative	0.745	3.083***
	(0.528)	(0.717)
Number of cases	2,942	2,919
Pseudo R^2	0.290	0.406

Note: Standard errors in parentheses. All other control variables from table 7.1 were also included in the model but not shown in the table.
*$p < 0.10$, **$p < 0.05$, ***$p < 0.01$, two-tailed tests
Source: Cooperative Campaign Analysis Project, 2012.

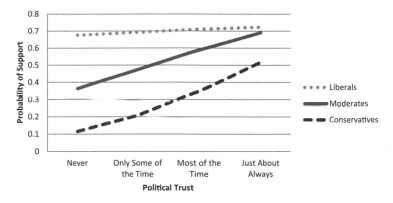

FIGURE 7.2. Effect of political trust on willingness to run a deficit by ideology

allow both trust and ideology to vary in order to estimate their effects depending on the value of the other. We present these results graphically in figure 7.2. For liberals, it is clear that trust makes almost no difference at all, with the slope of the line very flat. This is as expected: liberals do not need trust to support deficit spending because such support requires no ideological sacrifice of them. For moderates, trust makes about a 30 percentage-point difference across its range, which is a substantial effect indeed. It is substantively meaningful, too. Among distrusting moderates, our model calculates predicted probabilities of supporting deficit spending below 0.5. We would classify them as not supporting. However, among trusting moderates, our model calculates predicted probabilities above 0.5, which would move them into the supporting category. The line for conservatives is slightly steeper than it is for moderates. Among those in this group who report never trusting the government, there is only a 0.117 point chance that our simulated respondent would support deficit spending over balancing the budget. But if that same conservative trusted the government to do what is right just about always, the predicted probability rises to 0.522, more than a 40 percentage-point difference.

Although the effects for trust are quite large in the deficit equation, they are even larger in the support-for-additional-government-spending equation. These results appear in the second column of table 7.3. We find the expected sign on all the variables of interest, and each achieves statistical significance. The effect of political trust itself is positive and large, which again means that moderates need to trust government to support

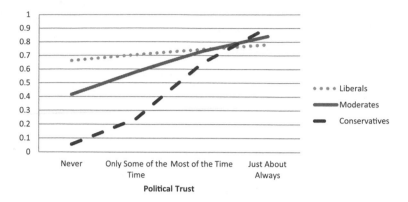

FIGURE 7.3. Effect of political trust on support for increased spending by ideology

increased government spending. The interaction between trust and being a conservative is positive and significant as well, which suggests the effect of trust is much larger for conservatives than for moderates. Finally, the interaction between trust and being a liberal carries a negative sign and is statistically significant, which suggests that the effect of trust is smaller for liberals than for moderates.

How do these estimated effects manifest themselves in our simulation? We can assess them graphically in figure 7.3. The effect for liberals is again almost nonexistent because, as theory would predict, they do not need trust to support more spending because no ideological sacrifice is required of them. For moderates, however, the effect is substantial, as evidenced by the relatively steep line in the figure. Those who say they "never" trust the government have a 0.416 probability of supporting increasing government spending as a stimulus measure.[13] Among those who trust "just about always," that probability jumps to 0.841, more than a 40 percentage-point difference.

But it is among conservatives that trust's effect is most pronounced. If conservatives profess trusting government either "never" or "only some of the time," which is almost universal in the present day, there is little chance that they will support increased government spending as an economic stimulus measure. The predicted probabilities in our simulation are 0.056 for those who never trust government and 0.241 for those who trust government only some of the time. If a substantial percentage of trusting conservatives existed, however, it would make a big difference in support for spending increases. The predicted probability among conservatives who say they trust the government "most of the time" is 0.642, and for those who say "just about always" it is 0.906. Put another way, the effect of trust across its range among conservatives is a staggering 85 percentage points.

A Coda on Economic Stimulus

We can glean one last interesting bit of information from the survey on economic stimulus. It points out how messaging can make a big difference in support for a policy. Respondents to our 2012 survey expressed mixed support for the stimulus package that was actually enacted in 2009. Specifically, the survey asked whether enacting the stimulus package in 2009 was the right or wrong thing for the government to do: 53 percent said it was the right thing to do, whereas 47 percent said it was the wrong thing to do. We can use people's responses to this question to help us understand what type of stimulus people were thinking about when they were asked to evaluate the economic stimulus of 2009. Of course, the stimulus was made up of somewhat close to equal parts spending increases and tax cuts, so it is plausible that people could have had either or both forms of fiscal stimulus on their minds when asked to evaluate it. The question itself made no reference to the specific components of the stimulus.

To assess what form of stimulus people were thinking about when asked about the stimulus package in general, we estimate correlations between this item and their support for the two specific types of fiscal stimulus: tax cuts and spending increases. If people's opinions about the 2009 stimulus package are positively correlated with their support for tax cuts as stimulus, it would suggest that people have tax cuts on their minds when they are asked to evaluate stimulus in general. If people's opinions about stimulus are positively correlated with support for spending increases as a stimulus measure, it would suggest that they have spending increases in mind. If opinions about stimulus are correlated with both, then they have both components in mind.

The results suggest that, when asked about stimulus in general, people are thinking about stimulus only in terms of spending increases. The correlation between support for the 2009 stimulus package and support for more government spending to stimulate the economy is a very strong 0.56. A correlation this strong does not suggest that people's views on the 2009 stimulus package and spending increases are one and the same, but it is a very strong correlation indeed. To provide some perspective, consider that the correlation between partisanship and ideology is about the same in most recent ANES samples. In contrast, support for tax cuts and support for the 2009 stimulus package are *negatively* correlated at −0.30.

Of course, these positions ought to be strongly a function of partisanship and ideology, so the bivariate correlations might be misleading. To confront this problem, we can calculate partial correlations among these variables while holding ideology and partisanship constant. After applying these controls, the results continue to suggest that people connect the 2009 fiscal stimulus with spending increases, but they do not connect it to tax cuts. After controlling for party and ideology, support for the stimulus and support for spending increases are correlated at 0.32, a reasonably strong correlation when using survey data. Support for stimulus and support for further tax cuts are still negatively correlated, albeit only weakly, at −0.07.

These results should be instructive to liberal policy makers. The 2009 stimulus is not overwhelming popular despite its utility, in part, because people connect it only to the unpopular component of fiscal policy— namely, spending increases. Liberal elites could make stimulus much more palatable to the public by also connecting it with its more popular component—namely, tax cuts. It appears that the electorate is unlikely to connect tax cuts to fiscal stimulus otherwise.

Conclusion

Throughout the Great Recession of 2008–9, the health of the US economy was precarious. As public confidence in the economy plummeted, so, too, did public trust in the federal government. That citizens' economic perceptions shape their levels of political trust is hardly a novel observation. Less appreciated, however, is the fact that the nation's climate of political trust can have a profound impact on the government's ability to pursue policies to overcome economic downturns.

The results of this chapter demonstrate that, in the midst of a weak economy, a lack of political trust limits the flexibility of policy makers. Almost all economists believe that running budget deficits, at least in the short term, is necessary to provide stimulus during hard times. The problem, we find, is that political distrust weakens support for deficit spending. Since few people trust government when the economy is foundering, it depresses support for the very antidote to a flagging private sector economy. In addition, we find that the specific form of stimulus favored by Keynesians, increased government spending, is especially vulnerable to low political trust in that it is particularly strongly related to levels of trust in government. Public support for increased government spending falls precipitously when political distrust rises.

In contrast, we find no correlation between political trust and support for conservatives' favored form of economic stimulus, tax cuts. As a result, public support for tax cuts does not evaporate, like support for government spending does, in the face of political distrust. Moreover, our results make clear that many Americans have no appreciation for the fact that tax cuts, like increased government spending, increase deficits, too. Collectively, these two findings are essential to understanding why the stimulus package passed by a Democratic-controlled Congress and signed into law by a Democratic president in 2009 included such a high percentage of tax cuts relative to spending increases. Low levels of political trust undermined support for spending increases but had little impact on support for tax cuts. The asymmetric effects of trust in this case carry important implications for the formation of public policy. Conservatives enjoy a natural advantage over liberals in pursuing their favored policy goals during hard economic times.

CHAPTER EIGHT

Political Trust and Flagging Support for Obamacare

In the previous chapter, we demonstrated that low and polarized political trust likely contributed to the passage of a smaller and weaker fiscal stimulus than President Obama and congressional Democrats initially sought. The debate of the stimulus was only a precursor to a much more rancorous fight. In this chapter, we demonstrate that low levels of polarized trust sharpened the legislative battle over health care reform and continued to cast a long shadow long after its passage.

The road to passage of the Affordable Care Act (ACA) was plagued by great discord and difficulty. It was far from a textbook study in how a bill becomes a law. After months of hearings, heated rhetoric, and questionable side deals to bring all sixty Democrats in the Senate together, the wheels started to fall off in late 2009. Most critical, Senator Scott Brown (R-MA) won a shocking upset to fill Senator Edward Kennedy's (D-MA) seat after Kennedy's untimely death, which robbed the Democrats of their filibuster proof majority. It subsequently appeared that passage of the health care law was in jeopardy. If all forty-one Republican members of the Senate stood together on cloture, they could stop the Senate from even considering the bill. In a last gasp effort, Senate Democrats resorted to budget reconciliation, a rarely employed device ordinarily used only for appropriations bills. Under budget reconciliation rules, a cloture vote is not required to end a filibuster, so only a majority vote on final passage is required. As a result, Senate Democrats no longer needed sixty votes to end debate before a vote on final passage could occur. For procedural reasons, the Senate version of the bill could not be amended in the House before being sent to the president for his signature. The move earned increased Republican ire, although it was unlikely that it decreased Republican support. In the end, only one House Republican member voted for the bill on final passage, Representative Anh Cao of Louisiana. No Republican senators did.

As always, public preferences are in the backs of members' minds when they decide on legislative strategy. In that sense, changes in public opinion during the health care reform debate played an indirect role in creating the circumstances that caused Democrats to follow the path they ultimately did. Had health care reform been wildly popular with the public, Obama and his congressional allies could have "gone public" (Kernell 1986) to pressure recalcitrant Republican lawmakers into backing the package by highlighting the support the ACA enjoyed in members' districts. Although health care reform *had* been popular when President Obama took office, it was no longer so a year later. In early 2009, clear majorities supported the "health care proposals being discussed in Congress" and believed "the country as a whole would be better off" if Congress and the president would enact them. By early 2010, however, clear majorities expressed unease about many of the provisions in the health care bill and opposed the overall bill. Whereas 59 percent thought health care reform would be good for the country in February 2009, only 42 percent did in January 2010. On the eve of the final votes in Congress, a Gallup poll revealed that 41 percent supported the health care reform package, which was not much different from the percentage that supported Bill Clinton's plan when his Administration abandoned it in July 1994 (Jacobs and Shapiro 2000, 144).

Since the bill became more unpopular as time passed, Democrats could not use the public to pressure Republican lawmakers. Instead, they had to initiate a bruising endgame to the process just to get the bill to the president's desk. The process that played out has continued to haunt the ACA long after its final passage. As with most sweeping initiatives, it contains some weaknesses and outright errors that policy makers would have liked to have fixed during the original legislative process or, alternatively, during the law's rollout. But legislative fixes were not possible then, nor are they possible now. In holding fifty-four votes to *repeal* the ACA between 2011 and 2014, majority House Republicans have made clear that there will be no fine-tuning through legislative tinkering.

In this chapter, we explore what caused public support for the ACA to deteriorate. Not surprisingly, political trust figures prominently in our explanation. Using tracking poll data from the Kaiser Foundation, we reveal the importance of three complementary trends. First, Americans' trust in government collapsed from early 2009 to early 2010. By the time health care reform came to a final vote in Congress, barely 20 percent of Americans said they trusted the federal government in Washington to do what was right either "most of the time" or "just about always," a 13 percentage-point decline from the beginning of the health care debate. The drop was particularly consequential among conservatives, the group called upon to make the ideological sacrifice necessary to back a liberal initiative like health care reform. Second, the percentage of self-identified conservatives increased over the time period. As a result, the percentage of people who would most need trust to support the policy was increasing at the same time that this group's level of trust was cratering. Third, more Americans came to believe that health care reform would require them to make a material sacrifice, with the percentage who thought their family would be harmed by health care reform tripling between February 2009 and January 2010 (Kaiser Family Foundation 2010). In sum, substantially lower levels of political trust combined with increasing percentages of people who believed sacrifices would be required led to the collapse of public support for health care reform.

In the next section, we develop our theory about why political trust is so important in building and sustaining public support for initiatives like health care reform. We also explain why the effects of trust are tied to individuals' perceptions of ideological and material sacrifice. Next we describe the tracking polls that we analyze in this chapter. Then we report the results of an empirical analysis in which we examine the effects of trust, ideological sacrifice, and material sacrifice on public support for a variety of health care reform proposals. We conclude by discussing our principal findings and by discussing their broader implications for liberal and conservative policy initiatives.

Political Trust and Health Care Reform

As we have made clear, political trust is a simple heuristic or decision rule that allows citizens to make policy judgments in a less effortful and more efficient manner. Instead of having to sort through the complex details of a policy proposal, such as health care reform, the trust heuristic enables people to simplify their decision-making process by basing policy judgments on whether or not they trust government.

The trust heuristic is particularly likely to be activated when (1) policy outcomes are uncertain and (2) the outcomes may be equally desirable or undesirable in nature (Rudolph and Popp 2009). Health care reform satisfies these conditions. Health care reform is a quintessential example of a risk-laden policy. There was great uncertainty about the likely consequences of enacting health care reform before, during, and even several years after the legislative debate ended. Many argued that health care reform would produce desirable consequences, such as greater access to care, greater affordability of care, and, ultimately, longer life expectancy. Others argued that it would lead to undesirable consequences, such as rationed care, increased costs, less freedom to choose one's doctor, and even "death panels."

In addition to risk, the salience of a policy area is central to understanding the preferences political trust ought to affect at a given time. As shown in chapters 3, 5, and 6, people think about different parts of the government when asked to evaluate it. The part of government they are thinking about has a powerful effect on support in that policy realm. We saw this in the lab in chapter 5 and in President George W. Bush's foreign policy successes and failures in chapter 6.

Health care reform was definitely on Americans' minds in 2009–10, with media coverage nearly ubiquitous for much of the period. In fact, a Pew Research Center Excellence in Journalism study found that health care reform filled fully 18 percent of the total news hole in the third quarter of 2009, making it the top issue on the media agenda. Moreover, it continued to garner more than 10 percent of the news hole for two subsequent quarters (Pew Research Center 2010b).[1] These numbers do not even begin to take into account the spinoff coverage the ACA generated on ideological news programs on cable stations. As a result of all this media attention, there is every reason to believe that Americans had in mind the parts of government that might administer health care reform when surveys asked them to evaluate the government during this period. Taken together, the health care debate of 2009–2010 satisfies the theoretical parameters for us to expect that political trust should have an important effect on driving the dynamics of the public's preferences on this issue during the period.

With a liberal initiative sponsored by a liberal congressional party and backed by a liberal president, conservatives would be required to make ideological sacrifices to support the ACA. Liberals would not need to trust government to support it because no ideological sacrifice is required of them. In addition, health care reform is a challenging issue for which to maintain support because a relatively high percentage of people are at least reasonably happy with their existing health coverage. As it relates to the universality of coverage, opponents could easily argue that Obama's health care proposal might require those who are satisfied with their coverage to sacrifice their happiness to benefit others. Thus supporting health care reform might require ideological and (at least perceived) material sacrifice as well.

In addition to having differing effects among different types of *people* (liberals vs. conservatives, insured vs. uninsured), we also expect that the size of political trust's effect will vary across *policy proposals*. Specifically, we expect that proposals suggesting more obvious intervention by government into the existing health care system will require more trust than those for which government intervention will be more limited. For example, one needs to trust government less to support it providing tax credits to small businesses to help them underwrite costs than to support it administering the health care system along the lines of a government-run single-payer system. Others have provided evidence that the effect of trust is at least partially determined by how profoundly government intervenes in an area. For example, Hetherington and Globetti (2002) show that the effect of trust is larger on racial policy preferences in the race conscious domain (e.g., affirmative action in hiring, college admission quotas) than in the equal treatment domain (e.g., supporting government efforts in school integration). We expect that health care preferences should follow the same arc. If we are correct, it is substantively important. It would suggest that, on health care, policy makers would have many more options in a high-trust environment than in a low-trust environment (see Hacker 2010).

Our task below is to demonstrate how political trust and the various forms of sacrifice interacted to explain why support for health care reform plummeted, producing the ugly endgame to the legislative process that ultimately transpired. We find that trust was dropping, while, at the same time, perceptions of material and ideological sacrifice—the two variables that make trust important—were increasing, making trust matter to an increasingly large segment of the population. Although panel data are not available for the period in question, a set of rolling cross sections allows us to track the magnitude of such increases and decreases and, in turn, to estimate their effects on preferences about health care reform.

Data and Measurement

The data we analyzed in this study are taken from portions of the Kaiser Health Tracking Poll. Sponsored by the Henry J. Kaiser Family Foundation and conducted by Princeton Survey Research Associates International, the Kaiser Health Tracking Poll is a collection of bimonthly and monthly surveys designed to monitor public sentiment toward health care and health insurance reform. In all, twelve nationally representative samples were drawn and surveyed between February 2009 and March 2010.[2] When describing longitudinal trends in public support for health care reform, we make use of data from all twelve of these surveys. When subjecting our hypotheses to multivariate analysis, we focus on the one survey that contains the requisite measures of political trust and support for health care reform (April 2009).[3] These data were collected approximately one year before Congress enacted health care reform.

To gauge public sentiment toward health care reform, respondents were asked how strongly they favored or opposed eight specific reform proposals. We classify each proposal according to whether it requires high, moderate, or low levels of government involvement in the health care system. Recall that trust should have the largest effect when government involvement is high and the smallest effect when government involvement is low. We classify three of the eight proposals as requiring high levels of government involvement: (1) having a national health plan in which all Americans would get their insurance from a single government plan, (2) creating a public health insurance option to compete with private health insurance, and (3) creating a public health insurance option similar to Medicare to compete with private health insurance plans. We classify four proposals as requiring moderate levels of government involvement: (4) expanding Medicare to cover people between the ages of fifty-five and sixty-four who do not have health insurance, (5) expanding state government programs for low-income people, such as Medicaid and the Children's Health Insurance Program, (6) requiring employers to offer health insurance to their workers or pay money into a government fund that will pay to cover those without insurance, and (7) requiring all Americans to have health insurance, either from their employer or from another source, with financial help for those who can't afford it. Finally, one of the eight proposals requires only minimal government involvement: (8) offering tax credits to help people buy private health insurance.

Preferences about these eight items will serve as the dependent variables in the analyses to follow.

The data provide us measures of both material and ideological interests. To measure material sacrifice, we rely on a question that asked respondents if they and their families would be better off or worse off if the president and Congress passed health care reform. Supporting health care reform would require greater material sacrifice from those who believe that they and their family would be worse off. To capture ideological sacrifice, we employ measures of ideological self-identification. Given principled ideological differences concerning the proper role of the federal government, supporting health care reform requires the greatest amount of ideological sacrifice from conservatives.

To measure political trust, we use the core American National Election Study (ANES) question designed to tap public trust in government again: how much of the time people trust the government in Washington to do what is right, ranging from "just about always" to "never." We created a four-point political trust scale in which higher values denote higher levels of trust in government. To test whether the effects of political trust depend on people needing to make material or ideological sacrifices, we form interactions between political trust and (1) our measures of perceived family impact (material sacrifice) and (2) ideological identification (ideological sacrifice), respectively. Our statistical models also include measures of respondents' education, sex, and party identification.

Results

Leveraging the rolling cross sections available to us, we first establish systematically how public opinion changed during the year that health care reform dominated the political stage. It is important to note that not all the provisions in the package were unpopular. In fact, many of the components of health care reform remained popular through final passage. For example, three-fifths or more of the public said the following items would make them more likely to support health care reform legislation: tax credits to small business, a health care exchange for those without access to group plans, an expansion of Medicaid, extending coverage to dependents through age twenty-five, and closing the Medicare "doughnut hole." Indeed, the only parts of the final bill that were particularly unattractive to Americans were the mandate that all Americans carry health insurance and the price tag ($871 billion over ten years). Clearly, the mandate and cost were central to people in deciding support for the overall bill.

The results for trust and our measures of sacrifice, which are key to our explanation for deteriorating support for health care reform, appear in figure 8.1. The first of the tracking polls, which was taken in April 2009, reveals that 32 percent of Americans trusted the government to do what was right "just about always" or "most of the time." Indeed, more than 20 percent of self-identified conservatives expressed trust in government, not much below the historical norm for conservatives during a Democratic presidency despite the fact that the country was experiencing miserable economic times. Although none of the Kaiser surveys taken after April 2009 asked a trust question, a CBS News/*New York Times* poll taken on the eve of the ACA's final passage found that the percentage of trusting Americans had fallen to 19 percent overall. Worse yet for proponents of the ACA, the percentage of self-identified conservatives who expressed trust in government dropped to 15 percent in this survey (Faber 2010). Very few, at that point, would be inclined to make the ideological sacrifice necessary to support health care reform. Politically speaking, this is particularly consequential because it would be these voices that conservative lawmakers would care about most, since they are central to securing lawmakers' reelections. With no pressure from their reelection constituency, conservative elites could do what party leaders asked them to do without fear of electoral fallout.

Not only was trust dropping, but the percentage of people who would theoretically need trust to support health care reform—those perceiving the need to make sacrifices—was increasing. The Kaiser data reveal that the percentage of self-identified conservatives increased from 31 percent to 36 percent, and the percentage of people who perceived that health care reform would hurt their family tripled, from 11 percent to 33 percent. We believe that, taken together, the nexus of these variables and their change over time helps explain the public opinion environment surrounding health care reform and hence the troubling legislative conclusion to the battle.

Impact of Trust and Material Sacrifice

We begin our analysis by examining the joint role that political trust and material sacrifice play in shaping public support for health care reform. Earlier, we hypothesized that material sacrifice should moderate the

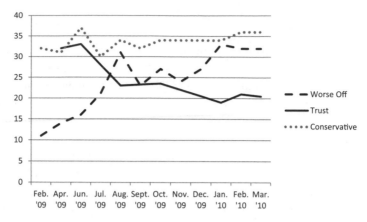

FIGURE 8.1. Percent trust, conservatism, and belief that family will be worse off

Source: Data on health care attitudes and ideology are taken from Kaiser Family Foundation, Kaiser Health Tracking Poll, 2010. Data on trust are taken from twelve national polls (see chapter 3 for more details on the trust data). Months with multiple trust readings are averaged and months with missing values are interpolated.

TABLE 8.1 **Material sacrifice and public support for health care reforms, April 2009**

8.1A. Proposals with "high" or "low" government involvement

	National plan (high)	Public option (high)	Public option like Medicare (high)	Tax credits (low)
Family worse off	−1.33**	−1.14**	−1.54**	−0.12
	(0.18)	(0.17)	(0.17)	(0.15)
Political trust	0.73**	0.55*	0.67**	0.18
	(0.24)	(0.24)	(0.22)	(0.22)
Political trust × Family worse off	1.49*	2.50**	1.41*	0.51
	(0.67)	(0.63)	(0.59)	(0.56)
Education	−0.50**	−0.17	−0.01	−0.06
	(0.19)	(0.19)	(0.18)	(0.17)
Female	−0.04	0.30**	−0.01	0.05
	(0.11)	(0.11)	(0.10)	(0.10)
Republican	−0.13	−0.18	−0.26*	−0.10
	(0.15)	(0.14)	(0.14)	(0.13)
Democrat	0.45**	0.10	0.36**	−0.11
	(0.13)	(0.13)	(0.13)	(0.12)
Conservative	0.03	−0.34**	−0.37**	−0.04
	(0.13)	(0.12)	(0.13)	(0.12)
Liberal	0.35**	0.36**	−0.09	−0.06
	(0.15)	(0.15)	(0.14)	(0.13)
χ^2	193.4**	75.1**	228.0**	4.9
Log likelihood	−525.1	−190.6	−551.2	−654.4
Number of cases	459	461	497	495

TABLE 8.1 (*continued*)

8.1B. Proposals with "moderate" government involvement

	Individual mandate	Employer mandate	Expand Medicare	Expand state programs
Family worse off	−1.03**	−1.04**	−1.28**	−1.14**
	(0.17)	(0.12)	(0.17)	(0.17)
Political trust	0.35	0.65**	0.21	0.42
	(0.24)	(0.17)	(0.23)	(0.24)
Political trust ×	1.83**	0.70*	1.32*	1.26*
Family worse off	(0.62)	(0.43)	(0.60)	(0.63)
Education	−0.34*	−0.37**	−0.66**	−0.43*
	(0.19)	(0.13)	(0.19)	(0.19)
Female	0.20*	0.17*	0.09	0.12
	(0.11)	(0.07)	(0.11)	(0.11)
Republican	0.04	−0.13	−0.06	−0.07
	(0.14)	(0.10)	(0.14)	(0.14)
Democrat	0.52**	0.21*	0.16	0.51**
	(0.14)	(0.09)	(0.13)	(0.14)
Conservative	−0.08	−0.29**	−0.14	−0.05
	(0.13)	(0.09)	(0.13)	(0.13)
Liberal	0.12	0.12	0.36**	0.14
	(0.15)	(0.10)	(0.15)	(0.15)
χ^2	144.1**	277.3**	160.3**	158.2
Log likelihood	−512.5	−1094.8	−534.9	−495.2
Number of cases	464	948	503	465

Note: Table entries are ordered probit coefficients with standard errors in parentheses. Cut points are not shown to conserve space.
* $p < 0.05$, ** $p < 0.01$, one-tailed tests.

Source: Kaiser Family Foundation: Kaiser Health Tracking Poll, 2010.

effects of political trust on attitudes toward reform such that trust matters more among those who believe that reform will make one's family worse off. To test this hypothesis, we use data from the April 2009 Kaiser survey and estimate ordered probit models for each of the eight health care reform proposals. We report the results of those models in table 8.1. The top portion of the table (8.1A) presents the results for policies requiring "high" or "low" government involvement. The bottom half of the table (8.1B) presents the results for policies involving "moderate" involvement.

If our theory holds, we should observe a positive interaction between political trust and the belief that reform will make one's family worse off, and that is precisely what we find. In seven of the eight statistical models, the coefficient in question (Political trust *x* Family worse off) is both positive and statistically significant. Only in the case of tax credits does the interaction fail to reach statistical significance. This provides strong evidence that trust is more consequential as a determinant of reform attitudes among those who believe such reforms will make their family worse off than among those who believe the reforms will make their family better off.

To illustrate the magnitude of these effects, figure 8.2 visually depicts the interaction for each of the eight reforms. Among those who believe that health care reform will make their family better off, the slope for political trust is essentially flat in each panel. This implies that trust is inconsequential among those for whom supporting reform requires no material sacrifice. By contrast, among those for whom supporting reform does require a material sacrifice (i.e., those who believe their family will be worse off), the slope for trust is positive and visibly steeper for seven of the eight reforms. Here a one-unit increase in political trust raises support for a national government plan, a public option, and a public option like Medicare by 56, 70, and 51 percentage points, respectively. A similarly sized shock in political trust heightens support for individual mandates, employer mandates, expanding Medicare, and expanding state programs by 43, 40, 40, and 45 percentage points, respectively.

Impact of Trust and Ideological Sacrifice

We continue our analysis by examining the joint role that political trust and ideology play in shaping public support for health care reform. We again expect the effect of trust to depend on a person's ideological predisposition. Liberals are not required to make an ideological sacrifice for health care reform, while conservatives must. Hence trust should be more important for conservatives, which will manifest itself as a positive and significant effect on the interaction between trust and conservatism. Table 8.2 reports the results of eight ordered probit models. Again, the top portion of the table (8.2A) presents the results for policies requiring "high" or "low" government involvement. The bottom half of the table (8.2B) presents the results for policies involving "moderate" involvement.

Consider first public support for the three health care reforms requiring high levels of government involvement. The coefficient for political trust, which captures the effect of trust for those who identify themselves as moderates, is statistically insignificant in two cases and only marginally significant in the third. These results indicate that trust has a small or negligible effect among self-identified moderates. We calculate the effects of political trust among liberals and conservatives by testing the null hypothesis that $\beta_{trust} + \beta_{trust \, x \, [\text{ideological category}]} = 0$. Among liberals, political trust has no impact on support for a national government plan ($\chi^2_{1df} =$

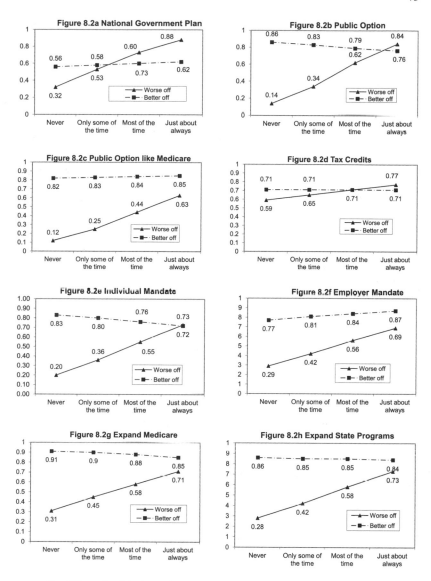

FIGURE 8.2. Effect of political trust by material sacrifice and reform proposal, April 2009

0.46, $p > 0.49$) or on support for a public option ($\chi^2_{1df} = 0.03, p > 0.87$). It has a modest impact on support for a public option like Medicare but, as evidenced by the insignificant interaction between trust and liberalism, the effect among liberals is indistinguishable from that among moderates ($\chi^2_{1df} = 1.38, p > 0.23$).

TABLE 8.2 **Ideological sacrifice and public support for health care reforms, April 2009**

8.2A. Proposals with "high" or "low" government involvement

	National plan (high)	Public option (high)	Public option like Medicare (high)	Tax credits (low)
Conservative	−0.59**	−0.97**	−0.78**	−0.21
	(0.23)	(0.23)	(0.22)	(0.21)
Liberal	0.54*	0.67*	−0.33	−0.13
	(0.31)	(0.31)	(0.28)	(0.28)
Political trust	0.51	0.44	0.56*	−0.14
	(0.35)	(0.35)	(0.30)	(0.30)
Political trust × Conservative	1.05*	1.29**	0.80*	0.27
	(0.52)	(0.51)	(0.48)	(0.47)
Political trust × Liberal	−0.20	−0.37	0.63	0.09
	(0.58)	(0.57)	(0.53)	(0.51)
Education	−0.74**	−0.47**	−0.36*	−0.06
	(0.18)	(0.17)	(0.17)	(0.16)
Female	−0.14	0.21*	0.01	0.04
	(0.10)	(0.10)	(0.10)	(0.10)
Republican	−0.22	−0.28*	−0.45**	−0.08
	(0.14)	(0.13)	(0.13)	(0.12)
Democrat	0.48**	0.24*	0.48**	−0.09
	(0.14)	(0.12)	(0.12)	(0.12)
χ^2	130.2**	135.5**	141.5**	3.2
Log likelihood	−598.6	−585.9	−645.6	−707.5
Number of cases	490	489	535	537

8.2B. Proposals with "moderate" government involvement

	Individual mandate	Employer mandate	Expand Medicare	Expand state programs
Conservative	−1.01**	−0.58**	−0.55**	−0.58*
	(0.23)	(0.16)	(0.22)	(0.23)
Liberal	0.11	0.42*	0.60*	0.43
	(0.33)	(0.21)	(0.30)	(0.23)
Political trust	−0.26	0.73**	0.40	0.39
	(0.36)	(0.24)	(0.31)	(0.37)
Political trust × Conservative	2.04**	0.51	0.68	0.89*
	(0.52)	(0.35)	(0.49)	(0.51)
Political trust × Liberal	0.22	−0.44	−0.54**	−0.24
	(0.59)	(0.40)	(0.56)	(0.60)
Education	−0.60**	−0.60**	−0.93**	−0.70**
	(0.18)	(0.12)	(0.17)	(0.18)
Female	0.13	0.08	0.10	−0.07
	(0.11)	(0.07)	(0.10)	(0.10)
Republican	−0.05	−0.23**	−0.20	−0.18
	(0.13)	(0.09)	(0.13)	(0.13)
Democrat	0.68**	0.31**	0.31**	0.55**
	(0.13)	(0.09)	(0.12)	(0.13)
χ^2	107.2**	193.3**	102.6**	107.9
Log likelihood	−570.9	−1231.2	−616.6	−561.2
Number of cases	494	1,024	545	497

Note: Table entries are ordered probit coefficients with standard errors in parentheses. Cut points are not shown to conserve space.

$*p < 0.05$, $** p < 0.01$, one-tailed tests

Consistent with theoretical expectations, however, political trust has a positive and statistically significant effect among conservatives. Among conservatives, trust increases support for a national government plan ($\chi^2_{1df} = 16.5, p < 0.01$), support for a public option ($\chi^2_{1df} = 20.6, p < 0.01$), and support for a public option like Medicare ($\chi^2_{1df} = 13.1, p < 0.01$). These results suggest that political trust matters, but only among those for whom supporting the health care proposal requires an ideological sacrifice. Moreover, it is of consequence that the percentage of conservatives who expressed trust in government dropped precipitously during the period in question, making trust particularly important in understanding opinion dynamics.

The fourth data column in Table 8.2A presents the determinants of support for tax credits to buy private insurance, the only reform requiring little government involvement. As before, the coefficient for political trust is statistically indistinguishable from zero, again implying that trust has no effect among moderates. Political trust has no impact among liberals ($\chi^2_{1df} = 0.07, p > 0.79$) or conservatives either ($\chi^2_{1df} = 0.63, p > 0.42$). At first glance, this null result among conservatives might appear to run afoul of our theory. Yet recall that our theory predicts that trust will matter most among those for whom supporting a given policy requires ideological (or material) sacrifice. Tax credits, in contrast to the other reform proposals, do not require much ideological sacrifice on the part of conservatives, particularly since the tax credits in question would be used to help purchase private, rather than public, insurance. From this perspective, the absence of a significant interaction between political trust and conservative ideology is quite consistent with our theory.

We turn next to an analysis of public support for reform proposals with moderate levels of government involvement. Among moderates, political trust has no effect on support for individual mandates ($\chi^2_{1df} = 0.53, p > 0.46$), expanding Medicare ($\chi^2_{1df} = 1.68, p > 0.19$), or expanding state programs ($\chi^2_{1df} = 1.16, p > 0.28$), but it does have a positive and significant effect on support for employer mandates ($\chi^2_{1df} = 9.6, p < 0.01$). Among liberals, political trust has no impact on support for individual mandates ($\chi^2_{1df} = 0.01, p > 0.93$), employer mandates ($\chi^2_{1df} = 0.83, p > 0.36$), expanding Medicare ($\chi^2_{1df} = 0.09, p > 0.76$), or expanding state programs ($\chi^2_{1df} = 0.10, p > 0.74$). Only among conservatives does trust consistently have a positive and significant influence. Among conservatives, trust increases support for individual mandates ($\chi^2_{1df} = 21.1, p < 0.01$), employer mandates ($\chi^2_{1df} = 22.1, p < 0.01$), expanding Medicare ($\chi^2_{1df} = 8.1, p < 0.01$), and expanding state programs ($\chi^2_{1df} = 12.5, p < 0.01$).

TABLE 8.3 **Effect of political trust by ideological sacrifice and reform type, April 2009**

Health care reform proposal	Low trust	High trust	First difference
High government involvement			
National government plan	0.14	0.68	0.54
Public option	0.23	0.83	0.60
Public option like Medicare	0.31	0.80	0.49
Moderate government involvement			
Individual mandate	0.29	0.89	0.60
Employer mandate	0.37	0.82	0.45
Expand Medicare	0.48	0.85	0.37
Expand state programs	0.43	0.87	0.44
Low government involvement			
Tax credits	0.63	0.73	0.10

Note: Table entries are predicted probabilities of policy support among conservatives at the specified levels of political trust. Policy support is defined as those who somewhat or strongly favor the policy. "Low trust" values reflect the belief that government can "never" be trusted. "High trust" values reflect the belief that it can be trusted "just about always." Party identification and sex are fixed at independent and male. Education is fixed at its mean.

Finally, we can turn to a discussion of whether the effects of political trust are contingent on the type of health care reform. We focus this discussion on the effect of trust on conservatives because it is conservatives who must make ideological sacrifices to support health care reform. Earlier, we suggested that the effect should increase with the level of government involvement. To test this hypothesis, we calculated the predicted probability of support for each of the eight reform proposals at different levels of political trust, which we report in table 8.3.

Political trust has no appreciable effect on health care reform attitudes when the proposed reform entails little government involvement. A one-unit increase in political trust increases public support for tax credits by only 10 percentage points. When government involvement is high, by contrast, the magnitude of trust's influence is, as expected, much greater. Here the same one-unit increase in political trust heightens public support for a national government plan, a public option, and a public option like Medicare by 54 percentage points, 60 percentage points, and 49 percentage points, respectively. The magnitude of trust's impact generally falls somewhere in between for reforms that involve moderate levels of government involvement. When trust increases from its minimum to its maximum value, support for expanding Medicare, employer mandates, and expanding state programs increases by 37 percentage points, 45 percentage points, and 44 percentage points, respectively. The effect on support for individual mandates is somewhat larger at 60 percentage points. In sum, political trust is a powerful predictor of attitudes toward health care reform among conservatives, particularly if the proposed reform entails greater federal involvement.

Replication: Attitudes after Final Passage

As promising as our results have been, the data collection we are relying on comes from spring 2009, before much of the health care reform debate had occurred. One might wonder whether the debate itself affected preferences and their ingredients in meaningful ways. Unfortunately, we found no survey data that included each of our key items (measures of trust and sacrifice) gathered in early 2010. We did, however, include the necessary items on the 2010 Cooperative Congressional Election Study (CCES), which was administered in October 2010. Although the timing of this survey is also less than ideal, given that the ACA was enacted more than six months before, we work under the assumption that the residue of this debate still existed. Given that health care reform emerged as a key midterm election issue, it seems reasonable to believe that these data will serve our purposes well.

The CCES noted to respondents in its pre-election study that "Congress considered many important bills over the past two years. For each of the following, tell us whether you support or oppose the legislation in principle." One of the items was the "Comprehensive Health Reform Act," which was accompanied by several of its specific provisions. On the Vanderbilt University module of the CCES, we also included an item asking people whether they thought the health care reform would make their family's health care situation better, worse, or whether it would not make much difference. We used this question to tap material sacrifice. In addition, the CCES included a five-point ideology scale. We coded those who identified themselves either "somewhat" or "very" conservative as conservatives to tap the notion of ideological sacrifice.

In our one-thousand-person module, 52 percent said they supported the health care law. This percentage is somewhat higher than the percentage found by other survey houses asking similar questions around the same time, likely because the CCES made explicit reference to the fact that the new law would "allow people to keep their current provider" and would "increase taxes on those making more than $280,000 per year," both popular provisions. In addition, 39 percent of Americans identified themselves as conservative, and 44 percent thought the health care law would be a net negative for their family. Finally, only about 15 percent of Americans expressed that they trusted the federal government either "most of the time" or "just about always." Of greatest consequence, only 4 percent of self-identified conservatives said they trusted government at least "most of the time," meaning that there was almost no one willing to make an ideological sacrifice.

The results of the replication appear in table 8.4. They are consistent with those from the Kaiser data. As it relates to material sacrifice alone, the results in the first column suggest that trust does not matter among those who believe that the new health care law made their family better off. This is manifested in the main effect of political trust, which is statistically insignificant. But among those who thought the health care law was injurious to their family, the effect of trust is large, which is manifested in the substantively large and statistically significant interaction between political trust and whether the respondent thought his or her family was harmed by health care reform.

We find the same pattern of corroborating results for ideological sacrifice. These results appear in the second column of table 8.4. Here the effect of political trust among self-identified moderates is statistically insignificant. It is manifested in the main effect of political trust. Similarly, the effect of political trust among liberals is also vanishingly small, evident in the insignificant interaction between trust and being a liberal. However, the effect of political trust among conservatives is quite large. This can be seen in the large and significant positive coefficient for the interaction between trust and being a conservative.

In the third column, we use the statistical power made available by a near one-thousand-person sample to account for both material and ideological sacrifice in the same model. Consistent with the results in the first two columns, trust's effect is not significant among nonsacrificers. But its effect is significant for sacrificers of both stripes. This can be observed in the positive and significant interactions between (1) trust and being a conservative and (2) trust and whether people thought their family would be worse off because of health care reform.

To provide a sense of the substantive effects of these variables, we again simulate predicted probabilities based on theoretically interesting values for the independent variables. We focus on the fully specified model

TABLE 8.4 **Support for health care law, 2010**

	Material sacrifice	Ideological sacrifice	Both material and ideological sacrifice
Political trust	−0.447	0.989	−0.828
	(1.088)	(0.831)	(1.288)
Family worse off	−3.866*	−2.813*	−3.702*
	(0.593)	(0.354)	(0.616)
Political trust x Family worse off	3.526* (1.528)	—	2.917* (1.596)
Conservative	−1.262*	−2.189*	−2.049*
	(0.296)	(0.495)	(0.511)
Liberal	0.004	−0.038	−0.003
	(0.285)	(0.510)	(0.525)
Political trust x Conservative	—	3.246* (1.432)	2.806* (1.452)
Political trust x Liberal	—	−0.057 (1.262)	−0.039 (1.274)
Republican	−0.233	−0.067	−0.090
	(0.340)	(0.340)	(0.345)
Democrat	1.438*	1.577*	1.550*
	(0.316)	(0.320)	(0.321)
Female	0.573*	0.535*	0.534*
	(0.221)	(0.221)	(0.222)
Education	0.228	0.209	0.198
	(0.448)	(0.449)	(0.451)
Constant	2.097*	1.579*	2.141*
	(0.510)	(0.44)	(0.549)
χ^2	607.237*	608.523*	611.797*
Log likelihood	−578.344	−577.057	−573.783
Number of cases	939	939	939

$*p < 0.05$, one-tailed tests

Source: CCES, 2010, Vanderbilt Module.

from the third column. Specifically, we chose a female, moderate independent with average education. We fix these characteristics and allow political trust and perceived material sacrifice to vary. Of course, we do not expect trust to make a substantive difference when people perceived that they were not making a material sacrifice. With the other characteristics fixed as described above, the most and least trustful participants who thought health care reform made their family situation better or that it made no difference differed by a mere 7 percentage points. The results of our simulation are displayed in figure 8.3a. When our simulated person thought health care reform hurt her family, however, the effect of trust is quite large. If we fix trust at its minimum, that person's probability of support is 0.28. If she said she trusted the government "some of the time," the probability jumps to 0.44. And if she said she trusted the government

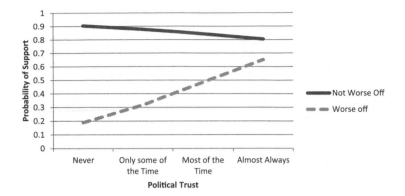

FIGURE 8.3a. Effect of political trust on health care policy preferences by material sacrifice

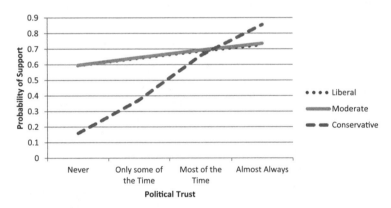

FIGURE 8.3b. Effect of political trust on health care policy preferences by ideological sacrifice

"most of the time," the probability increases beyond 0.5 to 0.615. In other words, we would predict that our simulated person would oppose health care reform if she reported trusting the government either never or only some of the time. But our model predicts that such a person who reported trusting the government most of the time would support it. Clearly, decreasing trust and increasing perceptions of material sacrifice diminished support for health care reform.

The same pattern holds for ideological sacrifice. If a person identifies as either a moderate or a liberal, holding all other variables at the simulated values described above and holding perceived material sacrifice at its midpoint, the effect of trust has no bearing on preferences about health care reform. As shown in figure 8.3b, however, among conservatives, trust matters. Under the simulated circumstances, a conservative who reports "never" trusting the government has only a 0.159 probability of support. And a conservative who only trusts the government "some of the time" has a 0.371 probability of support. In both cases, our model would predict opposition. In the very rare (4 percent) cases in which a conservative reported trusting the government "most of the time," however, our model predicts a 0.656 probability of support. With the percentage of conservatives increasing and levels of trust in government among conservatives plummeting, our model clearly suggests another reason support for health care reform was evaporating during this period.

Conclusion

From Harry Truman to Bill Clinton, progressives have attempted to implement comprehensive health care reforms with little success. Considering the public opinion environment, the serial failures are actually somewhat puzzling. Over the last several decades, Americans have often expressed more willingness to increase spending above present levels on health care than in any other policy area (Bartels 2008). Although Barack Obama and the Democrats ultimately succeeded in passing health care reform in 2010, it happened despite public opinion rather than because of it. By the end of the legislative process, public support for the final bill was weak, which surely contributed to the need for seldom-used legislative maneuvering to accomplish final passage. Some commentators suggest that the maneuvering contributed greatly to the Democrats' loss of sixty-three House seats and six Senate seats in the ensuing 2010 midterm elections. Senator Bayh (D-IN), for example, placed the blame for Democratic losses squarely on the shoulders of health care reform: "We . . . overreached by focusing on health care rather than job creation during a severe recession" (Bayh 2010).

Our analysis of rolling cross-sectional data taken during the months when the health care reform debate dominated American political discourse suggests that changing levels of trust in government, coupled with a marked increase in people's perception that reform would require either a material or ideological sacrifice, explains how the issue went from being a winner for Democrats to being a loser. Similar to 1994, opponents of

health care reform succeeded in convincing the public that the reform effort would require many to make material sacrifices, which, in turn, made
political trust relevant to more people in shaping their policy preferences.
In addition, the percentage of self-identified conservatives increased,
which made the vanishingly low levels of trust among those in this group
increasingly injurious to policy support. Had trust remained constant, our
results suggest that support for the final bill would have been much higher
than it was. Had support remained well above 50 percent, it surely would
have made lockstep opposition by Republicans in Congress much more
costly to them and perhaps would have led to a less acrimonious outcome.

In addition, our results explain how certain elements of the larger
health care reform package remained popular even as the full bill became
unpopular. Specifically, trust in government matters less when people
perceive government intervention to be less profound. For example, one
need not trust government too much to believe that insurance companies should provide coverage to people with preexisting conditions. Had
Democrats been more successful at connecting provisions like this to the
overall package rather than things like coverage mandates, the shape of
public opinion for the overall bill would have been much different.

Our results may also provide an indirect explanation for the Republicans' massive gains in the 2010 midterm elections. Although the conservative ideological label became somewhat more popular during the health
care debate (and beyond), the changes were on the order of about 5 percentage points. In contrast, our results suggest that the decrease in trust in
government was much deeper. Since trust in government is, most centrally,
a function of how well the government is performing (see, for example,
Chanley, Rudolph, and Rahn 2000; Citrin and Green 1986; Hetherington
1998; Weatherford 1984), the persistently poor economy during Obama's
first term was likely more important than public revulsion toward a massive new government initiative in explaining GOP gains. In that sense,
10 percent unemployment not only contributed directly to Democrats'
problems in 2010 but also made health care reform less popular by causing the public to think government was incapable of solving economic
problems and hence untrustworthy in the area of health care as well.

The results in this chapter provide further evidence that political trust
can have significant effects on important aspects of public opinion and,
in turn, public policy outcomes. Moreover, they appear to provide some
evidence that liberals may face higher policy implementation constraints
than conservatives do. Levels of trust tend to be lower when domestic

policy, as opposed to foreign policy, is salient (Hetherington and Rudolph 2008). But the Democratic Party is more inclined to talk about domestic issues than foreign issues because it is stronger with the public in these domains (see, for example, Petrocik 1996), which may help explain why the public expresses less trust in government when Democrats occupy the White House than Republicans (Pew Research Center for the People and the Press 2010). This also means that political trust will more often put a brake on liberal policy initiatives than conservative ones. Indeed, in the context of health care reform, final passage of the bill required rarely employed legislative maneuvering that further poisoned cross-aisle co-operation, something that might not have been necessary had the public maintained a more positive disposition toward the proposal.

CHAPTER NINE

Can Things Change?

The preceding chapters have advanced a common theme. Through a variety of data and designs, we have shown that both the levels and the consequences of political trust are, in part, products of what citizens are thinking about at a particular point in time and the political context in which they formulate their trust judgments. We have explained how these mechanisms have contributed to the polarization of political trust along partisan lines, which is central to understanding why the public is not a force that can be deployed by policy makers to overcome polarization in Washington. The public, in that sense, did not create the governing crisis, but the polarization of political trust reinforces it.

Chapters 6, 7, and 8 demonstrated some of the consequences of this new way of thinking about political trust, particularly in the context of its polarization by party. Trust began to polarize during the George W. Bush years, even as some of the more popular parts of government remained salient. This fact was central to understanding why the wars in Iraq became, in the public mind, partisan affairs. On the economy and health care, we found that Barack Obama faced even higher hurdles than Bush did, particularly because economic conditions were poor during much of his first two years in office, driving trust down. With political trust at historically low levels and Republican trust in government all but nonexistent, the president could not rely on public opinion to help him make his case to recalcitrant members of Congress. The result was often suboptimal policy outputs, bruising legislative endgames, or both. Indeed, we described the interlocking relationships between bad economies, low and polarized trust, and support for policy as a Gordian knot of sorts.

The legend of the Gordian knot suggests that thinking outside the box can produce a solution to what seems like an insuperable problem. Such is the aim of this chapter. Although we do not wish to flatter ourselves into thinking that our proposals are as promising as those of Alexander the Great, who solved the puzzle of the Gordian knot, we much more modestly provide some evidence that solutions may exist. Such solutions build on the results we have presented throughout the book—namely, that the amount of trust is contingent on what people are thinking about at a given moment. First, we believe that individuals' levels of political trust are not fixed over time and that initially distrustful citizens might be persuaded to trust government by reminding them of past government successes. Second, we suspect that if we cause people to think about the specific parts of government rather than the government as a whole, it might make a difference. Our thinking is driven by a simple—but we think critical— observation. Americans tend to say they hate the government, yet, when pushed about which parts they would like to shrink, they tend not to want smaller government after all. This is consistent with Ellis and Stimson's (2012) findings that people are symbolic conservatives but operational liberals.

We begin the chapter by exploring the pliability of political trust to see whether political trust can be restored. We report the results of an experiment designed to demonstrate whether we can persuade those who initially distrust government to express higher levels of political trust. We find evidence that reminding people of past government achievement can raise levels of trust in government, but the pattern of results is not altogether encouraging. Although trust increases when we present people with positive information about government, the increase comes entirely from Democrats and liberals. Because Republicans and conservatives do not respond the same way, positive information about government actually increases partisan and ideological differences. Moreover, it does nothing to boost the levels among those needing to make ideological sacrifices, the people we have shown need trust most.

We next take a different tack. Specifically, we expand our argument to show that the sources and consequences of political trust are contingent not only on the *issue domains* (e.g., environmental policy) that people are thinking about but also on the *parts of government* (e.g., Environmental Protection Agency) that people are thinking about. As the analyses in the preceding chapters have made clear, political trust is, in the American setting, most commonly measured by asking people how much of the time they feel they can trust "the government in Washington" to do what is right. In some respects, the target of evaluation in this instrument is quite clear. The phrase "government in Washington" clearly invites people to focus their trust judgments on the federal government and not on state or local governments. In other respects, the target of evaluation is much less certain. To some people, the government in Washington might mean the Congress or the presidency. To others, it might mean particular government agencies, such as the Environmental Protection Agency (EPA), the Department of Health and Human Services (HHS), or the Pentagon. Still others might attempt to make a global evaluation of the entire government.

We attempt to gain greater analytical control over this problem by developing and analyzing agency-specific measures of political trust. Rather than asking people how much they trust a global object such as "the government," we sharpen their evaluative focus by instead asking them how much they trust a series of specific government agencies. Such an approach helps to ensure that, in any given question, all respondents are evaluating the same part of the government. In some respects, we find strong evidence of partisan polarization in political trust, as Democrats and Republicans express systematically different levels of trust across specific government agencies. Surprisingly, however, we also find evidence of common ground, in that members of both parties consistently express greater trust in individual government agencies than they do in the government as a whole. Substantively, these evaluations of specific agencies are meaningful. In general, we find that support for a policy in a given domain (e.g., the environment) is more responsive to trust in the part of government (e.g., the EPA) that oversees that domain than it is to levels of trust in government as a whole.

Restoring Public Trust in Government

As we have demonstrated, political trust is an important ingredient in building and sustaining public support for certain types of government policies, particularly among policies that entail a high degree of government involvement. Moreover, we observed, people are more willing to sacrifice their own material or ideological interests when they trust the federal government. Such willingness helps reduce ideologically based policy differences in the mass public and forge policy consensus. Policy consensus among the mass public, in turn, has the potential to lessen legislative gridlock by encouraging lawmakers to reach consensus as well.

Given our findings that levels of political trust are persistently low and increasingly polarized along partisan and ideological lines, lawmakers appear to be facing some difficult challenges.

But what can be done, if anything, to restore public trust in government? As we observed in chapter 3, political trust is a dynamic concept that fluctuates over time in systematic ways that are, to some extent, predictable. Political trust tends to rise, albeit gradually, when economic performance is strong. Political trust also increases when the public perceives government processes to be fair and free of scandal. Exogenous shocks, such as the terrorist attacks on September 11, 2001, can also trigger a rising tide of political trust. Unfortunately for them, however, political leaders have little direct control over such factors. Although legislators can enact economic policies designed to promote economic growth, the effects of such policies are inexact and such policies do not always produce the intended results. Similarly, although lawmakers can strive to be transparent and fair in all procedural matters, they cannot ensure that government processes are perceived to be fair by members of the mass public. Finally, even if government officials could bolster political trust by increasing the likelihood of exogenous shocks such as terrorist attacks or international crises, it is most unlikely that they would wish do so for obvious normative reasons. In sum, government leaders appear to have little direct control over many of the factors known to increase public trust in government. This suggests that, over the long term, restoration of public trust is unlikely to occur naturally.

In the short term, though, are there more proximate things that government can do to restore public trust? Some of our results suggest that the answer to this question may be yes. First, the results of chapter 3 suggest that elites might be able to influence trust levels by focusing the public's attention in certain issue domains rather than others. Recall that political trust tends to be higher when the public is focused on international rather than domestic considerations. However, our results in chapters 5–8 suggest that such higher levels of trust would only help generate support in the foreign policy realm. A reservoir of trust built with foreign policy actors in mind would be of no help in generating support for domestic policy initiatives.

A second possibility, which we briefly explore here through a simple experiment, is to remind citizens of past government successes. In the 2012 Cooperative Congressional Election Study, we conducted a survey experiment in which we explored the pliability of political trust. We first collected a pretest measure of political trust from each respondent on a scale arrayed from one to four, with one meaning that respondents said they "never" trusted the government to do what is right and four meaning that they trusted the government in Washington "just about always." We then assigned respondents to one of six experimental conditions.

Respondents who initially expressed low levels of political trust were randomly assigned to one of three different "progovernment" conditions (efficiency, programmatic benefits, or regulatory protection). In the efficiency condition, for example, subjects were told that independent accountants estimate that waste makes up less than 5 percent of the federal budget. In the benefits condition, subjects were told that 55 percent of the federal budget goes toward programs that benefit nearly all Americans such as Social Security, Medicare, and national defense. Finally, in the regulatory protection condition, subjects were reminded that the federal government has made rules that ensure all Americans a minimum wage and safe-to-eat food. Each "progovernment" condition thus presented a unique positive argument about government.

Respondents who initially expressed high levels of political trust were randomly assigned to one of three different "antigovernment" conditions. Each "antigovernment" condition presented a unique negative argument about government. We concluded by collecting a posttest measure of political trust from each respondent. In the "government influence" condition, respondents received the message that some critics argue that campaign contributions to members of Congress buy interest groups too much influence. Respondents in the "government incompetency" condition received the message that some critics believe that the federal government is less capable of accomplishing its tasks than the private sector. Finally, respondents in the "government inefficiency" condition read a message suggesting that government is inefficient and wastes a lot of money.

At issue in this experiment is the question of pliability. Specifically, can the initially distrustful be persuaded to trust government? Can initially trustful individuals be persuaded to distrust it?

Our experimental results demonstrate that exposure to a variety of progovernment frames can increase citizens' trust in government, although the differences are often quite small. These results appear in table 9.1. That political trust rises in response to such messages is somewhat encouraging as it relates to considering means to overcome the governing crisis. Unfortunately, as it relates to our thinking, trust tends to in-

TABLE 9.1 **Effects of pro- and antigovernment frames on political trust**

Progovernment: protection frame

	Trust 1	Trust 2	Difference
All respondents	1.82	2.16	+ 0.34
Republicans	1.76	1.97	+ 0.21
Democrats	1.94	2.41	+ 0.47

Progovernment: benefits frame

	Trust 1	Trust 2	Difference
All respondents	1.78	1.87	+ 0.09
Republicans	1.79	1.86	+ 0.07
Democrats	1.90	1.93	+ 0.03

Progovernment: efficiency frame

	Trust 1	Trust 2	Difference
All respondents	1.83	1.95	+0.12
Republicans	1.82	1.87	+0.05
Democrats	1.89	2.09	+0.20

Antigovernment: influence frame

	Trust 1	Trust 2	Difference
All respondents	3.07	2.57	−0.50
Republicans	3.00	2.27	−0.73
Democrats	3.05	2.57	−0.48

Antigovernment: incompetency frame

	Trust 1	Trust 2	Difference
All respondents	3.05	2.91	−0.14
Republicans	3.13	2.69	−0.44
Democrats	3.01	2.96	−0.05

Antigovernment: inefficiency frame

	Trust 1	Trust 2	Difference
All respondents	3.16	2.91	−0.25
Republicans	3.03	2.94	−0.09
Democrats	3.17	2.93	−0.24

Source: Data taken from Cooperative Congressional Election Study, 2012.

crease in response to positive information much more among Democrats than Republicans, which only serves to exacerbate polarization between the two groups. In the "government protection" condition, for example, trust increased among Republicans by 0.21 points. Among Democrats, however, the same message was more than twice as effective, raising trust by 0.47 points. Similar results occur in the "government efficiency" condition. Here we observe that the effect of the efficiency message among Democrats was four times larger than it was among Republicans (0.20 vs. 0.05). Moreover, since conservatives tend to be Republicans, it does not appear as though positive information will do much to increase the percentage of citizens willing to make an ideological sacrifice for Barack Obama, the president at the time of our survey.

Worse still, our results further suggest that political trust is even more responsive to antigovernment rhetoric. The average decreases in trust in the bottom part of the table tend to be bigger than the average increases in trust in the top part of the table.[1] Furthermore, in two of the three frames, trust drops in response to negative information more among Republicans than among Democrats. This means that the net of negative and positive information will probably create less trust, a smaller pool of citizens willing to make ideological sacrifices, and greater polarization in political trust by party. Such partisan differences in pliability illustrate the difficulty in overcoming polarized trust.

Lessons from the Study of Political Tolerance

In this section, we invoke an analogy from the literature on political tolerance to motivate the need to develop content-controlled measures of political trust. Political tolerance has been defined as the "willingness to permit the expression of ideas or interests that one opposes" (Sullivan, Piereson, and Marcus 1982, 2). Early empirical work on the subject made some rather unsettling observations. In his seminal book, *Communism, Conformity, and Civil Liberties*, Stouffer (1955) found that levels of tolerance in the mass public were remarkably low. A majority of Americans, for example, agreed that communist teachers and clerks should be fired, that communists' citizenship should be revoked, and that books written by communists should be removed from public libraries. Perhaps most alarmingly, a majority of Americans agreed that communists should not be allowed to speak publicly (Stouffer 1955). The mass public exhibited somewhat lower yet still disturbingly high levels of intolerance toward suspected socialists and atheists.

Prothro and Grigg (1960) made another important discovery. They found that Americans were, in the abstract, quite supportive of basic principles such as commitment to democracy, majority rule, and the protection of minority rights. Indeed, more than 90 percent of respondents expressed support for these abstract democratic principles (Prothro and Grigg 1960). When it came time to apply these principles, however, Americans were far less committed to them. Fewer than 50 percent of respondents would allow a communist to speak in their city or run for mayor. More than half said that only taxpayers and the well informed should be allowed to vote in city referenda (Prothro and Grigg 1960). These findings reveal an important substantive lesson: there is often a large gap between tolerance attitudes in the abstract and tolerance attitudes in concrete political situations. For our purposes, this suggests the possibility of a gap between political trust in general and political trust toward particular parts of government.

During the 1970s, survey data began to show that Americans had become much more tolerant of communists, socialists, and atheists since the 1950s (Davis 1975; Nunn, Crockett, and Williams 1978). One study found, for example, that Americans were 30 percent more likely to permit communists to speak publicly, 30 percent more likely to permit communist authors to have their books on library shelves, and 35 percent more likely to permit communists to work as teachers (Nunn, Crockett, and Williams 1978). On the basis of such trends, some scholars concluded that the American public had become much more politically tolerant than just one generation prior.

John Sullivan and his colleagues identified the problem with such conclusions in a series of important papers (Sullivan, Piereson, and Marcus 1979, 1982; Sullivan et al. 1981). They argued that conventional measures of political tolerance did not make it possible to determine whether the public had become more tolerant generally or whether it had merely become more tolerant of communists, socialists, and atheists. To remedy this problem, they proposed an alternative measurement strategy premised on the belief that "tolerance can only be measured with reference to groups that people strongly dislike" (Sullivan, Piereson, and Marcus 1982, 60). To measure tolerance, they first employed a self-anchoring procedure in which respondents were asked to identify their least-liked group from a predetermined but diverse set of options. Respondents were then queried about their willingness to extend constitutional rights and liberties to members of their least-liked group. They describe their method as "content controlled" in the sense that all respondents were asked to evaluate "functionally equivalent" (i.e., least-liked) groups (Sullivan, Piereson, and Marcus 1982, 62–63).

Using their innovative measurement technique, Sullivan and colleagues found that the public had not truly become more tolerant. Although the public had become more tolerant of certain groups like communists and atheists, they remained highly intolerant of other controversial groups, such as the Ku Klux Klan. Similarly, research on public support for campaign finance reform has shown that citizens are less willing to support the political speech rights of interest groups that they dislike than they are to support the political speech rights of interest groups that they like (Grant and Rudolph 2003, 2004). Collectively, these findings provide us with a second important substantive lesson: when measuring political attitudes toward a political object, scholars must be sensitive to the fact that their measures can reflect both respondents' general attitudes as well as their feelings toward the target of evaluation. In the present context, this suggests the need for greater precision when specifying the target of evaluation during the measurement of political trust.

The Story of Three Government Agencies

Based on key insights we have gleaned from the political tolerance literature, we develop and analyze agency-specific measures of political trust. In this section, we describe the three government agencies on which our analysis will focus: the Environmental Protection Agency, the Department of Health and Human Services, and the Department of Defense (DOD).[2]

Environmental Protection Agency

The Environmental Protection Agency was established by President Nixon in the 1970s through executive order in order to consolidate federal oversight of environmental protection into a single government agency. The EPA seeks to promote a healthier environment through a variety of activities, including the monitoring of air and water quality, the regulation of fuel economy standards, the regulation of pollution control, and the enforcement of national environmental standards. Given its roles and responsibilities, the EPA tends to be viewed more favorably among groups and individuals who identify with the ideological left in the United States. One current debate that involves the EPA concerns a policy known as "cap and trade." Under typical cap-and-trade proposals, the government (i.e., the EPA) would limit, or cap, the amount of carbon emissions that a business could produce over a specified period of time. If businesses wish to exceed their emissions cap, they must buy additional permits on the open market from other businesses. Under most cap-and-trade proposals, the EPA would play an important role by issuing emissions permits and regulating their exchange.

Department of Health and Human Services

The Department of Health and Human Services, which began as the Department of Education and Welfare in 1953, describes itself as "the United States government's principal agency for protecting the health of all Americans and providing essential human services" (US Department of Health and Human Services 2014). HHS is a powerhouse among government agencies. It is responsible for the administration of more federal grant dollars than all other government agencies combined. It is also responsible for overseeing Medicare, which functions as the nation's largest health insurer. HHS has recently attracted considerable public attention for its role in the interpretation and administration of Obamacare. In a particularly controversial regulatory decision, HHS has ruled that private health insurance companies must cover contraceptive and reproductive services for women. This decision was sharply criticized by many religious groups and was ultimately struck down by the Supreme Court. Not surprisingly, HHS, like the EPA, tends to be a more popular part of government among the ideological left than it is among the ideological right. Given its regulatory and oversight functions, HHS will likely become the target of increased public scrutiny now that Obamacare has become fully operational.

Department of Defense

The Department of Defense, which began as the War Department, was established in 1789, making it one of the oldest departments in the US government. The Department of Defense is charged with organizing and supervising the nation's armed forces in an effort to preserve, protect, and defend the security of the United States. The DOD is a massive government agency. With more than three million employees, it is the largest employer in the world. It is the recipient of more federal money than any other government agency. In fact, its annual budget accounts for more than half of the entire federal discretionary budget. The military has, in general, often been viewed as one of the most successful and one of the most popular parts of the federal government. There is, of course, some heterogeneity in public attitudes toward the military. In contrast to the EPA and HHS, the military tends to be viewed more favorably by those who identify with the ideological right than by those who identify with the ideological left. From time to time, the DOD proposes new technologies or weapons systems, such as missile defense, to help it fulfill its duty of protecting national security.

Data

The data analyzed in this chapter are taken from the November 2011 iteration of the Vanderbilt University (VU) Poll. The VU Poll, which is sponsored by the Center for the Study of Democratic Institutions at Vanderbilt University, is based on a representative sample of voting-age adults who reside within the state of Tennessee.

Measuring Trust in Specific Government Agencies

The political tolerance literature offers two key lessons for the study and measurement of political trust. First, there is often a gap between general political judgments (i.e., in the abstract) and specific political judgments (i.e., applied to a particular group). Second, when measuring certain types of political judgments, it is important to make sure that all respondents have in mind comparable targets of evaluation. In the case of tolerance, this meant ensuring that all respondents were evaluating a least-liked group because tolerance requires a willingness to extend civil liberties to disliked groups. In the case of trust, we contend, this means ensuring that all respondents are evaluating the same part of government. When using traditional measures that ask people about their feelings toward "the government," scholars cannot always be certain whether people are thinking about specific parts of government (and, if so, which parts) or whether their response instead represents a global evaluation of government.

To address this challenge, we employ four different measures of political trust. The first is the now familiar trust instrument used by the American National Election Study (ANES) that asks, "How much of the time do you feel you can trust the government in Washington to do what is right: just about always, most of the time, only some of time, or never?" We also employ three variants of this question that are designed to elicit respondents' attitudes toward the government agencies discussed above:

EPA: How much of the time do you feel that you can trust the Environmental Protection Agency to do what is right: just about always, most of the time, only some of the time, or never?

HHS: How much of the time do you feel that you can trust the Department of Health and Human Services to do what is right: just about always, most of the time, only some of the time, or never?

DOD: How much of the time do you feel that you can trust the Department of Defense to do what is right: just about always, most of the time, only some of the time, or never?

We use individuals' responses to these three questions to create three agency-specific measures of trust. These measures are content controlled in the sense that we can be confident that all respondents are attending to the same part of government when they formulate their trust judgment. They are not content controlled in the sense that different respondents may differentially harbor positive or negative feelings toward different parts of government.

Levels of Trust in Government Agencies

The distribution of responses to the three agency-specific measures of trust is reported in table 9.2. For purposes of comparison, we also report the level of trust in "the government." Two observations are particularly worthy of note: First, consistent with contemporary surveys at the national level, trust in the government, as a whole, is remarkably low. Fewer than 15 percent of respondents in the sample indicated that they trusted government at least most of the time. By contrast, nearly 60 percent of respondents in the sample trusted government only some of the time, and more than 25 percent of respondents in the sample said that they *never* trust the government. On a scale ranging from one to four, the mean level of trust in the government is 1.89, well below the midpoint of the scale.

Second, we note that each of the three government agencies enjoys higher levels of public trust than does government as a whole. More than 37 percent of respondents trust the EPA at least most of the time. The mean level of trust in the EPA is 0.40 points higher than the mean level of trust in the government as a whole, a difference that is both substantively and statistically significant ($t = 14.2$, $p < 0.01$). More than 38 percent of respondents trust HHS at least most of the time. Mean trust in HHS is

TABLE 9.2. **Percent trust in government agencies**

	Trust in government	Trust in the EPA	Trust in HHS	Trust in the DOD
Just about always	1.8	7.9	7.8	13.3
Most of the time	12.5	29.7	30.8	38.0
Some of the time	58.8	46.0	48.7	41.9
Never	26.8	16.4	12.6	6.7
Number of cases	1,475	1,448	1,459	1,459
Mean trust (1–4)	1.89	2.29	2.34	2.58

Note: Table entries are the percentage of respondents who voice the specified level of trust in the specified government agency. Mean trust scores range from one to four.
Source: Data taken from Vanderbilt University (VU) Poll, November 2011.

0.45 points greater than mean trust in the government ($t = 16.7, p < 0.01$). Of the agencies explored, the DOD enjoys the highest levels of trust. A majority of respondents (51.3 percent) in the sample trust the DOD at least most of the time. The mean level of trust in the DOD is 0.69 points larger than mean trust in government ($t = 24.9, p < 0.01$). It is also greater than trust in the EPA ($t = 9.5, p < 0.01$) and trust in HHS ($t = 7.9, p < 0.01$).

Because the ideological composition of our sample of Tennessee residents is a bit more conservative than the national electorate, it is perhaps not surprising that the DOD would enjoy greater trust than HHS and the EPA. What is striking, however, is that all three government agencies, whether they tend to be popular among the ideological right (the DOD) or the ideological left (the EPA and HHS), receive greater public trust than does the government as a whole. The finding that people trust specific parts of government more than they trust the whole of government comports well with previous findings by public opinion scholars. Scholars have found, for example, that when government spending is framed in specific terms (i.e., with specific programs and target constituencies), public support tends to be much greater than when such spending is framed in very general terms (Jacoby 2000). Similarly, previous work has shown that the public is more confident in government's ability to run specific programs than it is in government's ability to run national programs "in general" (Lock, Shapiro, and Jacobs 1999).

Who Trusts Whom?

Do levels of trust vary by individual differences? To explore this question, table 9.3 reports the mean level of trust in each government agency by a variety of important subgroups.

TABLE 9.3 **Mean trust in government agencies by subgroups**

	Trust in government	Trust in the EPA	Trust in HHS	Trust in the DOD
Liberals	2.03	2.59	2.51	2.43
Moderates	1.96	2.47	2.47	2.54
Conservatives	1.82	2.06	2.17	2.67
Democrats	2.12	2.55	2.54	2.55
Independents	1.74	2.26	2.32	2.46
Republicans	1.81	2.07	2.17	2.76
Tea Party	1.73	1.94	2.14	2.66
Not Tea Party	2.04	2.55	2.49	2.52
Occupy	1.92	2.45	2.51	2.50
Not Occupy	1.82	2.05	2.19	2.63
Female	1.95	2.36	2.35	2.50
Male	1.83	2.22	2.33	2.66
African American	2.12	2.48	2.52	2.48
Non–African American	1.84	2.25	2.29	2.60
< High school	2.03	2.34	2.28	2.50
High school	1.85	2.35	2.39	2.54
Some college	1.88	2.22	2.27	2.59
College	1.86	2.25	2.29	2.63
Graduate school	1.97	2.28	2.44	2.62

Note: Table entries are mean levels of trust in the specified government agency for respondents who belong to the group specified in each row.
Source: Data taken from Vanderbilt University (VU) Poll, November 2011.

We organize our discussion into two parts: First, we examine between group differences within each column to show that individual differences strongly influence levels of trust toward each part of government. Second, we compare within group differences across each column to show that individual differences have little impact on individuals' tendency to trust specific parts of government more than government in general.

Consider first the effects of ideology and party identification on levels of trust. As shown in table 9.3, liberals and Democrats express higher mean levels of trust in government than do conservatives and Republicans. Liberals and Democrats also express greater trust in HHS and the EPA than do conservatives and Republicans. Trust in the EPA, for example, is 0.53 points higher among liberals than it is among conservatives and 0.48 points higher among Democrats than it is among Republicans. With respect to the DOD, however, the pattern is reversed. Conservatives and Republicans exhibit higher levels of trust in the Department of Defense than do liberals and Democrats. Trust in the DOD is 0.24 points higher among conservatives than it is among liberals and 0.21 points higher among Republicans than it is among Democrats. Clearly, levels of trust in specific government agencies differ significantly along partisan and ideological lines.

Next we consider whether levels of trust are associated with individuals' support for grassroots movements such as the Tea Party movement and the Occupy Wall Street movement. Consistent with the ideological effects noted above, we observe that people who support the Tea Party movement are less trusting of government than those who do not. Tea Party supporters are also less trusting of HHS and the EPA than non–Tea Party supporters. In the case of the DOD, however, trust is 0.14 points higher among Tea Party supporters than it is among nonsupporters. The opposite patterns are observed when we consider the Occupy Wall Street movement. Occupy supporters are more trusting of government, HHS, and the EPA than are nonsupporters. Occupy supporters are 0.13 points less trusting of the DOD than are nonsupporters.

Consider next the effects of demographic traits such as race, sex, and education on levels of trust. As table 9.3 makes clear, women tend to express higher levels of trust in the government, HHS, and the EPA than do men but lower levels of trust in the DOD. Similarly, African Americans voice greater trust in the government, HHS, and the EPA than do non–African Americans but lower trust in the DOD. Education appears to have little impact at all. Indeed, education is uncorrelated with trust in any of the specific agencies or in government as a whole.

Earlier, we reported that people tend to trust specific parts of government more than they trust government as a whole. The results in table 9.3 allow us to examine whether this finding is conditional on individual differences. Remarkably, the finding remains intact across all the subgroups. We observe, for example, that liberals express higher levels of trust in all three specific agencies than they do in government in general. Even the Department of Defense, which is more closely aligned with the ideological right, scores 0.40 points higher on the trust scale among liberals than does government as a whole. An identical pattern emerges among conservatives. Conservatives trust the DOD, HHS, and even the EPA more than they trust government. Although liberals and conservatives differ in terms of which agency they trust the most, they are similar in that they both trust "the government" least of all. There appears to be some common ideological ground as both liberals and conservatives trust specific parts of the government more than they trust the whole of government.

The story is much the same when we examine the relationship between trust and party identification. Democrats trust the EPA, HHS, and the

DOD more than the government overall by 0.43, 0.42, and 0.43 points, respectively. Among Republicans, the EPA, HHS, and the DOD are trusted by 0.26, 0.36, and 0.95 points more than is the government. This pattern is not limited to partisans. Self-identified independents trust the EPA, HHS, and the DOD more than the government by 0.52, 0.58, and 0.72 points, respectively. Regardless of party identification, it seems, people trust specific parts of government more than they trust the whole. The fact that each part of government inspires greater trust among Republicans and Democrats than does government as a whole could potentially provide a way to bridge the partisan polarization of trust. One should not be overly sanguine about this possibility, however, as trust in specific government agencies differs significantly along partisan and ideological lines. We observe a similar pattern within each of the subgroups. Among Tea Party supporters and nonsupporters, Occupy supporters and nonsupporters, men and women, African Americans and non–African Americans, and across all levels of education, respondents consistently express more trust in specific parts of the government than they do in government as a whole. Of course, it is also the case that none of the levels of agency-specific trust are particularly high either.

The Measurement of Policy Preferences

In the sections to follow, we will outline and test our hypotheses about the effects of agency-specific trust on public support for specific policy proposals. To do so, we included three policy questions in the VU Poll. Each of these policy questions was designed to gauge public sentiment toward an issue or issue domain in which one of the three specific government agencies described earlier has direct or indirect involvement. In the environmental domain, we queried respondents about their support for a "cap-and-trade" policy: "There's a proposal system called 'cap and trade' that some say would lower the pollution levels that lead to global warming. With Cap and Trade, the government would issue permits limiting the amount of greenhouse gases companies can put out. Companies that did not use all their permits could sell them to other companies. The idea is that many companies would find ways to put out less greenhouse gases, because that would be cheaper than buying permits. Would you support or oppose this system?" In the area of health, we inquired about respondents' opinions of recent health care reform legislation that was enacted in 2010: "As you may know, a health care reform bill was signed into law early last year. Given what you know about the health care reform law, do you have a generally favorable or generally unfavorable opinion of it?" Finally, in the area of national defense, we asked respondents about their views regarding the development of a space-based missile defense system: "Some people feel the U.S. should try to develop a ground and space based missile defense system to protect the U.S. from missile attack. Others oppose such an effort because they say it would be too costly and might interfere with existing arms treaties with the Russians. Which position comes closer to your view (Vanderbilt University 2011)?"

Hypotheses

This book has shown that trust is a potent predictor of public support for government action for those who must make ideological or material sacrifices. In chapter 5, we demonstrated that the effects of trust on policy preferences depended on the issues on which individuals were focused when they made their trust judgments. We found that the effects of trust on support for a given policy were most pronounced among people whose thoughts were focused on government action in that policy domain when they expressed how much they trusted government. In this chapter, we have argued for the need to develop agency-specific measures of political trust. We have already observed that people tend to express higher levels of trust in specific parts of government than they do in government as a whole.

We believe that agency-specific measures of trust will have distinct and meaningful consequences for domain-specific policy preferences. Our general expectation is that the effects of trust on policy preferences will be conditional on the degree of association between government agency and policy domain. From this expectation, we develop two sets of predictions: The first set includes our expectations about the effects of agency-specific trust relative to general political trust. The effects of trust in the EPA on support for cap-and-trade policies should be greater than the effects of trust in "the government"; the effects of trust in HHS on support for health care reform policies should be greater than the effects of trust in "the government"; and the effects of trust in the DOD on support for missile defense should be greater than the effects of trust in "the government." Our second set of predictions includes our expectations about the effects of one type of agency-specific trust relative to other types of agency-specific trust. Specifically, we expect that the effects of trust in the

EPA on support for cap-and-trade policies should be greater than the effects of trust in HHS or the DOD; the effects of trust in HHS on support for health care policies should be greater than the effects of trust in the EPA or the DOD; and the effects of trust in Defense on support for missile defense should be greater than the effects of trust in the EPA or HHS.

Results

We begin our analysis by examining the bivariate relationship between agency-specific trust and individuals' policy preferences. Table 9.4 presents the percentage of public support for each of the three policy proposals by level of trust. Consider first the relationship between trust and support for cap and trade. At first glance, there appears to be a positive correlation between trust in government and support for cap and trade. Among those who never trust the government, only 35.5 percent support cap and trade. Among those who trust government just about always, however, that figure rises to 60 percent, an increase of about 25 percentage points. Consistent with expectations, though, trust in the EPA has a bigger impact on cap-and-trade preferences than does trust in government. Only about 16 percent of people who never trust the EPA support cap and trade while almost 67 percent of those who just about always trust the EPA do so. This increase of more than 50 percentage points is double the size of the increase we observed for trust in government. As expected, trust in the EPA also appears to have a bigger impact on support for cap and trade than either trust in HHS or trust in the DOD.

Consider next the relationship between trust and support for health care reform. Once again, there appears to be a positive association between trust in government and support for health care reform. Among those who never trust government, approximately 21 percent support health care reform while more than 66 percent of those who just about always trust government do so, a difference of roughly 45 percentage points. We observe very similar results for trust in HHS. A similar change for trust in HHS boosts support for health care reform by about 41 percentage points. The bivariate correlation between trust in HHS and support for health care reform is 0.25, while the correlation between trust in government and support for health care reform is only slightly smaller at 0.22. Although this is consistent with our expectation, a more rigorous test will clearly require multivariate analysis. The results suggest that multivariate

TABLE 9.4 **Support for public policies by level of trust in government agencies**

Cap and trade

	Never	Some of the time	Most of the time	Just about always	Difference
Trust in government	35.5	47.1	57.5	60.0	+ 24.4
Trust in the EPA	15.8	43.4	61.3	66.7	+ 50.9
Trust in HHS	21.3	42.0	56.9	62.6	+ 41.3
Trust in the DOD	41.2	47.4	42.9	50.6	+ 9.4

Health care reform

	Never	Some of the time	Most of the time	Just about always	Difference
Trust in government	21.1	34.8	55.6	66.7	+ 45.6
Trust in the EPA	8.6	29.7	51.9	53.3	+ 44.7
Trust in HHS	13.0	28.7	46.3	54.1	+ 41.1
Trust in the DOD	24.2	36.2	31.8	37.1	+ 12.9

Missile defense

	Never	Some of the time	Most of the time	Just about always	Difference
Trust in government	61.3	58.0	49.1	52.2	− 9.1
Trust in the EPA	72.4	58.6	51.3	50.5	− 21.9
Trust in HHS	62.8	60.7	54.6	50.0	− 12.8
Trust in the DOD	45.7	54.0	62.0	64.0	+ 18.3

Note: Table entries are the percentage of respondents who the specified public policy at the specified levels of trust for each government agency.
Source: Data taken from Vanderbilt University (VU) Poll, November 2011.

analysis will also be needed to determine whether trust in HHS has a bigger influence on health care reform preferences than does trust in the EPA. Perhaps the reason these numbers are so close is because the part of government that people had in mind when asked to evaluate it in general was the part that dealt with health care, given how salient health care was in Obama's first term.

Last, we consider the relationship between trust in government and support for missile defense. Here we observe greater heterogeneity in the effects of trust. An increase in trust in government is actually associated with a 9 percentage-point reduction in public support for missile defense. When we examine trust in the Department of Defense, however, we observe the opposite relationship. An increase in trust in the DOD is associated with an 18 percentage-point increase in support for missile defense. As theorized, this effect is twice as large in magnitude. Trust in the EPA and trust in HHS are negatively associated with support for missile defense. Multivariate analysis will be needed to further determine whether the magnitude of these effects is smaller than those associated with trust in the DOD.

Multivariate Models: Consequences of Trust on Policy Support

To provide a more rigorous test of our hypotheses, we turn now to a multivariate analysis. Table 9.5 reports the results of three identically specified probit models in which policy support serves as the dependent variable. The models control for individuals' party identification and ideology, as well as demographic traits such as race and sex. Of primary interest in these models are the sign and significance of the coefficients representing trust in government or trust in one of the three specific government agencies. Using the coefficients obtained from estimating these models, we calculate and present some predicted probabilities of policy support in order to illustrate the magnitude of trust's impact. These probabilities tell us what impact changing trust levels might have on policy support for a typical individual. These predicted probabilities are displayed in figures 9.1, 9.2, and 9.3.

The first data column of table 9.5 reports the determinants of support for cap and trade. The results indicate that support for cap and trade is higher among women than it is among men. Support is lower among conservatives than it is among liberals and moderates. Of central interest, though, are the effects of trust. The coefficient for trust in government fails to reach statistical significance. This suggests that, controlling for the other variables in the model, trust in "the government" has no impact on cap-and-trade preferences. Consistent with expectations, the coefficient denoting trust in the EPA is positive and statistically significant. This means that trust in the EPA is a better predictor of support for cap and trade than is trust in government. The coefficient representing trust in HHS is also positive and significant but is smaller in size. The results suggest that trust in the DOD has no impact on support for cap and trade.

Figure 9.1 displays the predicted probabilities of support for cap and trade at all possible values of each type of trust.[3] We note first that the slopes representing both trust in government and trust in the DOD are essentially flat, confirming that neither type of trust exerts any appreciable influence on individuals' cap-and-trade preferences. The slope for trust in HHS, by contrast, is positive. Among those who never trust HHS, the probability of supporting cap and trade is 0.47. Among those who just

TABLE 9.5. **Determinants of support for public policies**

	Cap and trade	Health care reform	Missile defense
Political trust			
Trust in government	−0.06	0.10	−0.09
	(0.07)	(0.09)	(0.07)
Trust in the EPA	0.38***	0.27***	−0.21***
	(0.07)	(0.08)	(0.06)
Trust in HHS	0.14**	0.17**	−0.01
	(0.07)	(0.08)	(0.07)
Trust in the DOD	−0.03	−0.01	0.17***
	(0.06)	(0.07)	(0.06)
Political predispositions			
Democrat	0.17	0.50***	0.06
	(0.11)	(0.13)	(0.11)
Republican	−0.16	−0.60***	0.31***
	(0.11)	(0.14)	(0.11)
Liberal	0.02	0.09	−0.39***
	(0.13)	(0.15)	(0.13)
Conservative	−0.33***	−0.56***	0.17*
	(0.10)	(0.12)	(0.10)
Demographics			
Female	0.15*	−0.07	−0.02
	(0.09)	(0.10)	(0.08)
African American	−0.02	0.26**	0.04
	(0.12)	(0.13)	(0.11)
Constant	−1.05***	−1.43***	0.26
	(0.21)	(0.26)	(0.20)
Log likelihood	−605.98	−400.83	−642.18
Number of cases	989	851	1,006
Pseudo R^2	0.11	0.27	0.06

Note: Table entries are the coefficients and standard errors from identically specified probit models predicting support for a particular public policy.
*$p < 0.10$, **$p < 0.05$, ***$p < 0.01$
Source: Data taken from Vanderbilt University (VU) Poll, November 2011.

about always trust HHS, however, this likelihood climbs to 0.63, an increase of 16 percentage points. As expected, the slope for trust in the EPA is positive and is visibly steeper than any of the others slopes. The probability of supporting cap and trade among those who never trust the EPA is only 0.35. Among those who just about always trust the EPA, this likelihood rises to 0.78, an increase of 43 percentage points.

The second data column of table 9.5 reports the determinants of support for health care reform. As can be seen, the likelihood of support for health care reform rises among African Americans and Democrats but falls among Republicans and conservatives. The coefficient for trust in government once again fails to reach statistical significance. This means that, controlling for agency-specific trust and other factors, general trust has no effect on health care reform preferences. As predicted, the coefficient for trust in HHS is both positive and statistically significant, confirming that support for health care reform is a positive function of trust in HHS. Trust in the EPA also heightens support for health care reform while trust in the DOD has no effect.

To compare the relative magnitude of these effects, figure 9.2 reports the predicted probabilities of support for health care reform at different levels of trust. Recall our prediction that trust in HHS will exert more influence on support for health care reform than will trust in government. The results in figure 9.2 provide strong support for that expectation. Among those who never trust government, the probability of support for health care reform is 0.34. Among those who just about always trust government, that likelihood climbs to 0.45, an increase of 11 percentage points. The positive slope representing trust in HHS is much steeper. The same shock to trust in HHS heightens the probability of support for health care reform by 20 percentage points. As expected, trust in HHS is clearly a better predictor of health care preferences than is trust in the DOD. Contrary to expectations, however, the effects of trust in the EPA on health care reform preferences are slightly larger than the effects of trust in HHS.

The third data column of table 9.5 presents the determinants of support for missile defense. The results indicate that Republicans and conservatives are more likely to support missile defense, while liberals are less likely to do so. The coefficient denoting trust in government fails to reach

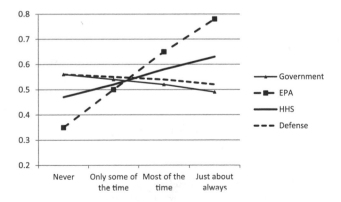

FIGURE 9.1. Effects of political trust on support for cap and trade

Note: Lines depict the predicted probabilities of supporting cap and trade at specified levels of trust in government.

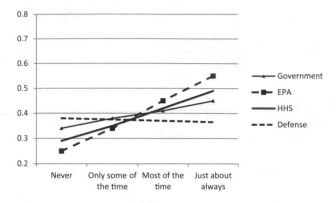

FIGURE 9.2. Effects of political trust on support for health care reform

Note: Lines depict the predicted probabilities of supporting health care reform at specified levels of trust in government.

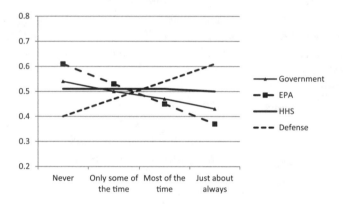

FIGURE 9.3. Effects of political trust on support for missile defense

Note: Lines depict the predicted probabilities of supporting missile defense at specified levels of trust in government.

statistical significance, suggesting that global trust has little influence on attitudes toward missile defense. The effects of trust in HHS are similarly insignificant. The results in table 9.4 show that, as expected, trust in the DOD raises support for missile defense among the mass public. The results further show that trust in the EPA depresses it.

To assess the magnitude of these results, we again examine the predicted probabilities of policy support at different levels of trust. As can be seen in figure 9.3, the slope for trust in government is relatively flat. As predicted, the slope for trust in the DOD is positive and steep. Among those who never trust the DOD, the probability of supporting missile defense is only 0.40. Among those who just about always trust the DOD, that likelihood rises 21 percentage points to 0.61. The slope for trust in HHS is indistinguishable from zero. The effects of trust in the EPA are negative but comparable in magnitude to those associated with trust in the DOD. Among those who never trust the EPA, the probability of support for missile defense is 0.61. Among those who just about always trust the EPA, that likelihood falls to 0.37, a decrease of 24 percentage points.

Conclusions

In this chapter, we have explored two avenues to changing the trust environment. The first was an experiment to see whether providing people information about what government accomplishes can increase trust. We were heartened to find that it is, in fact, possible to restore at least some political trust by reminding people that government does things that they like. Unfortunately, our experiment also reveals that reminding people of government failures actually does more to further erode trust than positive information does to increase it. In fact, the substantive outcome of such information is to polarize trust even more by party than it was before the experiment.

Our other approach to changing the trust environment might be a bit more promising. Specifically, we have argued in this chapter that trust and its consequences are products of what part of government individuals are attending to at the time they render their trust judgment. To explore this proposition, we developed and analyzed agency-specific measures of political trust. Then we examined the effects of trust in three specific government agencies (the EPA, HHS, and the DOD), contrasting them with the levels and consequences of global trust in government.

This analysis contributes several new substantive insights to the literature. First, our results indicate that citizens consistently trust specific parts of government more than they trust government globally. Levels of trust in the EPA, HHS, and the DOD all exceeded those of trust in government as a whole. Strikingly, we found that this conclusion holds across a variety of politically diverse subgroups. Conservatives and Republicans, for example, trusted all specific agencies, even agencies associated with the ideological left (i.e., the EPA and HHS), more than they trusted "the government." Liberals and Democrats also trusted all specific agencies, even those associated with the ideological right (i.e., the DOD), more than they trusted government as a whole.

Second, we found strong and consistent support for our hypotheses about the relative effects of global trust and agency-specific trust on policy preferences. In each of the three issue domains we examined, agency-specific trust outperformed global trust as a predictor of policy support. Trust in the EPA exerted far greater influence on support for cap and trade than did global trust. Similarly, trust in HHS was a better predictor of support for health care reform than was global trust. In addition, trust in the DOD had a bigger impact on citizens' attitudes toward missile defense than did global trust. These findings underscore the importance of recognizing what parts of government people are thinking about when they render trust judgments.

Third, we found strong but qualified support for our hypotheses about the relative influence of different types of agency-specific trust on policy preferences. As predicted, trust in the EPA outperformed both trust in HHS and trust in the DOD as a predictor of support for cap and trade. As expected, we found that trust in HHS outperformed trust in the DOD as a predictor of support for health care reform but, contrary to expectations, it failed to outperform trust in the EPA. Somewhat consistent with expectations, we found that the effects of trust in the DOD on support for missile defense were larger than those of trust in HHS and were comparable in magnitude to those of trust in the EPA. Collectively, these results suggest that individuals are discriminating when they incorporate different types of agency-specific trust into their policy preferences. It is not the case that each type of agency-specific trust influences individuals' degree of support for each type of policy. Rather, the strength of the relationship between agency-specific trust and policy support appears to be conditional on the degree of congruence between issue domain and the part of government that oversees that domain.

The results of this chapter have important implications for the role that political trust might play as an instrument of public opinion. First, because specific government agencies are consistently more trusted than government in general, public support for government-based efforts to solve social or economic problems is likely to be broader and deeper when those efforts are tied to particular government agencies. When public trust is needed to bolster public support for a policy, as we observed for health care reform in chapter 8, our results suggest that proponents of government action would be well advised to discuss that action in terms of the particular agencies involved (e.g., HHS) rather than in more global terms. Second, because the public's tendency to trust specific parts of government more than government globally occurs among all partisan and ideological groups, discussing government action in agency-specific terms may help to reduce the partisan polarization of trust. It is unlikely to eliminate such polarization entirely, however, as even trust in specific government agencies remains somewhat polarized along partisan lines.

CHAPTER TEN

Things Will Probably Get Better, but We Are Not Sure How

As professors, we teach young people for a living. Each year, we introduce ourselves to a couple hundred new faces and explain how the American political system works. On one level or another, we hope that some of these students will draw some inspiration from our lectures and discussions. Perhaps a few will be among the next generation of political leaders. As the polarization in Washington deepens with each passing year, our task gets a little more dispiriting. Optimistic and idealistic to our cores, we want our students to be the answer to the political system's ills. In writing this book, however, we have become increasingly concerned that solutions to the present situation in Washington are beyond the grasp of anyone's best efforts.

We began the book by noting the deep roots of dysfunction in the political class, citing a number of examples from the aftermath of the Great Recession (2008–9). An economic calamity of this magnitude might have brought the parties together to solve existing and looming problems. In the case of the Great Recession, however, partisan cooperation failed to materialize, at least after a complete collapse of the banking system was averted. Instead, partisan brinksmanship became the order of the day, resulting in a watered down stimulus in 2009, a debt ceiling crisis in 2011, sequestration in 2012, and a government shutdown in 2013. For better or worse, the same acrimonious spirit characterized foreign wars several years earlier. Political disagreements used to "end at the water's edge," but not in the early twenty-first century. Although Republicans and Democrats worked together in the immediate aftermath of 9/11, cooperation broke down quickly.

The extreme polarization that infects Washington resulted from two recent developments, both of which are likely to persist for the foreseeable future. The first is the emergence of more ideological parties. Ideologically focused, self-starting candidates became the norm after primary elections replaced party bosses as the conduit to party nominations (Aldrich 1995). Rather than securing patronage, office holders today are intense policy demanders who care deeply about policy outcomes (Cohen et al. 2008). Moreover, because primaries are low-turnout affairs dominated by the most ideologically committed voters in the electorate, would-be representatives have both personal *and* electoral incentives to be extreme. As a consequence, Democrats nominate liberals, Republicans nominate conservatives, and the ideological middle naturally disappears.

Once in Washington, further incentives exist that encourage lock-step party-line voting. No scholar has done more than Frances Lee (see especially 2009) to explain the role that close partisan margins play in understanding why we should not expect cooperation in Washington to flourish any time soon. When partisan margins are close, as they have been in both the House and Senate since 1994, both parties think the majority—along with all its perks and powers—can be theirs. To win the majority, however, the minority party must convince voters that the majority has failed. Cooperating and compromising with the majority might be good governance, but the legislative victories that emerge from that type of cooperation only serve to undermine the minority's case that the majority needs to be replaced at election time. Hence a better minority party strategy is to oppose and criticize the majority party relentlessly. Things were different in the post–World War II years. But as Lee points out, the main reason was that Republicans most often held so few seats, especially in the House, that they could never hope to control a majority. To get even half a loaf out of the legislative process, they had to compromise with majority Democrats.

Regardless of whether party-line voting is ideological or partisan in nature, its prevalence sends a message to partisans in the electorate that the other party is not to be liked, trusted, or followed. The details really do not matter. Indications of our thinking are ubiquitous, but rarely have they been clearer than in a skit on Jimmy Kimmel Live during the government shutdown in September 2013. Kimmel sent out a camera crew to ask people whether they preferred "Obamacare" or the "Affordable Care Act (ACA)." Person after person lauded the latter and attacked the former (with the exception of the one African American who did the reverse) despite the fact that the two are synonymous. Survey data collected by Gallup during the period found significantly higher public support for the ACA than for Obamacare.[1] Of course, the explanation is that the name of a polarizing Democrat is attached to one label but not the other. Obama's name boosts support from Democrats, but it increases resistance from Republicans even more.

The mass public is the only player in the governing process that could alter the incentives of ideological members seeking to win the majority. Under the right circumstances, citizens could nudge Congress toward cooperation. The most likely way the public might play such a role is if a consensus about policy solutions emerged in the electorate. When that happens, members of Congress are most likely to come together to pass laws (Page, Shapiro, and Dempsey 1987). As we have detailed throughout the book, however, such consensus in the electorate is hard to come by these days. We have shown that a key reason for disagreement on issues across party lines in the electorate is the deep dislike and distrust that partisans have of government when the other party runs it. Without trust, out-party partisans are almost never willing to support the policy ideas of the governing party. As a result, minority-party members of Congress feel no pressure from their constituents to compromise. In the end, ordinary Americans are perfectly willing to put up with the ideological and partisan excesses of those in Washington despite the fact that they are not ideologically extreme themselves (Fiorina et al. 2005). Partisans in the electorate reinforce what their favored elites are doing rather than encouraging them to chart a different, more cooperative, course.

Affective versus Principled Polarization

Perhaps the most important finding in our book is that political trust has polarized along party lines, with its polarization rooted in negative affect toward partisan out-groups rather than in principled differences in policy preferences. Put more simply, the nature of polarization in the electorate is based on feelings rather than a philosophy about the proper role of government. What implication does this have for the future?

Pundits routinely decry the dangers of *ideological* polarization. Obviously, it does not promote compromise. When the distance between the parties' ideological outlook widens, it becomes more difficult to bring people together. That said, ideological differences are at least rooted in a philosophy about governance. Perhaps the parties cannot work together on *certain* fundamental issues. But not all issues that government deals with are structured by ideological conflicts. It seems to us that things like reauthorizing a highway bill, having the president talk to school kids about working hard and staying in school, and scores of other matters fall outside ideological boundaries. Such matters can be dealt with through compromise and legislative logrolling in Congress, yet even that rarely happens anymore.

We think the reason for this is that partisans seem to flat out hate their counterparts. Indeed, according to the 2012 American National Election Study (ANES), Republicans in the electorate gave a higher average feeling thermometer score to atheists than they did to the Democratic Party.[2] When negative feelings are at the root of political disagreements, it can cause even worse problems than if it were ideology. When out-party partisans deeply dislike the governing party, they are not even likely to listen to what those in the governing party have to say, much less to believe that their side's representatives should make deals with them. When you deeply dislike your adversary, you do not want anything at all—big or small—to come to his or her benefit. In fact, you want things to go wrong. When Rush Limbaugh said in 2009, "I hope Obama fails,"[3] he was surely not alone.

Such thinking can have terrible consequences for the health of a nation. In baseball, it is not dangerous for Boston Red Sox fans to absolutely hate the New York Yankees, because the failure of the Yankees does not fundamentally affect people's well-being. Strong negative affect directed toward a party that runs the national government, however, has the potential to do just that. Do ardent partisans stop rooting for the country to succeed when the other party is in power? Survey research cannot provide a definitive answer to this question because people know enough to say that, of course, they want America to succeed whether or not, in their heart of hearts, they feel that way. But we suspect if we could have hooked up polygraphs to Democrats after George W. Bush ordered more troops to go to Iraq in 2007, more than a few would have revealed a preference that the "surge" should fail. Failure, in this case, would have meant the loss of hundreds, maybe thousands, of Americans' lives—quite a cost to further one's party's political ambitions. Similarly, it seems reasonable to believe that a sample of polygraphs would have revealed a substantial chunk of Republicans in 2009 rooting against a dramatic recovery from the Great Recession. Republicans might have viewed a dramatic recovery as a less than ideal outcome because it would have suggested Democrats were doing a good job, the plight of the long-term unemployed be damned.[4]

Unlike ideology, negative feelings have the potential to infect just about anything or any issue. Our reasoning is rooted in social psychology. People's feelings about people or groups are central to how they process information that is connected to those people or groups. For example, there is a growing body of literature on what psychologists call "implicit attitudes" (Bargh, Chen, and Ambady 1996; Fazio et al. 1986, 1995; Payne et al. 2005). Such attitudes have been linked to a variety of social groups, including race, ethnicity, gender, the elderly, and political candidates (see Perez 2013 for a review). The notion of implicit attitudes is based on the presumption that most people harbor deeply felt, yet sometimes unspoken, attitudes toward people or groups that are automatic and thus lie beyond their cognitive awareness and control. Those who express particularly negative feelings about certain groups tend to have particularly strong implicit biases against them.

Importantly, these implicit biases exist at a "precognitive" level. People do not even have to be consciously thinking about them for them to affect their evaluations and judgments. The biases are, instead, automatic. Such biases can negatively color anything that is associated with the group for whom one holds implicit attitudes. Because feelings are automatic and not always subject to cognitive control, their influence on decision making is difficult to regulate.

Operation at the precognitive level is key for our purposes. We believe it is this that causes the Colorado woman we described in chapter 1, who cried at the prospect of President Obama speaking on video to her children about the importance of hard work and staying in school, to consider keeping her kids home that day. It does not matter to her what the topic of the speech is. It does not matter to her what the message of the speech is. Before knowing any of that, she has made up her mind that exposing her child to President Obama is dangerous. His ideas, and by extension his party's ideas, are anathema to goodness and righteousness no matter how substantively uncontroversial they might be. The consequences for this kind of polarization are much worse than a polarization based on ideology.

One might like to think that people can rise above these instincts for the good of the country. But consider the application of our thinking to everyday life. Consider, for example, a work relationship in which you have come to dislike and distrust a coworker. Regardless of how the feelings developed, once present, they condition how you perceive everything about him or her. You automatically question the coworker's motives, even when the motives are, to a neutral observer, clearly benign. Negative feelings might make it hard to discern when the coworker is reaching out in a way that might mitigate the existing dislike and distrust. Without being able to recognize such efforts, it is difficult to start a process of *rapprochement*. As a result, bad feelings will tend to persist, whether justified or not, and continue to color (negatively) every future interaction and assessment. In the real world, a situation fraught with negative feelings could benefit from a neutral arbiter. Relationship counseling is built on this premise. A neutral arbiter could allow the contestants to acknowledge mistakes and to encourage forgiveness. In politics, however, no neutral arbiter exists. Even if one did, we do not see Barack Obama and John Boehner sitting down together with that person for a *kumbaya* moment any time soon.

Perhaps we overdramatize a bit the extent of the effects of affective polarization. Maybe it is not really "worse" than ideological polarization. Regardless, we feel extremely confident in the core role that negative feelings plays in our story. If minority-party partisans intensely dislike and deeply distrust the majority party, they will put little pressure on their favored representatives to compromise with the other party on much of anything. Partisans do not want their members of Congress to compromise with the devil. It is possible that these same people will complain that politics is not working. But the theories of motivated reasoning we have deployed throughout the book suggest people will target their dissatisfaction with politics at the majority party, not their own.

Finally, we think it is critical to note that because Americans do not know much about politics, the philosophical difference between the parties in Congress probably matter less to them than political observers tend to assume. The ACA again helps make our point. Americans expressed support for most of its main features. People liked extending coverage to children under twenty-five years of age. They liked not allowing insurance companies to refuse coverage due to preexisting conditions. The one clear exception to the rule was the individual insurance mandate, requiring most Americans to buy health insurance. Indeed, when asked just a couple months after President Obama signed the ACA into law, about two-thirds of Americans thought the individual mandate should be repealed, according to a February 2012 poll from the Kaiser Foundation. A staggering 86 percent of Republicans favored repeal of this provision.

Recall from chapter 2, however, that the individual mandate was a conservative idea that came out of a conservative think tank (the Heritage

Foundation) during debate about the Clinton health care initiative. Only after Democrats adopted the idea more than a decade later did ideologically conservative leaders in Washington decide it was anathema to the American way of life. Their partisans in the electorate dutifully followed their lead. Was ideology at the core of the reasoning of either leaders or followers? The evidence suggests otherwise. Instead, opposition was driven, as is often the case in politics, by the wish to deny political opponents a victory. Little wonder then that polarization in the electorate is not about policy or ideology but rather about feelings.

On the Current Climate of Political Trust

These increasingly negative feelings about the parties manifest themselves in the political system through low levels of political trust, particularly among out-party partisans. The current climate of political trust in the United States is not healthy and has several distinguishing features. First, consistent with previous research, we find that levels of political trust in the United States are remarkably low by historical standards. Gone are the days when three-quarters of the American people trusted government to do what is right at least most of the time. Since 2010, usually less than one-fifth of citizens express that level of trust in their government.

Second, we find that levels of political trust fluctuate in response to political and economic circumstances, but the effects are asymmetric relative to good and bad news. We observe some modest gains in political trust when the economy is doing well. As we found in chapter 3, however, strong economies only raise trust levels about one-fourth as much as weak economies lower them. The government gets disproportionate blame relative to credit. We also found that trust increases when the public is focused on international rather than domestic concerns. That can help governments respond to external threats, but these higher levels of trust have no bearing on domestic policy preferences. The story is actually quite grim as it relates to domestic policy. In chapter 7, we demonstrated that trust tends to be lowest when the country most needs to the government to act—namely, during an economic downturn. This hamstrings the government's best efforts to mitigate domestic crises.

Finally, our study indicates that political trust has polarized along partisan lines. There has always been a modest relationship between partisanship and trust in government (Keele 2005). Scholars have long observed that self-identified Republicans trust government more when a Republican rather than a Democratic president occupies the White House. The reverse pattern occurs for self-identified Democrats. But these differences have increased dramatically of late. In fact, it is not rare for fewer than 15 percent of out-party partisans to express that they trust the government in Washington to do what is right "most of the time." Our analysis not only demonstrates a marked increase in the polarization of political trust but also identifies when that polarization began to accelerate: the early 2000s. By 2010, we observed in chapter 4, trust had become more polarized along partisan and ideological lines than ever before.

On the Sources of Political Trust

Why do so few Americans trust government, and why has trust become so polarized? The analyses in this book help to answer these questions by providing new insights into the sources of political trust. In chapter 3, we showed that trust levels are, in part, a function of partisan polarization. Simply put, polarization depresses trust. This makes sense because polarization makes contentious partisan processes even more intense and ugly, which drives down trust (Hibbing and Theiss-Morse 1995). Polarization also undermines congressional productivity (Binder 2003, 2014), which ought to cause people to believe that government is performing poorly. Such perceptions also lower trust.

In addition, the results in chapter 3 demonstrated that trust levels vary with public attention to certain issues. When the mass public is focused on international concerns, political trust tends to rise. Since the days of "duck and cover" in the early 1960s, the public has seldom focused as long and intensely on international concerns, which has depressed contemporary trust levels. The importance of salience also resonates in our results from chapter 9. Here we showed that the amount of trust that people express depends on the part of government they are evaluating. People like certain parts of government a lot more than others. Interestingly, we find that individuals tend to trust all the specific government agencies we asked about more than the government considered as a whole.

One implication of these findings is that political elites can influence both the levels and the consequences of political trust by strategically drawing public attention to particular issues or particular parts of government. During the course of a campaign or a policy debate, strategic priming by competing partisan elites has the potential to lead members of different parties to base their trust judgments on very different sets of information. This, in turn, creates the potential for political trust to polarize along partisan lines.

Indeed, this is just what we found in chapter 4. Partisans update their trust judgments by relying on different pieces of information, and their choices about what pieces of information to weight heavily when updating their trust judgments are not random. Partisans have a propensity to update their trust judgments using the informational criteria most beneficial to their political allies and most harmful to their opponents. Such bias in information processing has made it increasingly difficult to raise levels of political trust among out-of-government partisans.

On the Consequences of Political Trust

Chapters 5–8 demonstrate the consequences of these lower and more polarized trust levels. Our experimental analysis in chapter 5 showed that manipulating individuals' issue attention can prime them to think about trust-policy linkages in a range of different ways. This means that trust might have a much wider range of effects than scholars have previously thought. In chapter 6, we replicate this finding from the lab using nationally representative survey data, comparing opinions in the pre- and post-9/11 worlds.

As we observed in chapters 7 and 8, political trust played a substantial role in shaping public support for health care reform and economic stimulus during the Obama years. In the context of health care reform, trusting individuals were more likely to support government-sponsored health care reform. Importantly, though, the effects of trust were moderated by three factors. First, the effects of trust were moderated by perceptions of material sacrifice. Among people who believed that health care reform would have a negative financial impact on their family, political trust was a more powerful determinant of support for reform. Second, the effects of trust were moderated by ideology. Trust was a critical determinant of support among conservatives but not among liberals, as only the former needed to sacrifice ideological principles in order to support reform. Finally, the effects of trust were moderated by level of government involvement. Trust had its greatest impact on support for policies that entailed the greatest amount of direct government involvement. Collectively, our results suggest that had political trust not been so low and so polarized, public opinion may have enabled the government to enact a much more sweeping and comprehensive form of health care reform than it did. Put differently, a climate of political distrust may have constrained the policy options that were available to lawmakers during the debate over health care reform. Given the herculean legislative maneuvering (i.e., reconciliation) that was needed to ultimately pass the Affordable Care Act, it would seem that a climate of political distrust may also limit the procedural options that are available to lawmakers.

In the economic realm, we observed a strong relationship between political trust and public attitudes toward some—but not all—forms of economic stimulus. In the wake of the Great Recession (2008–9), people who trusted government were much more likely to support traditional Keynesian approaches to stimulating the economy, such as running deficits and increasing government spending, than were those who distrusted government. Support for stimulating the economy through tax cuts, by contrast, was unaffected by levels of political trust. Moreover, the effects of trust on support for running deficits and increasing spending were moderated by ideology. Among conservatives, political trust was essential to bolster support for Keynesian forms of stimulus. Our simulations indicate that trusting conservatives would have supported running deficits and increasing government spending. Had political trust been a little higher, particularly among conservatives, our results suggest that both the size of Obama's economic stimulus plan and its balance between spending increases and tax cuts would likely have been substantially different.

The policy implications of these findings are significant. First, our findings suggest that political trust is a critical resource that helps build and sustain public support for government action under conditions of risk. In the case of both health care reform and economic stimulus, trusting citizens are the ones who are most likely to endorse government action. Second, given the nature of the interaction between political trust and ideology, political trust is an important tool that can help bridge ideological differences and forge policy consensus. As we observed with public attitudes toward health care reform in chapter 8, public trust in government has the potential to attenuate ideologically based differences in policy support between liberals and conservatives. Ideologues who trust government are the people who are most willing to sacrifice their own ideological preferences for the sake of consensus. Without such trust, ideological sacrifices are less likely to be made, and policy consensus is less likely to be achieved. Finally, our findings suggest that low-trust environments are particularly challenging to those who favor liberal or progressive approaches to public policy. Democrats, for example, are typically more likely than Republicans to propose initiatives that use government as a vehicle to achieve their social and economic goals. The nature of the link between political trust and support for government action under conditions of risk places Democratic initiatives at a competitive disadvantage when political trust is low but offers a competitive advantage when political trust is high.

During prolonged periods of political distrust, it can be exceedingly difficult for Democrats to build public support for their policy initiatives. From this perspective, low levels of political trust would seem to benefit Republicans. Indeed, Republican candidates have sometimes been known to actively promote distrust of the federal government. Yet, on occasion, Republicans do wish to use government as a vehicle for social and economic change. During George W. Bush's presidency, for example, Republicans sought to use government as an agent of change in the case of the Bush tax cuts and the case of Social Security privatization. In both instances, researchers have found, political trust was positively associated with support for tax cutting and privatizing Social Security (Rudolph 2009; Rudolph and Popp 2009). Although political trust may be understood as a resource that generally benefits support for liberal policy initiatives, its potential to buoy support for conservative initiatives should not be overlooked.

Other Alternatives?

Our results from chapter 9 provide us with some hope; evaluations of the specific parts of government are much better and less polarized than are evaluations of the government as a whole. However, we are concerned that such evaluations of specific agencies would not remain less polarized for long. Once the battleground about the government's involvement in Americans' lives shifted from being about the government as a whole to, say, the Department of Health and Human Services, we suspect that evaluations of the specific departments and agencies would come to look a lot like those for trust in the federal government. Worse, the results in chapter 9 are even less satisfying from the perspective of trying to increase trust and shrink polarization. Although we find that we can increase trust by reminding people of government successes, increases are greatest among those who identify with the president's party. That does not increase the pool of Americans prepared to make ideological sacrifices. Providing out-party partisans with information that might make government more attractive does little to increase their trust or reduce the polarized trust environment. Instead, out-party partisans seem particularly susceptible to negative information about government, more readily lowering their trust scores in response to it than in-party partisans do.

Perhaps what is required is a partisan stepping out of line with the usual approach taken by his or her party to provide a cue to partisans in the electorate that they ought to follow a different course. Could something similar to Nixon going to China provide an effective cue in this polarized environment to signal to fellow partisans that the old party orthodoxy needs to be changed? Recall that when staunch anticommunist Richard Nixon opened relations to China and initiated a policy of détente with the Soviet Union, he sent a message to anticommunist Republicans and conservatives that a change in approach might be warranted. Enough of them changed positions when Nixon took an unexpected position on an issue to produce a new policy direction (Cukierman and Tommasi 1998).

Unfortunately, the scholarly literature suggests that today's more polarized political environment relative to Nixon's day might short-circuit this "strange bedfellows" approach. In fact, Nicholson (2012) finds that when a partisan politician is involved in giving cues to the public, it might make the opinion environment even worse. Specifically, he found that when he cued people with information that George W. Bush had a position on immigration reform that was the opposite of his party's, it did not attract many Republicans to be more proimmigration reform. Instead, it motivated more Democrats to be anti-immigration reform, producing less, not more, overall support. This was not just a George Bush phenomenon either. Nicholson found the same pattern of results when politicians like Barack Obama and John McCain were presented as the cue givers. When he attributed positions to them that were the opposite of their party's orthodoxy, it did not attract too many of their copartisans. Instead, it repelled a lot of partisans of the other stripe.

It appears, then, that Nixon can no longer go to China. But partisans are not the only political actors who might take surprising positions on an issue that might, in turn, affect the opinions of ordinary people. In fact, seemingly nonpartisan actors might have more success because they would not cue up the remarkably negative feelings that partisans have about the other party, which is probably the source of the boomerang effect that Nicholson finds in his studies. But what actors, if not politicians, might be involved in these strange bedfellows relationships? The scholarly literature on cue taking suggests that effective cue givers need two characteristics: trustworthiness and expertise (Lupia and McCubbins

1998). We have found throughout the book that out-party partisans do not trust the government, further suggesting why low trust undermines support for government involvement in programs. But out-party partisans do trust other institutions. For instance, pretty much everyone, but especially conservatives, trusts the US military these days. What if it endorsed a "surprising" policy course? Would it attract more supporters?

In particular, our strange bedfellows theory suggests that the military might be effective in narrowing polarization on efforts to combat climate change. Not only is the military trusted by most Americans, but it is also working to develop expertise in climate change mitigation (see, for example, CNA Military Advisory Board 2007, 2014; Pumphrey 2008; US Navy 2010). Research suggests that such steps are in the military's best interest. More conflicts happen in warm years than cool ones (Hsiang, Meng, and Cane 2011), suggesting that the warming of the Earth might make the US military busier than it wishes. Moreover, many of the least stable places in the world, particularly in the Middle East and West Africa, are particularly vulnerable to the effects of climate change. As a result, the military has a flourishing alternative energy program (McMichael 2007; Broder 2009). Since the US military is also one of the world's most notorious polluters, it would probably be surprising to most Americans that the military cares about climate change. What if they knew?

Hetherington and Kam (n.d.) provide evidence that it might matter a lot. When they told people of the military's involvement in climate change mitigation, public support for a fictional $2 billion program to develop new technologies to combat climate change increased by 20 percentage points compared with when people were told the "federal government" was involved. The increases were, not surprisingly, almost completely driven by changing preferences among self-identified conservatives and Republicans, two groups who like and trust the military a great deal but also dislike and distrust the federal government a lot.

Perhaps other strange bedfellows could be similarly effective. To use another example involving the climate, many environmental groups believe that nuclear power is central to the mix of energy sources required to make carbon-based fuels less important. Given that Americans connect environmentalists with liberal causes but are more likely to think about nuclear power with past liberal objections in mind, this position would likely qualify as surprising. What if liberals actually knew of this shift in the thinking of environmental groups, groups that they tend to esteem? We suspect it would increase support a lot among those who would otherwise be most resistant to nuclear power. Although conservatives do not like environmentalists very much, they already like nuclear power. Just as liberals would not turn against climate change mitigation if the military were involved, we suspect that conservatives would not be repelled by environmentalists endorsing nuclear power. In both cases, the key groups already believe in the policies.

Although we cannot be sure such approaches would work, our research certainly suggests that anything involving the "government in Washington" is poison. And anything connected to a partisan politician is fast becoming poison to partisans of the other stripe. It is not that partisans love their own side's ideas. Instead, the key to understanding politics today is realizing how deeply partisans dislike and distrust their opponents. This is why consensus on issues of policy no longer develops in the public opinion. As a consequence, the public does little to encourage polarized politicians to rise above their basest and most partisan instincts. Public opinion did not create the polarization that has caused Washington to grind to a halt, but it does reinforce it. Unless something changes or new approaches to building policy consensus are adopted, we suspect that more hyper-partisanship in Washington will be in the offing, while the public mostly continues to sit by idly.

As for what this means for the future, it might be useful to consider what things were like in the late nineteenth century, the last time that measure of congressional voting approached those of today (Brady and Han 2006). Then as now, government did not produce much. Indicative of that, presidents of the era (Rutherford B. Hayes, James A. Garfield, Chester Arthur, Benjamin Harrison) are remembered more for their prodigious facial hair than their political accomplishments. A return to that past would not seem to be good news for the republic.

It is worth noting, however, that the late 1800s style of politics did not last forever. Instead, the 1896 election ushered in a new and more productive politics. After the 1901 assassination of William McKinley, one of the fixtures on Mount Rushmore, Theodore Roosevelt (TR), took the reins of government. TR's legend emphasizes his personal style and unmistakable charisma in getting what he wanted. Fewer than thirty years later, Franklin Delano Roosevelt (FDR) also established himself as one of the presidents whom historians usually identify as all-time greats. He, too, is well remembered for his political acumen in crafting and passing the New Deal legislative initiatives to cope with the Great Depression. Perhaps, then, all it takes to make Washington work is decisive and charismatic leadership to unify a fractured political system. Contemporary journalists on the White House and Capitol Hill beats suggest this all the time.

We are dubious that political skills alone are the key to overcoming polarization. Although Teddy Roosevelt bucked his own party's leaders at times, much of his success as president owed at least as much to his party's enormous congressional majorities (e.g., 250 to 136 in the House and 55 to 33 in the Senate after his election in 1904) as to his charisma. FDR's party enjoyed even more lopsided majorities than TR's had. After the 1932 election, the Democratic majority in the House was 313 to 117 seats and 59 to 36 in the Senate, majorities that would grow through the 1936 election and peak at a dumbfounding 334 to 88 advantage in the House and a 76 to 16 advantage in the Senate. Little wonder both administrations accomplished so much even though legitimate ideological differences existed between the parties. There simply were not enough minority party members to stand in the way.

Giant majorities that allow leaders to overcome partisan disagreements do not emerge from nowhere. Both these great presidencies—indeed, almost all the great presidencies—were presaged by economic calamity under the stewardship of the opposite party. This was true of Grover Cleveland and the Democrats' troubles with the Depression of 1894, as well as Herbert Hoover and the Republicans' troubles with the Stock Market Crash of 1929. Sometimes a different type of cataclysmic event, as was the case with the Civil War, can have the same effect. Perhaps circumstances at some point in the future will produce similarly large majorities for one party, and concerns about polarization will abate. It has happened regularly over the course of American history.

Yet neither 9/11 nor the Great Recession produced an enduring electoral tide.[5] If fundamental political change does not grow out of crises of this magnitude, then perhaps something has changed about our politics that prevents it. If that is true, elected leaders will continue to do what they are doing, with public opinion perhaps the only force that might be able to nudge parties in Washington together. We have shown, however, that because political trust has polarized, public opinion will not play that role. A lack of trust from out-party partisans causes them to think that all the majority party's ideas that become points of contestation are unworthy of support. This, in turn, allows out-party political leaders to place their short-term gains above the health of the country without risk of reprisal from their reelection constituency. And the beat goes on.

Notes

Chapter One

1. For a full account of the sequestration, see http://whitehouse.gov/omb/legislative_reports/sequestration.

2. For more information on the economic impact of the government shutdown, see http://money.cnn.com/2013/10/16/news/economy/shutdown-economic-impact.

3. The press release titled "Congressional Job Approval Stays Near Historical Low" from the Gallup Organization that contains these results can be accessed at http://www.gallup.com/poll/174806/congressional-job-approval-stays-near-historical-low.aspx.

4. It makes perfect sense that polarization in the electorate does not manifest itself in policy preferences or ideology. Decades of research suggest that most ordinary Americans do not tend to hold their policy preferences strongly (Converse 1964) and are "innocent of ideology," to borrow Herbert McClosky's (1964) wonderful turn of phrase. Looking for polarization in Americans' policy preferences or their ideological predispositions is almost certain not to turn up much (but see Abramowitz 2010 on health care).

5. See the article from the *New York Times* on the subject at http://www.nytimes.com/2009/09/04/us/04school.html.

6. The video can be viewed at http://www.cnn.com/2009/POLITICS/09/04/obama.schools/#cnnSTCVideo.

7. Including schools attended by the two children of one of the authors of this volume.

8. According to Politifact.com, some elected leaders did criticize Bush's effort to talk directly to students. But there was no wholesale movement not to show the address to students or to allow them to stay home from school that day as there was in 2009.

9. Of course, this doesn't happen all the time. Despite public consensus in favor of more gun control after a school shooting at Sandy Hook Elementary School in

Newtown, Connecticut, in late 2012, Republicans in Congress successfully quashed legislative gun control efforts. This is the exception, not the rule, however.

10. David Easton (1965) originally used the turn of phrase "reservoir of support." He had in mind support that leaders could draw on during bad times, so governments would not routinely collapse. Our take is slightly different. American democracy is strong enough that even a run of bad times should not cause institutional arrangements to collapse. Trust, instead, is important to facilitate cooperation across the political aisle.

11. We use ANES data for all presidents except for Obama because only one ANES survey has asked the trust-in-government question during his presidency to date; hence we take the average score of all media polls taken during his administration.

Chapter Two

1. See "Less than Half of Americans are Baseball Fans" at http://www.gallup.com/poll/102343/less-than-half-americans-baseball-fans.aspx.

2. See "The Ten Most Polarizing Foods" at http://www.huffingtonpost.com/2012/01/20/polarizing-foods_n_1216832.html.

3. Goldwater famously said at the 1964 Republican National Convention, "Extremism in the pursuit of liberty is no vice. And moderation in the pursuit of justice is no virtue" (Goldwater 1964). Voters liked this approach so much that Lyndon Johnson, Goldwater's opponent, won more than 61 percent of the vote, the highest percentage since James Monroe's victory in 1820.

4. Indeed, we suspect this increased tendency to express more constrained political views is *because* partisans today now have stronger affect about political actors. It seems unlikely to us that people changing their positions on these issues would cause them to have stronger feelings, given that they are probably changing their positions on issues that they do not care much about.

5. Although not depicted here graphically, the same pattern holds for the Senate. Indeed, with Republican and Democratic political elites pulling apart ideologically at this breathtaking pace, it has created the most polarized Congress since the early twentieth Century (McCarty, Poole, and Rosenthal 2006).

6. This was an observation made by several present and former members of Congress, including David Price, Mickey Andrews, and Tom Cole, at a conference on polarization held at Princeton University in 2004.

7. That was not always the case. For decades between the 1950s and the early 1990s, the minority party (House Republicans at the time) had so few seats that they had no hope of winning a majority. As a result, moderation and cooperation ruled the day. To get anything out of the legislative process, congressional Republicans had to negotiate with congressional Democrats.

8. This reference is a paraphrase of something Bob Luskin used to say about graduate students at the University of Michigan. We wish we could be similarly clever.

9. Thanks to Jason Reifler for making these data from his data collection available to us.

10. These 2010 scores may seem a little too low to be believed by a critical reader, and we share this concern. The 2012 ANES gives us some indication of how far off they might be. That year, the ANES conducted both its traditional face-to-face survey and an Internet-based survey like the one done by YouGov in 2011. In the face-to-face surveys, the average thermometer score that Republicans gave the Democrats was twenty-eight degrees, and the average score that Democrats gave the Republicans was thirty-one degrees. In both cases, these scores were about five degrees warmer than those found in the ANES's online surveys that were conducted at the exact same time. Even so, if we add five degrees to the average feeling thermometer scores we found in 2011, feelings that partisans had about the other party were still only around twenty-three degrees, by far the lowest reading since the questions debuted in 1978.

11. A semantic distinction is whether what we have presented here amounts to evidence of "polarization" or "partisan polarization." In this case, the distinction is immaterial. What we have presented in figure 4.2 amounts to what Fiorina et al. (2005) dubbed partisan polarization because we exclude pure independents from the analysis. We made this decision because our story is about how people perceive the other party, which requires them to have chosen a side themselves. Including the roughly 10 percent of respondents who are pure independents reveals evidence of what Fiorina et al. (2005) call polarization, too. This involves an entire population moving toward the poles. If we analyze all respondents, we find that the standard deviation for the Democratic Party and Republican Party thermometers has increased by 46 and 41 percent, respectively, between the first time the ANES asked these questions in 1978 and 2012.

12. This phrase is from Hebrews 11:1.

13. Some more recent research suggests that the opinions of the well off carry much more weight than the opinions of the middle class, with the opinions of the least well off carrying no weight at all with policy makers (see Gilens 2012; Gilens and Page 2014). In other words, when the opinions of the well off and the middle class differ, office holders tend to listen to the former at the expense of the latter. Although this argument makes good sense to us, it is beyond the scope of our inquiry to engage in the context of our thinking. What we can say, however, is the fact that consensus emerges less often in contemporary politics than it did before suggests that the well off will tend to get their way over the middle class with more frequency now than in years past.

Chapter Three

1. One caveat here: the present set of circumstances certainly increases the *negative* power of public opinion. Office holders can use public opinion to justify *blocking* action on policy matters, which suggests public opinion is powerful—just not in the way scholars have usually considered.

2. In addition to reflecting the public's concerns about process, congressional approval may also reflect public sentiment about government performance or scandal.

3. The most telling anecdote about the depth of Sax's fielding problems comes from a conversation between former Dodgers manager Tommy Lasorda and his struggling third baseman, Pedro Guerrero, in 1984. When Lasorda asked Guerrero what he could possibly be thinking when he was playing in the field, Guerrero said the following, "I'm only thinking about two things. First, I hope they don't hit the ball to me. Second, I hope they don't hit the ball to Sax" (qtd. in Garagiola 1988).

4. In the empirical analyses to follow, we assume that agenda setting has taken place and is manifested through the public's judgments concerning the national importance of particular issues. Our theory does not require that we posit a single source of agenda-setting effects. What is central to our theory is the proposition that these national importance judgments, once formed, are politically consequential and will shape political trust.

5. Our theory squares nicely with variation in individual-level findings. Specifically, Hetherington (1998) finds that retrospective economic evaluations had a significant effect on political trust in 1988 when the economy was fair but had no effect in 1996 when the economy was very good. Similarly, Citrin and Green (1986) find that these same economic perceptions had a significant effect on political trust in 1980 and 1982 when the economy was poor, but they had no effect in 1984 when the economy was again very good.

6. We examined all Gallup polls taken in 2004 that asked respondents whether they approved or disapproved of President Bush in multiple areas.

7. The link between public concern about international issues and political trust is not simply an aggregate-level phenomenon. In the 2004 ANES, for example, those who identified an international problem as most important expressed 50 percent more trust in government (mean = 0.37) than those who identified another issue (mean = 0.24).

8. Robert Hetherington, Scott's press secretary at the time, related this story to one of the authors.

9. Technical details concerning the "dyad ratios" algorithm are reported in appendix I of Stimson (1999). Initially designed to create a measure of policy mood, Stimson's method, which is publicly available on his website, has since been used to create a variety of time-series measures, including congressional approval (Durr,

Gilmour, and Wolbrecht 1997), political trust (Chanley, Rudolph, and Rahn 2000), public support for the Supreme Court (Durr, Martin, and Wolbrecht 2000), and racial policy preferences (Kellstedt 2000).

10. A potential criticism of the "most important problem" questions is that they may not faithfully reflect what is actually the most important problem facing the nation at any given point in time. For our purposes, however, these questions are particularly appropriate because they capture what the public perceives to be the most important problem. While these questions are certainly not without limitations as indicators of national importance judgments (Wlezien 2005), they are clearly the best available indicator over time.

11. At the individual level, Hibbing and Theiss-Morse (1995) also show a strong relationship between specific measures of process and congressional approval.

12. We accomplish this by separately regressing each approval series on consumer sentiment and saving the residuals.

13. Specifically, we use ordinary least squares to estimate a distributed lag model with a Koyck transformation. The underlying model is an infinite lag model with an exponential rate of decay, $Y_t = \alpha + \beta_0 X_t + \beta_0 \lambda X_{t-1} + \beta_0 \lambda^2 X_{t-2} \ldots + \varepsilon_t$. This means that more recent lagged values exert more influence than more distant lagged values. After the Koyck transformation, the effects of the lagged explanatory variables are expressed through the lagged dependent variable at a rate determined by the autoregressive parameter on lagged trust, λ. The direct effect of a one-unit change in X_t is simply β_0. The cumulative effect of a one-unit change in X_t is equal to $\beta_0/(1 - \lambda)$. The errors are assumed to be generated by an autoregressive process such that $\varepsilon_t = \lambda \varepsilon_{t-1} + u_t$ where $u_t \sim IID(0,\sigma^2)$. After the Koyck transformation, the model can be expressed as $Y_t = \alpha + \lambda Y_{t-1} + \beta_0 X_t + u_t$ where $u_t \sim IID(0,\sigma^2)$. Since our diagnostic tests reveal no serial correlation in the transformed model, OLS is consistent and efficient (Beck 1992; Pindyck and Rubinfeld 1998).

14. To increase confidence in causal inferences, we also performed a series of Granger causality tests. In a time-series setting, x is said to Granger cause y if lagged values of x help to predict y, even after controlling for lagged values of Y. One of our central claims is that polarization erodes political trust. This thesis implies two causal propositions. First, it implies that polarization has a causal effect on trust. Second, it implies that trust does not have a reciprocal causal effect on polarization. We test both propositions using Granger causality tests. We find strong evidence that polarization Granger causes political trust ($\chi^2 = 5.75$, $p < 0.02$). But we find no evidence that political trust has any reciprocal causal effect on polarization ($\chi^2 = 2.43$, $p > 0.10$).

15. A one-unit change is defined here as moving a variable from its minimum to its maximum value.

16. Recall that the cumulative effect of a variable depends on the expression, $\beta_0/(1 - \lambda)$, where λ is the coefficient for lagged trust. Since the effects of explanatory

variables persist over time at a rate determined by λ, the cumulative effect of a shock to congressional approval on political trust is 28.1 percent ($0.166/1 − 0.41 = 0.281$).

17. Using the formula from above, the calculation is ($0.084/1 − 0.38 = 0.081$).

Chapter Four

1. To be conservative, we use the adjusted mean score from 2011, which was gathered as part of an Internet poll. Recall from chapter 2 that the average scores for both Republicans and Democrats about the other party was eighteen degrees. However, when the ANES in 2012 asked both an Internet-based sample and their traditional face-to-face sample the same questions, they found the average score that partisans gave the other party was about five degrees warmer in the face-to-face sample than in the Internet sample. Hence, we add five degrees to the means found in the YouGov poll.

2. The questions were worded the following way: (1) "How much of the time do you think you can trust the government in Washington to do what is right: just about always, most of the time, or only some of time?" (2) "Would you say the government is pretty much run by a few big interests looking out for themselves or that it is run for the benefit of all the people?" (3) "Do you think that people in the government waste a lot of money we pay in taxes, waste some of it, or don't waste very much of it?" (4) "Do you think that quite a few of the people running the government are crooked, not very many are, or do you think hardly any of them are crooked?"

3. We use the four-item trust in government battery, since we have all four items available in all three waves of the panel.

4. This is an important point. Pundits and journalists often talk about the sky-rocketing percentage of Americans who call themselves independents. Indeed, this percentage moved above 40 percent in 2012. However, more than three-quarters of these supposed independents say that they actually lean toward one party or the other. Political science research demonstrates that these "partisan leaners" behave just like partisans do. They seem to want to call themselves independent from the parties because it sounds good. The percentage of people whom we exclude from this analysis, then, is about 10 percent of the whole sample, and these are by far the least participatory and politically engaged Americans.

5. Finally, it is also noteworthy that Republican women were significantly more likely to increase their trust levels than men, perhaps reflecting the concerns of so-called security moms after 9/11.

6. Oddly, it did ask nonpanel respondents these questions.

7. Our model also suggests that women Democrats and older Democrats were more likely to increase trust than men and younger Democrats.

8. Among other variables in the model, congressional approval and presidential approval also exerted significant effects. The more Republicans approved of

these Republican-led institutions, the more they tended to trust government. Interestingly, being a woman again had a statistically significant effect, but in the opposite direction this time, with Republican women's trust more likely than men's trust to drop during the period. Hence, any trust gains among Republican women between 2000 and 2002 were undone by a drop in trust among Republican women between 2002 and 2004.

9. The ANES did, in fact, carry out a panel survey during the time frame, but it did not include any of its trust in government items.

10. It is also possible that we are beating a dead horse in doing yet another test of the hypothesis.

Chapter Five

1. That is, unless generational replacement moves more like a Formula One race car than a steamship.

2. This result surprised us more than a little. In nationally representative samples, we catalogued in earlier chapters a tendency to express more trust when thinking about the foreign policy domain in particular. Our time-series model in chapter 3 confirms this result. We can think of at least a couple reasons for the null result. First, and most likely, the sample in this experiment is college students. This group almost certainly has relatively cooler feelings toward the military and foreign policy establishment than the population as a whole and more positive feelings toward the parts of government that might provide them health care and protect the environment. The other possibility is the foreign policy stimulus makes references to an external threat that the students did not express much enthusiasm for combatting. Regardless, we do not believe the pattern of results has any serious implications for the part of the experiment that follows—namely, testing whether the *effects* of political trust differ depending on salience.

Chapter Six

1. To tap this concept, we use the people's assessment of the importance of defense spending. More ideal would be how much threat people perceived from terrorism to tap differing reactions to the same context that all Americans were living in at the time (Berinsky 2009). Unfortunately, this variable is only available in the ANES panel.

2. To buttress these results, we also estimated simultaneous equation models for all six dependent variables in the 2004 ANES cross-section and political trust. These results also strongly support the causal flow we hypothesize.

3. Different levels of measurement among the dependent variables require different estimation techniques. The items about whether Iraq and Afghan wars

were worth the cost are dichotomous, so we use logistic regression. Preferences for spending on the war on terrorism, whether the war in Iraq reduced the threat of terrorism, and support for a strong military are measured on three- and four-point ordinal scales, so we use ordered probit. Support for defense spending is on a seven-point scale, which approximates an interval scale. Hence, we use ordinary least squares.

4. The other right-hand-side variables perform as expected. Party identification always plays an important role. Education has a consistently negative effect. In four of the six models, women are less hawkish than men. Those who score higher in patriotism, moral traditionalism, and those who identify defense spending as important are generally more hawkish. Although ideological self-placement and authoritarianism only achieve statistical significance once, both consistently carry the correct sign. Finally, race, age, and region are rarely statistically significant.

5. Specifically, we simulate a non–African American male who is from the South and is at the sample mean on all other characteristics.

6. When we replicate the models estimated by Hetherington and Globetti (2002) using 2004 data, the effect of political trust is statistically insignificant for both African Americans and non–African Americans.

7. Although there are several ways to measure salience, mentions by the mass media offer the best alternative. Niemi and Bartels (1985) identify the pitfalls of salience measures endogenous to the survey instrument, most notably that the survey itself makes certain issues salient (see also Rabinowitz, Prothro, and Jacoby 1982). This makes MIP questions particularly unattractive. Furthermore, issues can be salient to people without being identified as "most important." In contrast, more media coverage of an issue increases the probability that the issue provides an accessible consideration for people evaluating the political world around them, which matches our theory as it relates to issue salience and political trust.

8. If we drop authoritarianism from the 2004 cross-sectional models, it has no substantive impact on the effect of political trust, suggesting that its exclusion from the over-time model ought to make little difference to the results presented below.

9. Since we have an aggregate-level measure (salience) along with a set of individual-level characteristics, some might advocate for a multilevel model. The nature of our data suggests otherwise. Since multilevel models possess only attractive large-sample properties, the most commonly applied rule of thumb suggests the need for a minimum of thirty observations on both the aggregate and individual levels. With models that include cross-level interactions like ours, the minimum grows to fifty (Hox 1998). We follow the dominant strain in the literature in using ordinary least squares with clustered standard errors.

10. This result is not driven by the fact that Republican administrations make defense more salient. When we include an interaction between trust and the presence of a Republican presidential administration, it fails to approach significance, while the interaction between trust and salience remains significant.

11. As a check on our original data collection, we replicated the analysis below using PAP data, employing the following codes for race salience: social welfare, civil rights, community development and housing, and crime. The results follow the same pattern with the key interaction positive and significant. Since the PAP data return such a relatively small percentage of race cases, we favor our original content analysis.

12. We read a sample of articles returned by these counts, finding that they closely reflected the politics of each issue domain. The correlation between the content analysis we carried out for defense and the one from the PAP was 0.8. If we substitute the defense salience measure from our content analysis for the one using the PAP, the results follow the same pattern.

13. The specific question wording is as follows: "Some people feel that the government in Washington should make every possible effort to improve the social and economic position of blacks. . . . Others feel that the government should not make any special effort to help blacks because they should help themselves. Where would you place yourself on this scale, or haven't you thought much about it?"

14. If we estimate a separate model for African American respondents, the effect of trust is, as expected, never significant. We estimated the models separately by race to avoid the need for a three-way interaction, which streamlines interpretation.

Chapter Seven

1. These data come from the Pew Charitable Trusts article "The Impact of the September 2008 Financial Collapse," which can be accessed at http://www.pewtrusts.org/en/research-and-analysis/reports/2010/04/28/the-impact-of-the-september-2008-economic-collapse.

2. The shift also reflected how poorly McCain responded to the crisis. The Lehman collapse occurred just days before the first presidential debate was scheduled to occur. Echoing the sense of panic that was gripping policy makers at the time, McCain suggested postponing the debate and convening a meeting in Washington about the crisis. Political commentators and voters alike thought this was a silly idea. Ultimately, McCain was forced to participate in the debate. After Obama's strong showing, he widened his lead and never relinquished it.

3. The remaining 18 percent of the American Recovery and Reinvestment Act of 2009 was devoted to state and local fiscal relief.

4. Similarly, a Gallup/USA Today poll taken around the same time asked, "Regardless of whether you favor or oppose the economic stimulus bill that Congress passed, do you think it would have been better for the government to spend more money to stimulate the economy, better for the government to spend less money, or is the amount of spending in the bill about right?" The modal response was to spend less (Saad 2009).

5. Thanks to Larry Bartels for allowing us space on his part of the 2012 CCAP survey.

6. It also points to just how successful conservatives have been since the Reagan presidency in making Americans believe that they can have tax cuts without bearing any cost. As it relates to political trust's effect on tax cuts, it further suggests that trust will not be important. Many conservatives clearly do not perceive the need to make an ideological sacrifice—namely, allowing a budget deficit—to support tax cuts as stimulus.

7. Of course, the analysis we perform here and below is based on 2012 data. Unfortunately, we know of no data collected in early 2009 that included both economic stimulus items and a political trust item. Indeed, the only political trust item asked in the first months of 2009 was the Kaiser Health tracking poll we use in chapter 8. Trust was, indeed, relatively low and already deeply polarized even though President Obama had only assumed office four months before. Specifically, the percentage of trusting Americans was 32 percent, with 42 percent of liberals expressing trust and only 23 percent of conservatives. With trust so low among conservatives, the potential for ideological sacrifice was low, and hence, the chances of building consensus were very low.

8. Specifically, about 30 percent of Democrats fell into the two trusting categories, whereas only 9 percent of Republicans did.

9. Specifically, we fix the values of the other variables in the model as follows: a white, male independent who is an ideological moderate who thinks his personal financial situation is about the same as the year before and who thinks the economy is going to remain about the same. Most of these are modal categories in the data.

10. It is also worth noting that trust's effect is very large relative to other variables. If we fix trust at its mode (only some of the time) and leave the other variables as we did before, just allowing each of them to vary across their respective ranges one by one, we can compare trust's effect across its range with the effect of the other variables across their respective ranges. Our model suggests that the effect of being African American relative to being white is about 10 percentage points, a third of the size of trust's effect. The effect of being a woman relative to being a man is even smaller, about 6 percentage points. Moving from being an independent to being a Democrat increases the predicted probability of supporting deficit spending by a healthy 15 percentage points and moving from being an independent to being a Republican reduces the probability by about 10 percentage points. Combining the two party effects, the total effect of party identification—moving from being a Republican to being a Democrat—changes the predicted probability of supporting deficit spending by about 25 percentage points. While this effect is quite large, it is not as large as the effect of political trust across its range.

11. As preliminary evidence, only 4 percent of conservatives who distrusted government supported spending increases. Among the small handful of politically

trusting conservatives that existed in 2012, however, support was 50 percent. In other words, trust increased support among conservatives by 46 percentage points, without taking other potential causes into account. In contrast, trust apparently had little to do with liberals' preferences. Among distrusting liberals, 68 percent supported deficit spending. Among trusting liberals, a very similar 73 percent did.

12. As a reminder, we simulate the opinion of a white, male, independent, college graduate whose personal financial and national economic assessments are in the middle.

13. Of course, we have fixed at one a willingness to run budget deficits during hard times, which is why these probabilities are relatively high in general.

Chapter Eight

1. The study "What Americans Learned From the Media about the Health Care Debate" can be found at http://www.journalism.org/2012/06/19/how-media -has-covered-health-care-debate.

2. The dates and sample sizes for these twelve surveys are as follows: February 3–12, 2009 ($N = 1,204$), April 2–8, 2009 ($N = 1,203$), June 1–8, 2009 ($N = 1,205$), July 7–14 ($N = 1,205$), August 4–11, 2009 ($N = 1,203$), September 11–18, 2009 ($N = 1,203$), October 8–15, 2009 ($N = 1,200$), November 5–12, 2009 ($N = 1,203$), December 7–13, 2009 ($N = 1,204$), January 7–12, 2010 ($N = 1,202$), February 11–16, 2010 ($N = 1,201$), March 10–18, 2010 ($N = 1,208$).

3. Similar results are obtained when using data from the June 2009 survey. The response rates for the April and June 2009 surveys were 23 percent and 24 percent, respectively.

Chapter Nine

1. Exposure to the influence message lowered trust by 0.50 points, a decrease of 16.3 percent (3.07 vs. 2.57, $t = 6.87$, $p < 0.01$). Exposure to the incompetency message lowered trust by 0.14 points, a decrease of 4.6 percent (3.05 vs. 2.91, $t = 2.52$, $p < 0.02$). Exposure to the inefficiency message lowered trust by 0.25 points, a decrease of 7.9 percent (3.16 vs. 2.91, $t = 3.14$, $p < 0.01$).

2. We chose these three entities because all carry a high profile, so most Americans should be aware of them. We also wanted to make sure one department would be more attractive to conservatives than to liberals, so we asked about the Department of Defense. The Department of Health and Human Services is particularly relevant these days with the passage of the Affordable Care Act, so it, too, seemed a natural fit. Finally, no agency seems to elicit more heat from our experience in Tennessee than the Environmental Protection Agency.

3. To calculate such probabilities, all explanatory variables must be fixed at a given value. For the results shown in figure 9.1, we treat the hypothetical respondent in these calculations as a nonblack female who identifies as an independent and a moderate. Unless otherwise specified in figure 9.1, each type of trust is fixed at its mean value.

Chapter Ten

1. See "What's in a Name? Affordable Care Act vs. Obamacare" at http://polling matters.gallup.com/2013/11/whats-in-name-affordable-care-act-vs.html.

2. See Hetherington and Rudolph's contribution to the *Washington Post's* Monkey Cage blog in January 2014 at http://www.washingtonpost.com/blogs/monkey -cage/wp/2014/01/30/why-dont-americans-trust-the-government-because-the -other-party-is-in-power.

3. For a transcript of Limbaugh's remarks, see http://www.rushlimbaugh.com /daily/2009/01/16/limbaugh_i_hope_obama_fails.

4. Indeed, Mitch McConnell inartfully said in 2009 that his number-one priority was to make Obama a one-term president.

5. Obama and the Democrats had sixty Senate votes for a short time in 2009 and accomplished much during that period, but Republicans won big in 2010, returning the House to near its pre-2006 balance.

References

Abramowitz, Alan. 2010. *The Disappearing Center: Engaged Citizens, Polarization, and American Democracy.* New Haven: Yale University Press.

———. 2012. *The Polarized Public: Why Our Government Is So Dysfunctional.* New York: Pearson Longman.

Abramowitz, Alan I., and Kyle L. Saunders. 2008. "Is Polarization a Myth?" *Journal of Politics* 70(2): 542–55.

Achen, Christopher H. 1975. "Mass Political Attitudes and the Survey Response." *American Political Science Review* 69(4): 1218–31.

Adams, Greg D. 1997. "Abortion: Evidence of Issue Evolution." *American Journal of Political Science* 41(3): 718–37.

Aldrich, John H. 1995. *Why Parties? The Origin and Transformation of Political Parties in America.* Chicago: University of Chicago Press.

Alford, John R. 2001. "We're All in This Together: The Decline of Trust in Government, 1958–1996." In *What Is It about Government That Americans Dislike?*, John R. Hibbing and Elizabeth Theiss-Morse, eds., 28–46. Cambridge: Cambridge University Press.

Almond, Gabriel. 1950. *The American People and Foreign Policy.* Orlando: Harcourt Brace.

Altemeyer, Robert. 1996. *The Authoritarian Specter.* Cambridge, MA: Harvard University Press.

American National Election Study. 2010. "Time Series Cumulative Data File." Stanford University and the University of Michigan.

Ansolabehere, Stephen, and Brian Schaffner. 2012. "CCES Common Content, 2012." http://hdl.handle.net/1902.1/21447.

Bafumi, Joseph, and Michael Herron. 2010. "Leapfrog Representation and Extremism: A Study of American Voters and Their Members of Congress." *American Political Science Review* 104(3): 519–42.

Baker, William D., and John R. Oneal. 2001. "Patriotism or Opinion Leadership? The Nature and Origins of the 'Rally Round the Flag' Effect." *Journal of Conflict Resolution* 45(5): 661–87.

Bargh, John A., Mark Chen, and Nalini Ambady. 1996. "Automaticity of Social Behavior: Direct Effects of Trait Construct and Stereotype Activation on Action." *Journal of Personality and Social Psychology* 71(2): 230–44.

Barnes, Robert. 2011. "Obama Administration Clears Path for Faster Supreme Court Decision on Health Care Law." *Washington Post*. September 26, 2011. http://www.washingtonpost.com/politics/obama-administration-clears-the-way-for-a-faster-supreme-court-decision-on-health-care-law/2011/09/26/gIQAzSg3zK_story.html.

Bartels, Larry M. 1994. "The American Public's Defense Spending Preferences in the Post-Cold War Era." *Public Opinion Quarterly* 58(4): 479–508.

———. 2002. "Beyond the Running Tally: Partisan Bias in Political Perceptions." *Political Behavior* 24(2): 117–50.

———. 2008. *Unequal Democracy: The Political Economy of the New Gilded Age.* Princeton, NJ: Princeton University Press.

Bayh, Evan. 2010. "Where Do Democrats Go Next?" *New York Times*, November 2, 2010.

Beck, Nathaniel. 1992. "Comparing Dynamic Specifications: The Case of Presidential Approval." *Political Analysis* 3: 27–50.

Behr, Roy L., and Shanto Iyengar. 1985. "Television News, Real-World Cues, and Changes in the Public Agenda." *Public Opinion Quarterly* 49(1): 38–57.

Bennett, W. Lance, and David L. Paltez. 1994. *Taken by Storm: The Media, Public Opinion, and U.S. Foreign Policy in the Gulf War.* Chicago: University of Chicago Press.

Berinsky, Adam J. 2009. *In Time of War: Understanding American Public Opinion from World War II to Iraq.* Chicago: University of Chicago Press.

Binder, Sarah A. 2003. *Stalemate: Causes and Consequences of Legislative Gridlock.* Washington, DC: Brookings.

———. 2014. "How Political Polarization Creates Stalemate and Undermines Lawmaking." *Washington Post*, January 13, 2014. http://www.washingtonpost.com/blogs/monkey-cage/wp/2014/01/13/how-political-polarization-creates-stalemate-and-undermines-lawmaking.

Bloom, Howard S., and H. Douglas Price. 1975. "Voter Response to Economic Conditions: The Asymmetric Effect of Prosperity and Recession." *American Political Science Review* 69(4): 1240–54.

Brady, David W., and Harie C. Han. 2006. "Polarization Then and Now: A Historical Perspective." In *Red and Blue Nation*, Pietro Nivola and David W. Brady, eds., 119–51. Baltimore: Brookings/Hoover.

Broder, John M. 2009. "Climate Change Seen as a Threat to U.S. Security." *New York Times*, August 8, 2009. http://www.nytimes.com/2009/08/09/science/earth/09climate.html?pagewanted=all.

Brody, Richard A. 1991. *Assessing the President: The Media, Elite Opinion, and Public Support.* Stanford: Stanford University Press.

Campbell, Angus, Philip E. Converse, Warren E. Miller, and Donald E. Stokes. 1960. *The American Voter*. New York: John Wiley and Sons.

Carmines, Edward G., and James A. Stimson. 1989. *Issue Evolution: Race and the Transformation of American Politics*. Princeton, NJ: Princeton University Press.

Carson, Jamie L., Gregory Koger, Matthew J. Lebo, and Everett Young. 2010. "The Electoral Costs of Party Loyalty in Congress." *American Journal of Political Science* 54(3): 598–616.

CBS News. 2008. "CBS Poll: Thoughts On Economy Grow Darker." CBS News, March 19, 2008. http://www.cbsnews.com/news/cbs-poll-thoughts-on-economy-grow-darker.

Chanley, Virginia A. 2002. "Trust in Government in the Aftermath of 9/11: Determinants and Consequences." *Political Psychology* 23(3): 469–83.

Chanley, Virginia A., Thomas J. Rudolph, and Wendy M. Rahn. 2000. "The Origins and Consequences of Public Trust in Government." *Public Opinion Quarterly* 64(3): 239–56.

Citrin, Jack. 1974. "Comment: The Political Relevance of Trust in Government." *American Political Science Review* 68(3): 973–88.

Citrin, Jack, and Donald Philip Green. 1986. "Presidential Leadership and the Resurgence of Trust in Government." *British Journal of Political Science* 16(4): 431–53.

Citrin, Jack, and Samantha Luks. 2001. "Political Trust Revisited: Déjà Vu All Over Again?" In *What Is It about Government That Americans Dislike?*, John R. Hibbing and Elizabeth Theiss-Morse, eds., 9–27. Cambridge: Cambridge University Press.

Clinton, Joshua D. 2006. "Representation in Congress: Constituents and Roll Calls in the 106th House." *Journal of Politics* 68(2): 397–409.

Clinton, Joshua, Ira Katznelson, and John S. Lapinski. Forthcoming. "Where Measures Meet History: Party Polarization during the New Deal and Fair Deal." In *Governing in a Polarized Age: Elections, Parties, and Representation in America*, Alan Gerber and Eric Schickler, eds., New York: Cambridge University Press.

CNA (Center for Naval Analyses) Military Advisory Board. 2007. *National Security and the Threat of Climate Change*. Alexandria, VA: CNA.

———. 2014. *National Security and the Accelerating Risks of Climate Change*. Alexandria, VA: CNA.

Cohen, Marty, David Karol, Hans Noel, and John Zaller. 2008. *The Party Decides: Presidential Nominations before and after Reform*. Chicago: University of Chicago Press.

Converse, Philip E. 1964. "The Nature of Belief Systems in Mass Publics." In *Ideology and Its Discontents*, David E. Apter, ed., 206–61. New York: The Free Press of Glencoe.

Cook, Thomas D., and Donald T. Campbell. 1979. *Quasi-Experimentation: Design and Analysis Issues for Field Settings*. Boston, MA: Houghton Mifflin.

Cover, Albert D. 1986. "Presidential Evaluations and Voting for Congress." *American Journal of Political Science* 30(4): 786–801.

Crespin, Michael H., David W. Rohde, and Ryan J. Vander Wielen. 2013. "Measuring Variations in Party Unity Voting: An Assessment of Agenda Effects." *Party Politics* 19(3): 432–57.

Cukierman, Alex, and Mariano Tommasi. 1998. "When Does It Take a Nixon to Go to China?" *American Economic Review* 88(1): 180–97.

Davis, Darren W., and Brian D. Silver. 2004. "Civil Liberties vs. Security: Public Opinion in the Context of the Terrorist Attacks on America." *American Journal of Political Science* 48(1): 28–46.

Davis, James A. 1975. "Communism, Conformity, Cohorts, and Categories: American Tolerance in 1954 and 1972–73." *American Journal of Sociology* 81(4): 491–513.

Delli Carpini, Michael X., and Scott Keeter. 1996. *What Americans Know about Politics and Why It Matters*. New Haven: Yale University Press.

Downs, Anthony. 1957. *An Economic Theory of Democracy*. New York: Harper and Row.

Druckman, James N. 2004. "Priming the Vote: Campaign Effects in a U.S. Senate Election." *Political Psychology* 25(4): 577–94.

Druckman, James N., Erik Peterson, and Rune Slothuus. 2013. "How Elite Partisan Polarization Affects Public Opinion Formation." American Political Science Review 107(1): 57–79.

Durr, Robert H., John B. Gilmour, and Christina Wolbrecht. 1997. "Explaining Congressional Approval." *American Journal of Political Science* 41(1): 175–207.

Durr, Robert H., Andrew D. Martin, and Christina Wolbrecht. 2000. "Ideological Divergence and Public Support for the Supreme Court." *American Journal of Political Science* 44(4): 768–76.

Easton, David. 1965. *A Systems Analysis of Political Life*. New York: Wiley.

Edwards, George C., III, William Mitchell, and Reed Welch. 1995. "Explaining Presidential Approval: The Significance of Issue Salience." *American Journal of Political Science* 39(1): 108–34.

Ellis, Christopher, and James A. Stimson. 2012. *Ideology in America*. New York: Cambridge University Press.

Erbring, Lutz, Edie N. Goldberg, and Arthur H. Miller. 1980. "Front-Page News and Real-World Cues: A New Look at Agenda-Setting by the Media." *American Journal of Political Science* 24(1): 16–49.

Erikson, Robert S., Michael B. MacKuen, and James A. Stimson. 2002. *The Macro Polity*. New York: Cambridge University Press.

Faber, Dan. 2010. "Poll: 70 Percent Angry or Dissatisfied with Washington." CBS News, February 11, 2010. http://www.cbsnews.com/news/poll-70-percent-angry-or-dissatisfied-with-washington.

Fazio, Russell H. 1986. "How Do Attitudes Guide Behavior?" In *The Handbook of Motivation and Cognition: Foundations of Social Behavior*, R. M. Sorrentino and E. T. Higgins, eds., 204–43. New York: Guilford.

Fazio, Russell H., Joni R. Jackson, Bridget C. Dunton, and Carol J. Williams. 1995. "Variability in Automatic Activation as an Unobtrusive Measure of Racial Attitudes: A Bona Fide Pipeline?" *Journal of Personality and Social Psychology* 69(6): 1013–27.

Fazio, Russell H., David M. Sanbonmatsu, Martha C. Powell, and Frank R. Kardes. 1986. "On the Automatic Activation of Attitudes." *Journal of Personality and Social Psychology* 50(2): 229–38.

Federal Reserve Bank of Minneapolis. 2007. "The Recession and Recovery in Perspective." http://www.minneapolisfed.org/publications_papers/studies/recession_perspective/index.cfm.

Feldman, Stanley. 1983. "The Measure and Meaning of Political Trust." *Political Methodology* 9: 341–54.

Fiorina, Morris P. 1978. "Economic Retrospective Voting in American National Elections: A Micro-Analysis." *American Journal of Political Science* 22(2): 426–43.

———. 1981. *Retrospective Voting in American Elections*. New Haven: Yale University Press.

Fiorina, Morris, Samuel J. Abrams, and Jeremy C. Pope. 2005. *Culture War? The Myth of Polarized America, 1st Edition*. New York: Pearson Longman.

———. 2010. *Culture War? The Myth of Polarized America, 3rd Edition*. New York: Pearson Longman.

Fiske, Susan T., and Shelley E. Taylor. 1984. *Social Cognition*. New York: McGraw Hill.

Gaines, Brian J., James H. Kuklinski, Paul J. Quirk, Buddy Peyton, and Jay Verkuilen. 2007. "Interpreting Iraq: Partisanship and the Meaning of Facts." *Journal of Politics* 69(4): 957–74.

Gamson, William A., and Andre Modigliani. 1966. "Knowledge and Foreign Policy Opinions: Some Models for Consideration." *Public Opinion Quarterly* 30(2): 187–99.

Garagiola, Joe. 1988. *It's Anybody's Ballgame*. New York: G. K. Hall.

Gerber, Alan S., and Gregory A. Huber. 2010. "Partisanship, Political Control, and Economic Assessments." *American Journal of Political Science* 54(1): 153–73.

Gilens, Martin. 1999. *Why Americans Hate Welfare: Race, Media, and the Politics of Antipoverty Policy*. Chicago: University of Chicago Press.

———. 2012. *Affluence and Influence: Economic Inequality and Political Power in America*. New York: Russell Sage.

Gilens, Martin, and Benjamin I. Page. 2014. "Testing Theories of American Politics: Elites, Interest Groups, and Average Citizens." *Perspectives on Politics* 12(3): 564–81.

Goldwater, Barry. 1964. "Goldwater's 1964 Acceptance Speech." *Washington Post.* http://www.washingtonpost.com/wp-srv/politics/daily/may98/goldwaterspeech.htm.

Goren, Paul. 2002. "Character Weakness, Partisan Bias, and Presidential Evaluation." *American Journal of Political Science* 46(3): 627–41.

Grant, J. Tobin, and Thomas J. Rudolph. 2003. "Value Conflict, Group Affect, and the Issue of Campaign Finance Reform." *American Journal of Political Science* 47(3): 453–69.

———. 2004. *Expression vs. Equality: The Politics of Campaign Finance Reform.* Columbus: Ohio State University Press.

Greer, Jim. 2009. "Obama Going to Talk to Kids: Yikes!" *The Huffington Post,* October 21, 2009. http://www.huffingtonpost.com/mona-gable/obama-going-to-talk-to-ki_b_278215.html.

Grosskopf, Anke, and Jeffery J. Mondak. 1998. "Do Attitudes toward Specific Supreme Court Decisions Matter? The Impact of Webster and Texas v. Johnson on Public Confidence in the Supreme Court." *Political Research Quarterly* 51(3): 633–54.

Hacker, Jacob S. 2010. "The Road to Somewhere: Why Health Reform Happened or Why Political Scientists Who Write about Public Policy Shouldn't Assume They Know How to Shape It." *Perspectives on Politics* 8(3): 861–76.

Haidt, Jonathan, and Marc J. Hetherington. 2012. "Look How Far We've Come Apart." *New York Times,* September 17, 2012.

Hartz, Louis. 1957. "The Coming of Age of America." *American Political Science Review* 51(2): 474–83.

Herrmann, Richard K., Philip E. Tetlock, and Penny S. Visser. 1999. "Mass Public Decisions to Go to War: A Cognitive-Interactionist Framework." *American Political Science Review* 93(3): 553–73.

Hetherington, Marc J. 1998. "The Political Relevance of Political Trust." *American Political Science Review* 92(4): 791–808.

———. 2005. *Why Trust Matters: Declining Political Trust and the Demise of American Liberalism.* Princeton, NJ: Princeton University Press.

———. 2008. "Turned Off or Turned On: The Effects of Polarization on Political Participation, Engagement, and Representation." In *Red and Blue Nation? Volume 2,* David Brady and Pietro Nivola, eds., 1–33. Washington, DC: Brookings.

Hetherington, Marc J., and Suzanne Globetti. 2002. "Political Trust and Racial Policy Preferences." *American Journal of Political Science* 46(2): 253–75.

Hetherington, Marc J., and Jason A. Husser. 2012. "How Trust Matters: The Changing Political Relevance of Political Trust." *American Journal of Political Science* 56(2): 312–25.

Hetherington, Marc J., and Cindy D. Kam. n.d. "Institutional Cue-Giving and Persuasion: Enlisting the Military as Environmental Protector." Unpublished manuscript.

Hetherington, Marc J., and Michael Nelson. 2003. "Anatomy of a Rally Effect: George W. Bush and the War on Terrorism." *PS: Political Science and Politics* 36(1): 37–42.

Hetherington, Marc J., and Carolyn E. Roush. n.d. "It's Not Me, It's You: Why the Public Tolerates Elite Polarization." Unpublished manuscript.

Hetherington, Marc J., and Thomas J. Rudolph. 2008. "Priming, Performance, and the Dynamics of Political Trust." *Journal of Politics* 70(2): 498–512.

Hetherington, Marc J., and Jonathan Weiler. 2009. *Authoritarianism and Polarization in American Politics*. New York: Cambridge University Press.

Hibbing, John R., and Elizabeth Theiss-Morse. 1995. *Congress as Public Enemy*. Cambridge: Cambridge University Press.

———. 2002. *Stealth Democracy: Americans' Beliefs about How Government Should Work*. New York: Cambridge University Press.

Higgins, E. Tory. 1996. "Knowledge Activation: Accessibility, Applicability, and Salience." In *Social Cognition: Handbook of Basic Principles*, E. Tory Higgins and Arie W. Kruglanski, eds., 133–68. New York: Guilford.

Higgins, E. Tory, and King G. 1981. "Accessibility of Social Constructs: Information Processing Consequences of Individual and Contextual Variability." In *Personality, Cognition, and Social Interaction*, Nancy Cantor and J. Kihlstrom, eds., 69–121. Hillsdale, NJ: Erlbaum.

Hovland, Carl I., Irving L. Janis, and Harold H. Kelley. 1953. *Communication and Persuasion: Psychological Studies of Opinion Change*. New Haven: Yale University Press.

Hovland, Carl I., and Walter Weiss. 1951. "The Influence of Source Credibility on Communication Effectiveness." *Public Opinion Quarterly* 15(4): 635–50.

Hox, J. J. 1998. "Multilevel Modeling: When and Why." In *Classification, Data Analysis, and Data Highway*, I. Balderjahn, R. Mathar, and M. Schader, eds., 147–54. New York: Springer Verlag.

Hsiang, S. M., K. C. Meng, and M. A. Cane. 2011. "Civil Conflicts Are Associated with the Global Climate." *Nature* 476(7361): 438–41.

Hurwitz, Jon, and Mark Peffley. 1987. "How Are Foreign Policy Attitudes Structured? A Hierarchical Model." *American Political Science Review* 81(4): 1099–120.

———. 1990. "Public Images of the Soviet Union: The Impact on Foreign Policy Attitudes." *Journal of Politics* 52(1): 3–28.

Iyengar, Shanto, and Donald R. Kinder. 1987. *News That Matters*. Chicago: University of Chicago Press.

Iyengar, Shanto, Donald R. Kinder, Mark D. Peters, and Jon A. Krosnick. 1984. "The Evening News and Presidential Evaluations." *Journal of Personality and Social Psychology* 46(4): 778–87.

Iyengar, Shanto, G. Sood, and Y. Lelkes. 2012. "Affect, Not Ideology: A Social Identity Perspective on Polarization." *Public Opinion Quarterly* 76(3): 405–31.

Iyengar, Shanto, and Sean J. Westwood. 2014. "Fear and Loathing across Party Lines: New Evidence on Group Polarization." *American Journal of Political Science*. doi: 10.1111/ajps.12152.

Jacobs, Lawrence R., and Robert Y. Shapiro. 2000. *Politicians Don't Pander: Political Manipulation and the Loss of Democratic Responsiveness*. Chicago: University of Chicago Press.

Jacobson, Gary C. 2006. *A Divider, Not a Uniter: George W. Bush and the American Public*. New York: Pearson.

Jacoby, William G. 1994. "Public Attitudes toward Government Spending." *American Journal of Political Science* 38(2): 336–61.

———. 2000. "Issue Framing and Public Opinion on Government Spending." *American Journal of Political Science* 44(4): 750–67.

Johnston, Richard, Andre Blais, Henry E. Brady, and Jean Crete. 1992. *Letting the People Decide: Dynamics of a Canadian Election*. Stanford: Stanford University Press.

Jordan, Nehemiah. 1965. "The Asymmetry of Liking and Disliking: A Phenomenon Meriting Further Reflection and Research." *Public Opinion Quarterly* 29(2): 315–22.

Kaiser Family Foundation. 2010. "Kaiser Health Tracking Poll: January 2010." http://kff.org/health-reform/poll-finding/kaiser-health-tracking-poll-january-2010.

Keele, Luke J. 2005. "The Authorities Really Do Matter: Party Control and Trust in Government." *Journal of Politics* 67(3): 873–86.

———. 2007. "Social Capital, Government Performance, and the Dynamics of Trust in Government." *American Journal of Political Science* 51(2): 241–54.

Kellstedt, Paul M. 2000. "Media Framing and the Dynamics of Racial Policy Preferences." *American Journal of Political Science* 44(2): 245–60.

Kernell, Samuel. 1986. *Going Public: New Strategies of Presidential Leadership*. Washington, DC: Congressional Quarterly Press.

Kessler, Aaron M. 2011. "New U.S. Fuel Rules Delayed." *Detroit Free Press*, September 29, 2011. http://www.freep.com/article/20110929/BUSINESS01/109290478/New-U-S-fuel-rules-delayed.

Key, V. O. 1955. "A Theory of Critical Elections." *Journal of Politics* 17(1): 3–18.

———. 1966. *The Responsible Electorate*. Cambridge, MA: Harvard University Press.

Kinder, Donald R., and D. Roderick Kiewiet. 1979. "Economic Discontent and Political Behavior: The Role of Personal Grievances and Collective Economic Judgments in Congressional Voting." *American Journal of Political Science* 23(3): 495–527.

———. 1981. "Sociotropic Politics: The American Case." *British Journal of Political Science* 11(1): 129–61.

Klein, Ezra. 2012. "Why Republicans Oppose the Individual Health Care Mandate." *The New Yorker*, June 18, 2012.

Krehbiel, Keith. 2000. "Party Discipline and Measures of Partisanship." *American Journal of Political Science* 44(2): 212–27.

Krosnick, Jon. A., and Laura A. Brannon. 1993. "The Impact of the Gulf War on the Ingredients of Presidential Evaluations: Multidimensional Effects of Political Involvement." *American Political Science Review* 87(4): 963–75.

Krosnick, Jon A., and Donald R. Kinder. 1990. "Altering the Foundations of Support for the President through Priming." *American Political Science Review* 84(2): 497–51.

Krugman, Paul. 2014. "Knowledge Isn't Power." *New York Times*, July 31, 2014. http://www.nytimes.com/2014/08/01/opinion/paul-krugman-knowledge-isnt -power.html?partner=rssnyt&emc=rss&_r=0.

Kunda, Ziva. 1990. "The Case for Motivated Reasoning." *Psychological Bulletin* 108(3): 480–98.

Lau, Richard R. 1985. "Two Explanations for Negativity Effects in Political Behavior." *American Journal of Political Science* 29: 353–77.

Lauderdale, Benjamin E. 2013. "Does Inattention to Political Debate Explain the Polarization Gap Between the U.S. Congress and Public?" *Public Opinion Quarterly* 77(S): 2–23.

Lavine, Howard, John L. Sullivan, Eugene Borgida, and Cynthia J. Thomsen. 1996. "The Relationship of National and Personal Issue Salience to Attitude Accessibility on Foreign and Domestic Policy Issues." *Political Psychology* 17(2): 293–316.

Lee, Frances E. n.d. "Patronage, Logrolls, and 'Polarization." Unpublished manuscript.

———. 2009. *Beyond Ideology: Politics, Principles, and Partisanship in the U.S. Senate.* Chicago: University of Chicago Press.

Levendusky, Matthew. 2009. *The Partisan Sort: How Liberals Became Democrats and Conservatives Became Republicans.* Chicago: University of Chicago Press.

Lock, Shmuel T., Robert Y. Shapiro, and Lawrence R. Jacobs. 1999. "The Impact of Political Debate on Government Trust: Reminding the Public What the Federal Government Does." *Political Behavior* 21(3): 239–64.

Lodge, Milton, and Charles Taber. 2000. "Three Steps toward a Theory of Motivated Reasoning." In *Elements of Reason: Cognition, Choice, and the Bounds of Rationality*, Arthur Lupia, Mathew D. McCubbins, and Samuel L. Popkin, eds., 183–213. New York: Cambridge University Press.

———. 2013. *The Rationalizing Voter.* New York: Cambridge University Press.

Luker, Kristin. 1985. *Abortion and the Politics of Motherhood.* Berkeley: University of California Press.

Lupia, Arthur, and Mathew D. McCubbins. 1998. *The Democratic Dilemma: Can Citizens Learn What They Need to Know?* New York: Cambridge University Press.

Luskin, Robert C. 1987. "Measuring Political Sophistication." *American Journal of Political Science* 31(4): 856–99.

MacKuen, Michael B. 1984. "Reality, the Press, and Citizens' Political Agendas." In *Surveying Subjective Phenomena*, Charles F. Turner and Elizabeth Martin, eds., 443–73. New York: Sage.

MacKuen, Michael B., and Stephen L. Coombs. 1981. *More Than News: Media Power in Public Affairs*. Beverly Hills, CA: Sage.

MacKuen, Michael B., Robert S. Erikson, and James A. Stimson. 1992. "Peasants or Bankers? The American Electorate and the U.S. Economy." *American Political Science Review* 86(3): 597–611.

Mann, Thomas E., and Norman J. Ornstein. 2008. *The Broken Branch: How Congress Is Failing America and How to Get It Back on Track*. New York: Oxford University Press.

———. 2012. *It's Even Worse Than It Looks: How the American Constitutional System Collided with the New Politics of Extremism*. New York: Basic.

Mazzetti, Mark, Eric Schmitt, and Robert F. Worth. 2011. "Two-Year Manhunt Led to Killing of Awlaki in Yemen." *New York Times*, September 30, 2011. http://www.nytimes.com/2011/10/01/world/middleeast/anwar-al-awlaki-is-killed -in-yemen.html?_r=1&hp=&pagewanted=print.

McCarty, Nolan, Keith Poole, and Howard Rosenthal. 2006. *Polarized Politics: The Dance of Ideology and Unequal Riches*. Cambridge, MA: Massachusetts Institute of Technology Press.

McClosky, Herbert. 1958. "Conservatism and Personality." *American Political Science Review* 52(1): 27–45.

———. 1964. "Consensus and Ideology in American Politics." *American Political Science Review* 58(2): 361–82.

McClosky, Herbert, and Alida Brill. 1983. *Dimensions of Tolerance: What Americans Believe about Civil Liberties*. New York: Russell Sage Foundation.

McMichael, William H. 2007. "Report: Climate Change a Major Military Issue." *Army Times*, April 16, 2007.

Mendelsohn, Matthew. 1996. "The Media and Interpersonal Communication: The Priming of Issues, Leaders, and Party Identification." *Journal of Politics* 58(1): 112–25.

Merolla, Jennifer, and Elizabeth J. Zechmeister. 2009. *Democracy at Risk: How Terrorist Threats Affect the Public*. Chicago: University of Chicago Press.

Miller, Arthur H. 1974. "Political Issues and Trust in Government: 1964–1970." *American Political Science Review* 68(3): 951–72.

Miller, Arthur H., and Stephen A. Borrelli. 1991. "Confidence in Government during the 1980s." *American Politics Quarterly* 19(2): 147–73.

Miller, Joanne M., and Jon A. Krosnick. 2000. "News Media Impact on the Ingredients of Presidential Evaluations: Politically Knowledgeable Citizens Are Guided by a Trusted Source." *American Journal of Political Science* 44(2): 301–15.

Miller, Warren E., and Donald E. Stokes. 1963. "Constituency Influence in Congress." *American Political Science Review* 57(1): 46–56.

Montopoli, Brian. 2008. "Polls Find Widespread Pessimism about U.S." CBS News, October 14, 2008. http://www.cbsnews.com/news/poll-finds-widespread -pessimism-about-us.

Mueller, John E. 1970. "Presidential Popularity from Truman to Johnson." *American Political Science Review* 64(1): 18–34.

———. 1973. *War, Presidents, and Public Opinion.* New York: Wiley.

Mutz, Diana C., and Byron Reeves. 2005. "The New Videomalaise: Effects of Televised Incivility on Political Trust." *American Political Science Review* 99(1): 1–15.

Nicholson, Stephen P. 2012. "Polarizing Cues." *American Journal of Political Science* 56(1): 52–66.

Niemi, Richard G., and Larry M. Bartels. 1985. "New Measures of Issue Salience: An Evaluation." *Journal of Politics* 47(4): 1212–20.

Nunn, Clyde Z., Harry J. Crockett, and J. Allen Williams. 1978. *Tolerance for Nonconformity.* San Francisco, CA: Jossey-Bass.

Obama, Barack. 2009. "President Barack Obama Makes Historic Speech to America's Students." http://www2.ed.gov/admins/lead/academic/bts.html.

Onaran, Yalman. 2008. "Fed Aided Bear Stearns as Firm Faced Chapter 11, Bernanke Says." *Bloomberg*, April 2, 2008. http://www.bloomberg.com/apps/news ?pid=newsarchive&sid=a7coicThgaEE.

Page, Benjamin I., Robert Y. Shapiro, and Glenn R. Dempsey. 1987. "What Moves Public Opinion?" *American Political Science Review* 81(1): 23–44.

Parker, Suzanne L. 1995. "Toward an Understanding of 'Rally' Effects: Public Opinion in the Persian Gulf War." *Public Opinion Quarterly* 59(4): 526–46.

Payne, B. Keith, Clara Michelle Cheng, Olseya Govorun, and Brandon D. Steward. 2005. "An Inkblot for Attitudes: Affect Misattribution as Implicit Measurement." *Journal of Experimental Social Psychology* 89(3): 277–93.

Peffley, Mark, and Jon Hurwitz. 1992. "International Events and Foreign Policy Beliefs: Public Response to Changing Soviet-U.S. Relations." *American Journal of Political Science* 36(2): 431–61.

Perez, Efren O. 2013. "Implicit Attitudes: Meaning, Measurement, and Synergy with Political Science." *Politics, Groups, and Identities* 1(2): 275–97.

Petrocik, John R. 1996. "Issue Ownership in Presidential Elections, with a 1980 Case Study." *American Journal of Political Science* 40(3): 825–50.

Pew Research Center. 2010a. "Most Americans don't know, or seem to care, about Supreme Court." http://www.pewresearch.org/2010/08/03/the-invisible -court.

———. 2010b. "Six Things to Know about Health Care Coverage." http://www .journalism.org/2010/06/21/six-things-know-about-health-care-coverage.

———. 2014. "Political Polarization in the American Public: How Increasing Ideological Uniformity and Partisan Antipathy Affect Politics, Compromise and Everyday Life." http://www.people-press.org/2014/06/12/political-polarization-in -the-american-public.

Pew Research Center for the People and the Press. 2006. "Bush a Drag on Republican Midterm Prospects." http://www.people-press.org/2006/02/09/bush-a-drag-on-republican-midterm-prospects.

———. 2010. "Public Trust in Government: 1958–2010." http://www.people-press.org/2014/11/13/public-trust-in-government.

Pindyck, Robert S., and Daniel L. Rubinfeld. 1998. *Econometric Models and Economic Forecasts, 4th Edition.* Boston: McGraw-Hill.

Price, Vincent, and David Tewksbury. 1997. "News Values and Public Opinion: A Theoretical Account of Priming and Framing." In *Progress in the Communication Sciences, Volume 13*, G. A. Barnett and F. J. Boster, eds., 173–212. Greenwich: Ablex.

Prior, Markus. 2013. "Media and Political Polarization." *Annual Review of Political Science* 16: 101–27.

Prothro, James W., and Charles W. Grigg. 1960. "Fundamental Principles of Democracy: Bases of Agreement and Disagreement." *Journal of Politics* 22(2): 276–94.

Pumphrey, Carolyn, ed. 2008. *Global Climate Change: National Security Implications.* Carlisle, PA: Strategic Studies Institute. http://www.strategicstudies institute.army.mil/pdffiles/pub862.pdf.

Rabinowitz, George, James W. Prothro, and William Jacoby. 1982. "Salience as a Factor in the Impact of Issues on Candidate Evaluation." *Journal of Politics* 44(1): 41–63.

Radcliff, Benjamin. 1994. "Reward without Punishment: Economic Conditions and the Vote." *Political Research Quarterly* 47(3): 721–31.

RealtyTrac. 2011. "Foreclosures Frozen in February." *Realtytrac.com*, March 9, 2011. http://www.realtytrac.com/content/press-releases/foreclosure-activity-decreases-14-percent-in-february-6420.

Redlawsk, David. 2002. "Hot Cognition or Cool Consideration: Testing the Effects of Motivated Reasoning on Political Decision Making." *Journal of Politics* 64(4): 1021–44.

Roberts, Joel. 2007. "Poll: Most Doubt Iraq Peace, Iran Threat." CBS News, February 12, 2007. http://www.cbsnews.com/news/poll-most-doubt-iraq-peace-iran-threat.

Rohde, David W. 1991. *Parties and Leaders in the Postreform House.* Chicago: University of Chicago Press.

Rokeach, Milton. 1973. *The Nature of Human Values.* New York: Free Press.

Rothgerber, Hank. 1997. "External Intergroup Threat as an Antecedent to Perceptions of In-Group and Out-Group Homogeneity." *Journal of Personality and Social Psychology* 73(6): 1206–12.

Rudolph, Thomas J. 2002. "The Economic Sources of Congressional Approval." *Legislative Studies Quarterly* 27(4): 577–99.

———. 2006. "Triangulating Political Responsibility: The Motivated Formation of Responsibility Judgments." *Political Psychology* 27(1): 99–122.

————. 2009. "Political Trust, Ideology, and Public Support for Tax Cuts." *Public Opinion Quarterly* 73(1): 144–58.

Rudolph, Thomas J., and Jillian Evans. 2005. "Political Trust, Ideology, and Public Support for Government Spending." *American Journal of Political Science* 49(3): 660–71.

Rudolph, Thomas J., and Elizabeth Popp. 2009. "Bridging the Ideological Divide: Trust and Support for Social Security Privatization." *Political Behavior* 31(3): 331–51.

Saad, Lydia. 2009. "Americans Endorse Obama's Approach, but Wary of Debt." Gallup, February 20–22, 2009. http://www.gallup.com/poll/116086/Americans -Endorse-Obama-Approach-Wary-Debt.aspx.

Scheufele, Dietram A., and David Tewksbury. 2007. "Framing, Agenda Setting, and Priming: The Evolution of Three Media Effects Models." *Journal of Communication* 57: 9–20.

Shapiro, Robert Y., and Harpreet Mahajan. 1986. "Gender Differences in Policy Preferences: A Summary of Trends from the 1960s to the 1980s." *Public Opinion Quarterly* 50(1): 42–61.

Sinclair, Barbara. 1997. *Unorthodox Lawmaking: New Legislative Processes in the U.S. Congress.* Washington, DC: CQ Press.

Smith, Tom W., Michael Hout, and Peter V. Marsden. 2012. "General Social Survey, 1972–2012 [Cumulative File]. ICPSR34802-v1." Storrs, CT: Roper Center for Public Opinion Research, University of Connecticut. http://doi.org/10.3886 /ICPSR34802.v1.

Sniderman, Paul M., Richard A. Brody, and Philip E. Tetlock. 1991. *Reasoning and Choice: Explorations in Political Psychology.* New York: Cambridge University Press.

Snyder, Michael. 2013. "29 Incredible Facts Which Prove That Poverty in America Is Absolutely Exploding." *The Economic Collapse Blog*, October 27, 2013. http://theeconomiccollapseblog.com/archives/29-incredible-facts-which-prove -that-poverty-in-america-is-absolutely-exploding.

Stimson, James A. 1999. *Public Opinion in America.* Boulder: Westview.

————. 2004. *Tides of Consent: How Public Opinion Shapes American Politics.* New York: Cambridge University Press.

Stimson, James A., Michael B. MacKuen, and Robert S. Erikson. 1995. "Dynamic Representation." *American Political Science Review* 89(3): 543–65.

Stokes, Donald E. 1962. "Popular Evaluations of Government: An Empirical Assessment." In *Ethics and Bigness: Scientific, Academic, Religious, Political, and Military*, Harlan Cleveland and Harold D. Lasswell, eds., 61–72. New York: Harper and Brothers.

Stouffer, Samuel. 1955. *Communism, Conformity, and Civil Liberties.* New York: Doubleday.

Sullivan, John L., George E. Marcus, Stanley Feldman, and James Pierson. 1981. "The Sources of Political Tolerance: A Multivariate Analysis." *American Political Science Review* 75(1): 92–106.

Sullivan, John L., James Piereson, and George E. Marcus. 1979. "An Alternative Conceptualization of Political Tolerance: Illusory Increases, 1950s–1970s." *American Political Science Review* 73(3): 233–49.

———. 1982. *Political Tolerance and American Democracy*. Chicago: University of Chicago Press.

Swann, Christopher. 2014. "GDP and the Economy: Advance Estimates for the Fourth Quarter of 2008." US Bureau of Economic Analysis, February 2009. http://www.bea.gov/scb/pdf/2009/02%20February/0209_gdpecon.pdf.

Taber, Charles S, and Milton Lodge. 2006. "Motivated Skepticism in the Evaluation of Political Beliefs." *American Journal of Political Science* 59(3): 755–69.

Terkel, Amanda. 2012. "112th Congress Set to Become Most Unproductive since 1940s." *The Huffington Post*, December 28, 2012. http://www.huffingtonpost.com/2012/12/28/congress-unproductive_n_2371387.html.

Theriault, Sean M. 2008. *Party Polarization in Congress*. New York: Cambridge University Press.

Treier, Shawn, and D. Sunshine Hillygus. 2009. "The Nature of Political Ideology in the Contemporary Electorate." *Public Opinion Quarterly* 73(4): 679–703.

Tversky, Amos, and Daniel Kahneman. 1974. "Judgment under Uncertainty: Heuristics and Biases." *Science* 184(4157): 1124–31.

———. 1981. "The Framing of Decisions and the Psychology of Choice." *Science* 211: 453–58.

US Bureau of Labor Statistics. 2014. "Labor Force Statistics from the Current Population Survey." http://data.bls.gov/timeseries/LNS14000000.

US Department of Health and Human Services. 2014. "About HHS." http://www.hhs.gov/about.

Uslaner, Eric M. 2012. *Segregation and Mistrust: Diversity, Isolation, and Social Cohesion*. New York: Cambridge University Press.

US Navy. 2010. "Navy Climate Change Roadmap." http://www.navy.mil/navydata/documents/CCR.pdf.

Vanderbilt University. 2011. "Vanderbilt University Poll." http://www.vanderbilt.edu/csdi/november2011poll.php.

Weatherford, M. Stephen. 1984. "Economic 'Stagflation' and Public Support for the Political System." *British Journal of Political Science* 14(2): 187–205.

Williams, John T. 1985. "Systemic Influences on Political Trust: The Importance of Perceived Institutional Performance." *Political Methodology* 9: 125–42.

Wlezien, Christopher. 2005. "On the Salience of Political Issues: The Problem with 'Most Important Problem.'" *Electoral Studies* 24(4): 555–79.

Yamagishi, Toshio, Karen S. Cook, and Motoki Watabe. 1998. "Uncertainty, Trust, and Commitment Formation in the United States and Japan." *American Journal of Sociology* 104(1): 165–94.

Yang, Jin, and Gerald Stone. 2003. "The Powerful Role of Interpersonal Communication in Agenda Setting." *Mass Communication and Society* 6(1): 57–74.

Zaller, John R. 1992. *The Nature and Origins of Mass Opinion*. Cambridge: Cambridge University Press.

Zeleny, Jeff, and Megan Thee-Brenan. 2009. "Survey Reveals Broad Support for President." *The New York Times*, February 23, 2009. http://www.nytimes.com/2009/02/24/us/politics/24poll.html?hp.

Index

ABC News poll on government's trustworthiness, 54–55
abortion rights, polarization and, 27–28
Abscam scandal, 63
abstract democratic principles, American support for, 193
accessibility, priming and, 52
accessibility heuristic, 103
Affordable Care Act (ACA). *See* Obamacare
Afghanistan, war in, 7, 8, 10, 86, 119, 120; political trust and, 123
African Americans: political trust of, in the government, 200; salience hypothesis and aid to, 135–38; support for health care reform, 206; support for spending increases as economic stimulus, 155
agency-specific trust, bivariate relationship between individual policy preferences and, 203
agenda setting: priming and, 52; role of mass media in, 51–52
Alexander the Great, 187
American International Group (AIG), bankruptcy of, 141
American National Election Study (ANES): assessing performance in both economic and foreign policy domains, 79–80; average feelings on military in, 54; cumulative data collection by, 44; exploration of trust and policy preferences, 121–22; feeling thermometer scale of, 74–77; ideological self-identification by party identification and, 16; leverage

from using the 2012, 91; measurement of political trust, 49, 170, 196–97, 215; on people on welfare, 54; questions on public trust in, 8–9; trust-in-government question in, 151–52
American politics, as dysfunctional, 1
Americans: aversion to taxes, 146; collapse of trust in government, 166; feelings on Obama speech on education in 2009, 3–4; as moderate, 1; support for basic principles, 192–93
American Voter, 100
antigovernment conditions, political trust and, 190, 191
Arthur, Chester, 225
asymmetric effect of political trust, 131–32
atheists, Republican rating of, over Democrats, 215
attitude instability and causation, 99–102
authoritarianism: effect of, 134; in tapping attitudes about force, 122
Awlaki, Anwar al-, killing of, 108

banking industry, insufficient regulation of, 141
baseball fans, 41; Gallup Poll on, 17–18
Bayh, Evan, on 2010 midterm election losses, 183
Bear Stearns: failure of, 146–47; merger with J. P. Morgan, 146–47
Berlin Wall, fall of, 51
"big government" initiatives, effect of political trust on support for, 119
bill markups, 57

Chicago Studies in American Politics

A SERIES EDITED BY BENJAMIN I. PAGE, SUSAN HERBST,
LAWRENCE R. JACOBS, AND ADAM J. BERINSKY

Series titles, continued from front matter:

THE TIMELINE OF PRESIDENTIAL ELECTIONS:
HOW CAMPAIGNS DO (AND DO NOT) MATTER *by
Robert S. Erikson and Christopher Wlezien*

LEARNING WHILE GOVERNING: EXPERTISE
AND ACCOUNTABILITY IN THE EXECUTIVE
BRANCH *by Sean Gailmard and John W. Patty*

ELECTING JUDGES: THE SURPRISING EFFECTS
OF CAMPAIGNING ON JUDICIAL LEGITIMACY *by
James L. Gibson*

FOLLOW THE LEADER? HOW VOTERS
RESPOND TO POLITICIANS' POLICIES AND
PERFORMANCE *by Gabriel S. Lenz*

THE SOCIAL CITIZEN: PEER NETWORKS AND
POLITICAL BEHAVIOR *by Betsy Sinclair*

THE SUBMERGED STATE: HOW INVISIBLE
GOVERNMENT POLICIES UNDERMINE AMERICAN
DEMOCRACY *by Suzanne Mettler*

DISCIPLINING THE POOR: NEOLIBERAL
PATERNALISM AND THE PERSISTENT POWER OF
RACE *by Joe Soss, Richard C. Fording, and
Sanford F. Schram*

WHY PARTIES? A SECOND LOOK *by John H.
Aldrich*

NEWS THAT MATTERS: TELEVISION AND
AMERICAN OPINION, UPDATED EDITION *by
Shanto Iyengar and Donald R. Kinder*

SELLING FEAR: COUNTERTERRORISM, THE MEDIA,
AND PUBLIC OPINION *by Brigitte L. Nacos,
Yaeli Bloch-Elkon, and Robert Y. Shapiro*

OBAMA'S RACE: THE 2008 ELECTION AND THE
DREAM OF A POST-RACIAL AMERICA *by Michael
Tesler and David O. Sears*

FILIBUSTERING: A POLITICAL HISTORY OF
OBSTRUCTION IN THE HOUSE AND SENATE *by
Gregory Koger*

IN TIME OF WAR: UNDERSTANDING AMERICAN
PUBLIC OPINION FROM WORLD WAR II TO
IRAQ *by Adam J. Berinsky*

US AGAINST THEM: ETHNOCENTRIC
FOUNDATIONS OF AMERICAN OPINION *by
Donald R. Kinder and Cindy D. Kam*

THE PARTISAN SORT: HOW LIBERALS BECAME
DEMOCRATS AND CONSERVATIVES BECAME
REPUBLICANS *by Matthew Levendusky*

DEMOCRACY AT RISK: HOW TERRORIST THREATS
AFFECT THE PUBLIC *by Jennifer L. Merolla and
Elizabeth J. Zechmeister*

AGENDAS AND INSTABILITY IN AMERICAN
POLITICS, SECOND EDITION *by Frank R.
Baumgartner and Bryan D. Jones*

THE PRIVATE ABUSE OF THE PUBLIC
INTEREST *by Lawrence D. Brown and
Lawrence R. Jacobs*

THE PARTY DECIDES: PRESIDENTIAL
NOMINATIONS BEFORE AND AFTER REFORM *by
Marty Cohen, David Karol, Hans Noel, and
John Zaller*

SAME SEX, DIFFERENT POLITICS: SUCCESS
AND FAILURE IN THE STRUGGLES OVER GAY
RIGHTS *by Gary Mucciaroni*